DIGNITY RIGHTS

DEMOCRACY, CITIZENSHIP,
AND CONSTITUTIONALISM

Rogers M. Smith and Mary L. Dudziak, Series Editors

DIGNITY RIGHTS

COURTS, CONSTITUTIONS,
AND THE WORTH OF THE HUMAN PERSON

UPDATED EDITION

ERIN DALY

Foreword by
Aharon Barak

PENN

UNIVERSITY OF PENNSYLVANIA PRESS

PHILADELPHIA

Published by
University of Pennsylvania Press
Philadelphia, Pennsylvania 19104-4112
www.upenn.edu/pennpress

Printed in the United States of America
on acid-free paper
2 4 6 8 10 9 7 5 3 1

Library of Congress Cataloging-in-Publication Data

Daly, Erin.
    Dignity rights : courts, constitutions, and the worth of
the human person / Erin Daly.—updated ed.
        p.   cm.—(Democracy, citizenship, and constitution-
alism)
    ISBN 978-0-8122-2475-7 (updated edition)
Includes bibliographical references and index.
    1. Respect for persons—Law and legislation. 2. Dignity.
I. Title. II. Series: Democracy, citizenship, and constitutionalism.
K3249.d35   2012
342.08'5   2012007873

For Bobby Lipkin, who helped me set sail

For David, Jasper, and Alex, who keep me afloat

CONTENTS

Erin Daly

Dignity rights are an idea whose time has come. And not a moment too soon.

This book is the story of a relationship between two powerful ideas. On one side there is human dignity—the intrinsic and equal worth of every "member of the human family," as the Universal Declaration of Human Rights (UDHR) reminds us.[1] On the other side, the idea of rights—the notion that people are entitled to make claims against those who hold power over them. When these two come together, the effect is revolutionary.

Dignity gives rights meaning and purpose. Dignity is why we have the right to have and to claim rights, to paraphrase Hannah Arendt.[2] And it is the very reason why we insist on rights: we want decent housing or a healthy environment or we want to express our opinions or vote. We insist on rights because we are being abused or demeaned or treated as something less than human and we believe—because our dignity tells us so—that that we are entitled to more or better than mere existence.

Rights, in turn, give dignity power. For most of human history, dignity existed as an idea, an article of faith, a sense that there is something distinctively important about the human person. But it had no legal effect. Then, in the early dawn after the dark night of World War II, dignity was yoked to human rights. And the story of dignity changed forever.

The Charter of the United Nations reaffirmed faith in "the dignity and worth of the human person"[3] and three years later, the Universal Declaration of Human Rights would recognize "the inherent dignity and of the equal and inalienable rights of all members of the human family."[4] Its first article would go further: "All human beings are born free and equal in dignity and rights. They are endowed with reason and conscience and should act toward one another in a spirit of brotherhood."[5]

What a magnificent cluster of ideas lies in these few succinct phrases!

Every person everywhere who has ever lived or ever will live has human dignity just by virtue of being born. This marks the first time an international document said that *every person counts*. The universality of dignity admits of no exception: it doesn't matter where someone is born or under what circumstances or into which family or with which body. Nor does it matter when: generations past and generations yet to come are all equal in dignity. It is as if each person receives a valuable coin at birth that can never be lost. Despite all of our differences, in our dignity we are the same.

And this is so because we are fortunate enough to belong to a species that is endowed with reason and conscience, regardless of the individual differences among us. But the good fortune of reason comes with responsibilities: it imposes on us an obligation to act toward one another in a spirit of brotherhood (and sisterhood). That is, our dignity obligates us to recognize the dignity of others, to treat each other as members of the same human family. In the hands of the UDHR's drafters, dignity is more than the name given to human worth. And it is more than an entitlement to respect or privilege. That worth unlocks a set of legal rights that each person is entitled to claim. The UDHR doesn't explain why dignity and rights are twinned, it simply announces that everyone is born equal in both and then proceeds, in the remaining twenty-nine articles, to enumerate the rights that flow from the recognition of universal human dignity.

In the 1940s, the announcement of the relationship between dignity and rights had no legally binding effect. Neither the Charter nor the Universal Declaration imposed human rights obligations on the sovereign states of the world. But just as the Charter's mere mention of dignity led to the Declaration's fuller articulation of it, the Declaration in turn led to dignity's absorption into the fabric of human rights law. This began in earnest with the two International Covenants whose preambles both share the language of dignity: "Considering that, in accordance with the principles proclaimed in the Charter of the United Nations, recognition of the inherent dignity and of the equal and inalienable rights of all members of the human family is the foundation of freedom, justice and peace in the world."[6] Both covenants also refer to dignity, though sporadically, in the enumeration of rights, as do many other international human rights instruments, including the Convention on the Rights of the Child and the UN Declaration on the Rights of Indigenous People.

The UDHR may have been ahead of its time, but in the last few years, the world has shown that it's ready to catch up and get to work. In 2018, the Human Rights Committee of the United Nations recognized that the very right to life enshrined in the International Covenant on Civil and Political Rights "concerns the entitlement of individuals . . . to enjoy a life with dignity."[7] Because dignity represents an inherent human claim not just to life but to a certain quality of life, it both prohibits states from taking action that would violate human dignity and obligates them to take affirmative steps to ensure that people live with dignity. The committee explained:

> The duty to protect life also implies that States parties should take appropriate measures to address the general conditions in society that may give rise to direct threats to life or prevent individuals from enjoying their right to life with dignity. These general conditions may include high levels of criminal and gun violence, pervasive traffic and industrial accidents, degradation of the environment, deprivation of land, territories and resources of indigenous peoples, the prevalence of life threatening diseases, such as AIDS, tuberculosis or malaria, extensive substance abuse, widespread hunger and malnutrition and extreme poverty and homelessness.[8]

This is an important statement of the indivisibility of rights and their common source in the right to live with dignity. But while international law has enormous rhetorical power and can help galvanize nations into action, the process is slow and weak and it's largely unenforceable: it's almost impossible for people to realize their rights in international arenas.

Fortunately, the story of dignity rights did not end there. It traveled around the world to the constitutions of more than 160 nations that address dignity in one way or another.[9] Dignity shows up as a fundamental value, an inviolable right, or a right associated with certain vulnerable groups (children, people who are disabled, migrants or people with disabilities) or to protect against certain unjustifiable wrongs (torture, medical experimentation) or to ensure certain rights (education, fair employment). Increasingly, it shows up in constitutions in more than one guise. One exhaustive study found that the average age of constitutions that refer to dignity more than eight times is twenty-one years, while the average age of those that don't refer to it at all is nearly fifty years, suggesting that newer constitutions are increasingly paying attention to the importance of human dignity in law.[10] Indeed, all forty-nine constitutions adopted since 2003 include at least one reference to dignity.[11]

Still, the concept of dignity can feel rather abstract. Empty, elastic, useless—some have said—or, on the other hand, "flabby from overuse," as Ronald Dworkin once wrote. Perhaps dignity is nothing more than a unicorn—beautiful to imagine but without substance on earth. And so it might remain were it not for the constitutional courts of countries around the world who are pressing dignity into service. Perhaps the more apt zoologic metaphor, as James Ingram suggests, is not a unicorn but a mule. And, as he explains, "the essential difference between a unicorn and a mule is not that the mule exists, but that it will work."[12]

This book tells the remarkable story of how judges throughout the globe are making dignity work. In case after case, courts are writing dignity into the language of rights and thereby helping to bring the promise of human dignity to life—or rather, to people's lives. These cases are helping people to exercise agency over their lives, to live according to their own values, to be respected by others "as a person," and to live in sufficient comfort to be able to enjoy other rights. This global blossoming of dignity law is transforming the very relationship between people and their governments, in real time, before our eyes.

In the last fifteen years, we have seen an undeniable turn toward dignity rights in courts around the world. Perhaps the most notable feature of the global jurisprudence of dignity rights is that courts in all regions of the world and from all legal traditions have patriated dignity, not because it is foundational to international law but because it is at the foundation of their own constitutional culture as they define it for themselves. Sometimes, this has taken on a religious tone. Courts in Pakistan have rooted dignity in the Quran, while courts in Israel have found it consistent with Jewish teachings, while courts in the west have found it consistent with Christian traditions, and for some African courts it reinforces the principle of ubuntu. For others, it is, as it was for the United Nations, simply an article of secular faith. It is not that dignity is the chameleon of rights because it doesn't change as it passes through each court's hands. Rather, it has the capacity to focus attention on what is most important and what is common to all humanity, regardless of language, tradition, or creed.

A related feature of dignity law is the substantive diversity of issues addressed in the cases. Courts have found dignity relevant in cases dealing with every type of right: personal matters relating to identity (name, gender identity, religious and cultural identity, professional ambitions, language, choice of family structure), matters relating to the quality of life (involving claims for adequate housing, food, water, education, environmental quality), pro-

tection from discrimination and humiliation (particularly in situations involving custody or dependence), and rights of participation in democratic
governance (involving freedom of speech, association, the franchise, and so
on). These cases are filling in dignity's broad contours, giving it context, substance, and meaning.

Even more remarkable than the diversity of cases is the fact that in most
of these cases, recourse to dignity is not necessary. Courts deciding these
cases rely on some other provision of the constitution in question, whether
express or implied. There is, of course, the rare case that is inexplicable on
any basis other than dignity. For instance, courts in Pakistan and in Uganda
have invalidated legislation meant to protect people with disabilities because
the statutory language is offensive. A court in China wrestled with the dignity implications of a couple's decision to give their child a poetic surname
rather than the surname of one of the parents, as is the rule. Courts in Canada and Europe have resisted the claim that the human body can be patented
simply because it is *human*. These are nothing more and nothing less than
dignity interests—the human need to be special, the interest of a person to
have agency over essential aspects of their life and to have the respect of others in doing so. In most cases, however, courts do not *have* to rely on dignity
to reach their conclusions. But they choose to do so anyway. Throughout the
caselaw, dignity is being strategically pressed into service not because it is the
exclusive basis for the ruling in question but in order to build an irrefutable
foundation for what the court is doing.

Sometimes, dignity supports the very nature and function of rights because it is recognized as a foundational principle on which rights rest. Cases
from Peru, South Africa, Germany, India, Israel, and other countries too
numerous to mention have repeatedly recalled that dignity is the source or
"mother right" that gives birth to all other rights,[13] the central premise on
which the institution of rights and the rule of law, or the nation itself, rests.

Other times, dignity's work is directed at more particular interests, invoked to reinforce or give definition to the right at issue in the case or to provide the measure of a remedy. In cases involving discrimination, some courts
have explained that a distinction among people becomes unconstitutionally
invidious at the point at which it harms the dignity of the oppressed person
or group. In cases involving pension levels and prison conditions, courts have
described the requisite level of protection as that which is necessary to maintain or ensure human dignity. The quality of the environment has been defined by the ability of people to live in it with dignity and sustainably. Dignity

in these cases is the measure of law's success: it is the thing that determines how close law is to justice.

*   *   *

In the years since this book was first published, the landscape of dignity rights has evolved in important ways. It has spread to more countries and become more firmly entrenched in the fabric of law at the international, regional, and domestic levels. And it has reached more diverse areas of law—meeting new technologies and new challenges.

One area that has seen a dramatic shift of attention to dignity rights is environmental protection.[14] This is in part a product of the convergence of human rights and environmental rights that we have seen at the international level and in domestic constitutions[15] and in part a recognition of the growing importance of environmental protection to the ability of people to enjoy lives of dignity and to exercise all other rights.[16] When the first edition of this book was written, there was hardly a case about environmental dignity rights. Now, we see it in the Indian subcontinent, Latin America, South Africa, and elsewhere insisting that the right to live with dignity (whether explicitly protected in the constitution or not) demands a healthy and sustainable environment. The American Bar Association has recently established a new project to advance environmental dignity..

A few examples illustrate the trend. In a series of decisions in 2015 and 2018, the High Court of Lahore in Pakistan established a climate commission in response to the government's failure to protect the constitutional dignity rights of the people of Pakistan from the ravages of climate change.[17] The Supreme Court of Nepal struck down a permit for marble mining, holding that it would violate the right of the people to live with dignity and freedom, which requires a healthy environment.[18] On the other side of the world, the Constitutional Court of Colombia has been equally emphatic about the fundamental place of dignity in the country's constitutional scheme based on the "social rule of law" and on the indivisibility of human and environmental rights including the right to dignity: in determining that one of Colombia's most important rivers, the Rio Atrato, was entitled to juridical personhood, the court in 2016 held that "generating significant environmental pollution affects, as a whole, the rights to life, human dignity, health, water, food security, the health of the environment, to the culture and territory of the ethnic communities that inhabit the basin of the Atrato River."[19] More and more, the right to life is deemed to mean the right to live with dignity, which includes all manner of social, cultural, economic, environmental, civil, and political rights. And, as the cases say, courts are increasingly finding that the right to live with dignity is not restricted to human beings, but may extend to all sentient beings and even to other parts of the planet's ecosystems.[20] This extension makes sense: dignity has always applied to what is important and what the law should protect, whether it be sovereigns or courts or human beings. Now nature is being recognized in the same way.

As described in the pages of this book, the United States has always been a bit of an outlier in dignity jurisprudence and in the jurisprudence of rights as a whole. Decrying the relative dearth of cases about dignity rights, this book was published months before the United States Supreme Court decided *Obergefell v. Hodges*, the landmark decision affirming the rights of all people to marry the partner of their choice. To date, this is the most important decision about the Constitution's commitment to human dignity, as expressed in the confluence of the equal protection and due process clauses.[21] While this development represents a milestone in American rights jurisprudence, it remains to be seen whether and when the principle of human dignity recognized in *Obergefell* will be applied in other contexts where it is needed: to alleviate environmental injustice, systemic racism, the continued oppression of indigenous people and people who migrate, educational failures and disparities, over-incarceration, the lack of national healthcare, and other social ills that impede people's ability to live with dignity.

Without these rights written into the Constitution, American lawyers are at a disadvantage when they try to persuade judges to consider the humanity and the dignity of the people whose rights are stake in their cases. It is therefore a welcome development that, in 2019, the American Bar Association adopted a Resolution affirming that "human dignity—the inherent, equal, and inalienable worth of every person—is foundational to a just rule of law; and [urging] governments to ensure that 'dignity rights'—the principle that human dignity is fundamental to all areas of law and policy—be reflected in the exercise of their legislative, executive, and judicial functions."[22] This resolution could have dramatic implications as lawyers bring attention to the need for courts to provide legal protection for the dignity of all people.

With the entrenchment of dignity jurisprudence in global law, it is not surprising that more scholars are becoming interested in the work that dignity can do in court. This book was the first monograph devoted to dignity rights, but shortly after its publication, two monographs and two collected editions about dignity law appeared[23] and new books are following suit at an accelerating rate.[24] The first casebook on the subject will be published in 2020.[25] The time has come.

                              *   *   *

The joining of the value of human dignity with the assertion of legal rights has become indelible in constitutions, laws, and court cases throughout the world and throughout this broad global jurisprudence, courts are pressing dignity into service to serve a variety of functions: to establish a humanitarian norm, to help explain the meaning of other rights, to reveal their fundamental indivisibility, to root the rule of law, to provide a measure for judicial remedies, and more. Throughout the caselaw, courts are finding that the very purpose of rights is to promote and protect the worth of the human person. And perhaps even more profound is the recognition that the very act of claiming these rights—the impulse to say *we are entitled to these things simply because we are human*—is itself an act of dignity.

The idea of human dignity has now become inextricably entwined with the idea of rights. This book is a study of how that relationship grew, so that the promise of dignity can become a reality for every person, everywhere.

Notes

1. Universal Declaration of Human Rights (UDHR). G. A. Res. 217 (III) A. UN General Assembly, 10 December 1948, Preamble.

2. Hannah Arendt, *The Origins of Totalitarianism* (New York: Schocken Books, 1951), 298.

3. United Nations, Charter of the United Nations, 24 October 1945, 1 UNTS XVI, Preamble.

4. UDHR, Preamble.

5. UDHR, Article 1.

6. International Covenant on Civil and Political Rights, New York, 16 December 1966, in force 23 March 1976, 999 *United Nations Treaty Series* 171, Preamble; and International Covenant on Economic, Social and Cultural Rights, New York, 16 December 1966, in force 3 January 1976, 993 *United Nations Treaty Series* 195, Preamble.

7. CCPR/C/GC/36 (adopted by the Committee at its 124th session [8 October to 2 November 2018]).

8. Id. at para. 26.

9. Doron Shulztiner and Guy E. Carmi, "Human Dignity in National Constitutions: Functions, Promises and Dangers," *American Journal of Comparative Law*, 62 (2014): 461–90, 465–66.

10. Id.

11. Id. at 465.

12. James D. Ingram, "What is 'The Right to Have Rights?' Three Images of the Politics of Human Rights," *American Political Science Review* 102.4 (2008): 401–416 at 402.

13. Aharon Barak, *Human Dignity: The Constitutional Right and its Daughter-Rights* (Tel Aviv: Nevo Publishing, 2014).

14. See James R. May and Erin Daly, "Environmental Dignity Rights," in James R. May and Erin Daly, *Human Rights and the Environment: Legality, Indivisibility, Dignity and Geography*, vol. 7, *Elgar Encyclopedia of Environmental Law* (Cheltenham: Edward Elgar Publishing, 2019).

15. John H. Knox and Ramin Pejan, *The Human Right to a Healthy Environment* (Cambridge: Cambridge University Press, 2018).

16. CCPR/C/GC/36 (adopted by the Committee at its 124th session [8 October to 2 November 2018]).

17. *Ashgar Leghari v. Federation of Pakistan*. No. W.P. No. 25501/2015 (Lahore High Court, 2015 and 2018).

18. *Pro Public v. Godavari Marble Industries Pvt. Ltd. and Others* (Supreme Court of Nepal, 2015).

19. *Center for Social Justice Studies et al. v. Presidency of the Republic et al.* ("Rio Atrato" Case), No. Judgment T-622/16 (Constitutional Court of Colombia, 2016).

20. *Animal Welfare Board v. A Nagaraja* (Supreme Court of India, 2014). See also STC4360-2018 Radicación n.° 11001-22-03-000-2018-00319-01 (Constitutional Court of Colombia 2018) (finding that the Colombian Amazon has juridical rights); and see *Islamabad Wildlife Management Board v. Metropolitan Corporation Islamabad* W.P. No.1155/2019 (Islamabad High Court 2019) (finding that elephants and other animals have rights).

21. *Obergefell v. Hodges*, 135 S. Ct. 2584 (2015).

22. Resolution of the American Bar Association, adopted 12 August 2019.

23. Catherine Dupré, *The Age of Dignity: Human Rights and Constitutionalism in Europe* (Oxford: Hart Publishing, 2015); Aharon Barak, *Human Dignity: The Constitutional Value and the Constitutional Right* (Cambridge: Cambridge University Press, 2015); Christopher McCrudden, ed., *Understanding Human Dignity*, repr. ed. (Oxford: Oxford University Press, 2014); Marcus Düwell, Jens Braarvig, Roger Brownsword, and Dietmar Mieth, eds., *The Cambridge Handbook of Human Dignity: Interdisciplinary Perspectives* (Cambridge: Cambridge University Press, 2014).

24. See e.g. Dina L. Townsend, *Human Dignity and the Adjudication of Environmental Rights* (Cheltenham: Edward Elgar, 2020); James R. May and Erin Daly, *Advanced Introduction to Human Dignity and Law* (Cheltenham: Edward Elgar, 2020).

25. Erin Daly and James R. May, *Dignity Law: Global Recognition, Cases and Perspectives* (Getzville, NY: William S. Hein, 2020).

FOREWORD

Aharon Barak

The twentieth century was a time of revolutionary developments in the area of human rights. At the center of those developments stands the revolution with respect to human dignity—a response, at least in part, to the Nazis' hideously brutal actions during the Second World War and the Holocaust. More than one hundred constitutions and dozens of international treaties include express references to human dignity.

Human dignity has a long history. It has been recognized in various religions and has served as the basis for a variety of philosophical outlooks. The essential nature of the concept is sharply debated. Some see it as a paramount constitutional value and a central constitutional right. Others see it as a concept void of any content and having no constitutional use. Against the background of these sharp disputes, Erin Daly's book comes as a breath of fresh air. It sets before the reader the broad comparative base, points out the key problems that arise, and outlines the principal lines of thought and their development.

Daly's book nicely shows that the fundamental distinction that must be considered—and is missing from comparative-law discourse on the subject—is the distinction between human dignity as a constitutional value and human dignity as a constitutional right. As a constitutional value, human dignity is the value of a person within the society. It is a value that is unique to each society and each constitution, and it expresses the society's fundamental religious, moral, and ethical concepts. As such, it is a value that depends on context and is subject to change in a changing world. That said, democratic-liberal-modern societies for the most part have a common approach to the constitutional value of human dignity. That value is anchored, explicitly or implicitly, in the constitution itself and serves as the basis for all the constitutional rights recognized therein, playing an important interpretive role in fixing the scope of the various rights. Within that framework of interpretation, the interpretive value functions as a regulative, organizational, and integrative principle for the constitutional text. It can be of use, for example, in interpreting the right to equality. Similarly, the constitutional value of human dignity has a role in interpretive balancing (in situations where constitutional rights conflict) and in constitutional balancing (in situations where a law limits the realization of a constitutional right).

What is the content of the constitutional value of human dignity? As Erin Daly's book nicely shows, comparative law provides no agreed- upon answer. The question arose in the Israeli High Court; in answering, I noted that

> Human dignity is a complex principle. In formulating it, one must avoid any attempt to adopt the moral outlook of one thinker or the philosophical concepts of another. Human dignity must not be made into a Kantian concept, nor should it be seen as expressing one or another natural law notion. The content of "human dignity" will be determined in accord with the perspectives of the enlightened public in Israel, in accordance will the purpose of Basic Law: Human Dignity and Liberty. At the base of this concept stands the recognition that man is a free creature, one who develops his body and mind as he sees fit, all within the social framework to which he belongs and on which he is dependent.[1]

In another case, I added:

> At the center of human dignity are the sanctity and liberty of life. At its foundation are the autonomy of the individual will, the freedom of choice, and the freedom of man to act as a free creature. Human dignity rests on the recognition of a person's physical and intellectual wholeness, one's humanity, one's value as a person—all without any connection to the extent of its utility for others.[2]

This concept of the value of human dignity is grounded in the humanity of man. Human dignity as a constitutional value reflects society's understanding of man's humanity within the society.

What is the content of human dignity as a constitutional right? It depends on the constitutional interpretation given it. The constitutional value expresses the constitutional purpose, but that purpose functions within the bounds of a constitutional text. The understanding of that text is determined on the basis of the constitution's structure, its architecture, the structure of the bill of rights it contains, and all the other interpretive considerations that bear on the scope of a constitutional right. Similarly, the content of the right is influenced by the rules of constitutional interpretation that prevail in the particular legal system. Human dignity interpreted in accord with its original meaning (following the doctrine of originalism) is not the same as human dignity interpreted in accord with its modern understanding (following the doctrine of "a living constitution"). Indeed, the type of normativity associated with the constitutional right to human dignity bears on its content.

So, for example, in German constitutional law, human dignity (Würde des Menschen) is an absolute right (that is, not subject to the rules of proportionality) and an eternal right (that is, not subject to constitutional amendments). Moreover, it constitutes part of a full constitutional bill of rights that covers—even without consideration of human dignity—all human behavior (primarily on account of the broad reach of the separate constitutional right to personal development). This sort of normativity led to a narrow interpretation of human dignity in German constitutional law. Israeli constitutional law, in contrast, treats the right to human dignity as relative (that is, subject to limitation by the rules of proportionality) and non-eternal (that is, subject to constitutional amendment); and it is embodied in a very limited constitutional bill of rights that, for historical reasons, covers only a small number of constitutional rights (preservation and protection of life, body, and dignity; property; privacy; travel to and out of Israel; liberty from imprisonment, arrest, extradition, or impairment of liberty "in any other way"; and freedom of occupation). The sort of normativity ascribed to human dignity in Israeli constitutional law led to a broad interpretation of human dignity in the Israeli Basic Law: Dignity and Liberty expressing fully the value of human dignity. On this interpretation, human dignity reflects man's humanity. It extends to, and precludes impairment of, the rights to equality, freedom of speech, and freedom of religion, as well as various social rights as long as those rights—which are progeny of the right to human dignity—reflect the human aspect of man.

With this distinction between the constitutional value of human dignity and the constitutional right to human dignity as its background, the great importance of Erin Daly's book becomes plainly evident. Now that the comparative law regarding human dignity has been set before us—both United States and Canadian case law, in which human dignity is a constitutional value rather than a constitutional right, and the case law of Germany, South Africa, Colombia, Peru, and Israel, in which human dignity is both a constitutional value and a constitutional right—we can examine the concept of human dignity. We can consider its links to other human rights, and we can

come to understand, through the approach to human dignity, the role of the
state and the interrelationship between human dignity and democracy. Erin
Daly's book treats all these matters comprehensively and clearly, making an
important and original contribution. It is my hope that in the wake of this
book, and on the basis of the intellectual platform it affords, we will be able to
pursue a comparative legal- constitutional discourse that will clarify human
dignity as a constitutional value and a constitutional right, determining its
scope and defining its limits.

Introduction

Most central of all human rights is the right to dignity. It is the source from which all other human rights are derived. Dignity unites the other human rights into a whole.

—Aharon Barak

Dignity is . . . the whole law in a nutshell. . . . Study it from every aspect, for everything is in it.

—Supreme Court of Israel

The meaning of human dignity needs no further definition.

—Hans Carl Nipperdey

Humanity talks to itself about itself, it judges itself, it invents the questions and answers, it alone worries about human dignity. There is no appeal beyond itself. But the discussion must go on because there are certain questions that must be answered, and can only be answered by reference to the idea of human dignity.

—George Kateb

Until the late twentieth century, there was no right to dignity. Dignity was an idea, a quality, something to aspire to, or something associated with high office or status. But it was not a right that law recognized. All that changed in the aftermath of the Second World War. Dignity is now recognized as a right in most of the world's constitutions, and hardly a new constitution is adopted without its explicit recognition. In the world's constitutions, it appears in many different guises: sometimes it is a stand-alone value of foundational stature; in other instances it is associated with particular interests (property, protection against medical experimentation) or with particular sectors of the population (women, workers, older people, or people with disabilities).

This book tells the story of how dignity evolved, over the last half century, from an inchoate idea to an enforceable right variously recognized through-out the world. This is not an argument for (or against) the right to dignity, but an investigation into the scope and significance of the right as it has de-veloped in the global constitutional jurisprudence of recent decades. Thus it is not a philosophical inquiry into the meaning of human dignity but asks instead what dignity means when it is rendered in law, and specifically in constitutional law. What does dignity mean *as a right*? The meaning or con-tent of dignity that is ultimately developed here goes only as far as the con-stitutional texts and judicial opinions will take us, and no further. Nor is this a traditional country-by-country analysis of comparative law; indeed, there is often as much variation within each country's jurisprudence as among the courts, which mitigates the value of making country- or court- or even cul-ture-specific generalizations. Rather, this book explores cases from around the globe to try to discern common themes.

If the right to dignity were simply window dressing, like so many pre-ambles, courts would be inclined to ignore it, knowing that it could not determine the outcome of any particular case that demands decision. But dignity has turned out to be one of the *least* ignored provisions in modern constitutional law. It has been invoked, interpreted, and applied by courts around the world in thousands of cases in the last few decades. Where it is written amply into a constitutional text (as in Germany, South Africa, and Colombia), it is given full force; where it is written narrowly (as in Israel and India), it is often emphasized as a fundamental or general value; and where it is written not at all, it is often inferred (as in Canada and, to some extent, the United States).

In fact, however modern human rights are conceived and categorized, courts have held that dignity is relevant throughout. If we associate rights with the principles of the French Revolution, dignity is implicated in cases dealing with liberty (such as in abortion cases and cases about sentencing), equality (discrimination, affirmative action), and fraternity (in cases dealing with reputation and civic responsibilities). If we think of rights in terms of generations, dignity has been determinative in cases dealing with first genera-tion civil and political rights (voting, expression, equality), second generation economic and social rights (housing, medical care, employment, pensions), and third generation solidarity rights (environmental, cultural rights).[1] So, if we think in the bifurcated terms of international human rights law, dignity is as relevant to civil and political rights as to socioeconomic rights.[2] And, as often happens with prominent constitutional concepts, as it becomes entrenched in a nation's developing constitutional law, its roots are spreading deeper into civic discourse. Still, this is an ongoing story: while some courts have developed a robust jurisprudence of dignity, others are just beginning to discern its vague contours and to give content and meaning to its form.

Why have constitution drafters and interpreters come to rely so heavily on the right to human dignity? Why, particularly given that in almost all cases the right is superfluous? Cases can be brought and decided under other enumerated rights, such as the right to life, the right to privacy, equality rights, the right to health or social security, the right against cruel or inhumane punishment, and so on. And yet, courts choose to focus on the right to dignity. But what is this right? What work is dignity doing in all these cases? These are the questions that animate this book.

One might argue that law has always been about promoting human dignity. Law establishes order and secures freedoms, both of which contribute to the enhancement of human dignity. But in the past, dignity has always played what David Luban has called "a cameo role,"[3] and if it was promoted through the development of law, it was no more than an unintended by-product. Now, dignity has come to the fore in both national and international realms. In some nations, constitutional law's very purpose is to promote human dignity; the success of the constitutional enterprise might legitimately be measured by the degree to which human dignity is enhanced. In Peru, the constitution affirms that respecting dignity is the "supreme purpose" of the state.[4] In other countries, courts have privileged dignity over all other constitutional rights.

With all this attention to dignity in legal circles, it is not surprising to see a backlash: has dignity become too exalted or elastic to be effective? Has it become too common to be meaningful? Are we expecting more out of dignity than it can deliver? Some argue that judicial reliance on dignity is a sign of intellectual laziness. Dignity's very plasticity has made it, in Ronald Dworkin's words, "debased by flabby overuse."[5] Because dignity has no "concrete meaning or consistent way of being defined," Man Yee Karen Lee has written, judges are led to "introduce their own moral standards amid competing claims of rights each of which has a plausible case of human dignity violation. The elusive nature of human dignity spells even greater challenges when it is evaluated across cultures."[6] Stéphanie Hennette-Vauchez warns against the current "infatuation" with the right to dignity.[7] And Susanne Baer has written that although "dignity surfaces all over the judicial globe . . . the concept seems to be functionalized rather than filled with independent content."[8]

So the questions begin to mount. Does the term have independent content? Does it mean the same thing in different factual contexts? Or is it simply an empty vessel into which peoples and courts have put their aspirations and hopes for human betterment?

Comparativism brings with it its own set of challenges, and dignity's parentage in international human rights law adds yet another layer of complexity to the analytic project. We should be wary of "lumping" together meanings of dignity that have evolved in dramatically divergent social, historical, and jurisprudential contexts.[9] We should not equate the concept of *Menschenwürde* as it is understood in German constitutional law with *la dignidad humana* as Colombians or Mexicans conceive of it. Nor should we succumb to the temptation to think that all the drafters of the Universal Declaration of Human Rights, or of the many international treaties since then that refer to human dignity, had a single concept in mind. But the comparativist project does not require finding identity. It is a welcome reality that regional variations persist, as domestic constitutional courts fashion an understanding of dignity that is useful and relevant to their particular constitutional and sociopolitical culture, whether or not it is identical to or shares common features with the understanding of dignity adopted in a neighboring country or a country a world away. Rice is found in diets throughout the world, and yet, in each culinary tradition, it is different: it looks different, it has different qualities, and it is used differently; in some places it is a staple, in others a luxury; in some countries it is a breakfast food and elsewhere a dessert; Vietnamese rice pancakes hardly resemble Costa Rican *gallo pinto*; they were developed for different reasons and serve different purposes. The interesting point is that it is fundamentally the same raw material transformed by each country's culinary culture. In the same way, dignity is fundamentally the same idea throughout the world—there is an identifiable emerging consensus that dignity is the bedrock value of human rights in any constitutional regime. Yet, in each court's hands, it is transformed by each country's constitutional culture, to produce a distinctive value suited to each society's needs. In Latin America, where the struggle for democracy has been building for centuries, it is about building a strong enough base on which democracy can stand to resist assaults, domestic or foreign. In Germany, where the postwar constitution spawned postwar jurisprudence, dignity makes the individual strong enough to withstand the threats of tyrannical powers that would dehumanize and deracinate him or her. In South Africa, it is the ever "widening gyre"[10] of the promise of self-fulfillment, where the fundamental evil of the apartheid state was to limit and control the possibility of self-realization. In India, whose democracy is relatively stable and whose threats are not existential, dignity is about grappling with irrepressible, pervasive, and deep poverty. In Israel, dignity is critical to keeping the balance between a democratic and free society on the one hand and the security needs of a state under constant existential threat on the other. Far from meaning all things to all people, dignity has a meaning that is particular to the history and present challenges of each culture. It is the "flip side of 'never again,'"[11] the customized magic weapon conjured to combat whatever demons are in each country's closet.

While there is no single understanding of what dignity means in all circumstances, the cases reveal that courts interpreting the concept of dignity and applying it to concrete factual situations have developed a sense of the word that is coherent and substantive, and not merely a product of each judge's idiosyncratic moral standards. Dignity, it appears, is no more amorphous or subject to interpretive personal whim than any other constitutional provision: there are situations to which it applies and situations to which it does not. The cases demonstrate that the right to dignity has content and boundaries. It means *something*, but not everything. And what it does mean is important. This book is an attempt to identify and explore the independent content with which the judicial globe has filled dignity.

In the pages that follow, I investigate two questions about this global jurisprudential phenomenon: what is it, and what work is it doing? The first question considers the cases like so many pieces of an unfamiliar puzzle and asks whether there are similarities and connections among the pieces from which we might begin to discern a pattern. In other words, is there any coherence to this cacophony of dignity chatter that courts around the world are engaging in? Although some have suggested that there is none—that dignity means different things to different jurists in different countries and has no substantive meaning[12]—my analysis indicates that there are, in fact, motifs that cut across geographic boundaries, factual settings, and legal categories. This is not to say that there is uniformity or even cohesion across or even within jurisdictions. There is no agreed-on working definition of dignity that the courts invoke, nor are there customs and usages of the trade that cabin discretion or direct when a court should or should not invoke or vindicate dignity rights. There has not been time for those customs to develop, though perhaps dignity's meaning will coalesce in the years ahead. In the meantime, although some patterns are discernible, dignity rights remain multifarious and include interests associated with equality, expression, due process, privacy, health,

family, work, and virtually every other sphere of life. Likewise, the language
the courts use to describe why dignity is important or what dignity secures
is diverse and scattered and at times may seem incongruous if not mutually
unintelligible. For instance, while some courts emphasize the importance of
each person's uniqueness, others think of dignity in terms of its equalizing
nature; while some courts think of dignity as a right that entitles the bearer to
goods, other courts view it as a protection against government over-reaching,
or even an obligation imposed on the dignity holder toward other people.
The cases do not create a uniform picture of dignity, and this book does not
attempt to impose order where there is none; at the end of the day, one can
not speak of *a right* to dignity, but of many *dignity rights*. The most that can be
fairly said is that some patterns emerge from the aggregation of cases, regardless of jurisdiction or legal tradition, and that these themes tell us something
important about the nature of dignity rights. What follows, then, is not a taxonomy of the cases or of the types of rights encountered, for such a catalog
would suggest a false sense of order and would not necessarily illuminate
the underlying value of dignity in contemporary constitutional law. Nor do I
present a comprehensive summary of dignity cases—with thousands already
decided and hundreds more decided every year, such a project would be almost impossible. Rather, the book focuses on the themes that emerge from
the cases and suggests what we might learn from this assemblage.

The second question—what work dignity is doing in modern constitutional law—is by necessity more hypothetical. It is clear that courts find dignity rights to be relevant even in cases where they are not necessary for the
disposition of the case. This is evident from the number of cases that involve
claims grounded in other provisions of a nation's constitution, such as the
right to work or the right to life, but where a court nonetheless rules on the
basis of or with emphatic reference to the right to dignity. This is true both
where the right to dignity is itself actionable, as in Germany and many Latin
American countries, and where it is not, as in India and Canada. It is also
striking how often the dignity claim is vindicated: when dignity is raised,
courts are very often sympathetic. And this is true even where courts might
otherwise be reluctant to get involved: courts often desist from finding violations of the right to health, for instance, if they would have to order wide-
ranging changes in health policy with broad financial implications, but where
the claim is converted into a violation of the right to dignity, courts are likely
to intervene on the claimant's behalf. And this becomes important as courts
are increasingly asked to vindicate second, third, and fourth generation rights,

which, although enumerated in constitutions around the world, are not easily amenable to judicial implementation. Alleged violations of a right to health or housing or to a clean environment often result in judicial demurrals, but allegations that the deprivation of health or housing or a clean environment violates the right to dignity often meet with greater success. It is as if the right to dignity implicitly converts a case involving social justice into one involving individual rights warranting primarily negative remedies, which is where many judicial traditions are more comfortable. In this way, courts use dignity to help define when a broader right has been violated: a right to housing becomes actionable when the denial of housing impairs the claimant's dignity.

Moreover, close analysis of the cases suggests that the judicial use of the concept of human dignity is strategic: courts are *choosing* to invoke human dignity in order to say something about deeper constitutional values and about the evolving nature of society. They are using the right to dignity to describe what human beings are entitled to just by virtue of being human; that is, the right to dignity is coming to describe what it means to be human in the modern world. And because courts are engaging in this discourse not in a philosophy classroom but in the context of real cases involving actual people asserting serious rights against the state, recourse to dignity is also describing the boundaries of state power: if the right to human dignity means that a person's bodily integrity must be protected, the state's power to torture or punish a person is to that extent limited. In the aggregate, this growing worldwide body of dignity jurisprudence is describing the relationship between the individual and the state in modern times, in a way that is simultaneously normative and descriptive: What are human beings entitled to? What must a state guarantee to the people? What must it refrain from imposing? The *right* to dignity is how we describe what legal claims people can assert to insist that their humanity be recognized.

It is possible, moreover, that this global phenomenon of dignity jurisprudence may have a broader sociological and political value as well. If, through the construct of the right to dignity, courts are empowering people to insist that their humanity be recognized, it may well be that the awareness that people have (whether individually or collectively) of their status vis-à-vis the state may evolve. This change may be gradual or fitful, sometimes perceptible and sometimes not. But one way or another, it seems likely that as the rhetoric and ideology of dignity seep into the public mind-set through the cases, people's relationship to the state will change. In particular, in nations with fledgling democracies, this evolving political self-awareness is likely to contribute to a more robust democratic praxis. Indeed, many of the judicial opinions explicitly recognize, if not foster, the correspondence between dignity and democracy, particularly in nations where democracy continues to be a work in progress, as in Latin American countries, South Africa, and India.

We begin, as lawyers must, with the texts. Chapter 1 sets the stage by exploring how dignity found its way into so many of the world's constitutions. In the chapters that follow, I analyze representative and distinctive cases interpreting those texts, and elucidate certain themes that emerge. The most prominent of these is the idea that dignity reflects and protects the part of each person that is individual and that entitles one to set one's own life course. This idea of individuation can be seen in cases ranging from abortion to burial, from mundane issues relating to the height of public service windows to core issues of personal identity relating to the choice of names, to cultural rights, and so on. The range of cases in which this aspect of dignity is recognized is stunning, and Chapter 2 provides a sampling of how courts think about it. The ability to set one's own life course, while central to the jurisprudential notion of dignity, may be compromised for those who depend on others to satisfy core needs. Chapter 3 takes up this variation in the cases, where courts seek to define the dignity of those who are not independent, whether as a matter of fact (such as in situations of extreme penury) or of law (such as where individuals live in custody in penal or other sorts of institutions). While these two chapters illustrate the substantive coherence of dignity jurisprudence across jurisdictions, it is worth noting that the United States is, as is often the case, an outlier. The United States Supreme Court has had an altogether different relationship with the constitutional idea of dignity: while there is no shortage of cases that mention dignity, the majority has concerned not human, but institutional and inchoate, dignity. Only recently has the U.S. Supreme Court seriously begun to entertain the notion that human dignity may be of value to American constitutionalism. These cases, then, merit their own chapter, but not only because the trajectory of the cases deviates so noticeably from the rest of the world's dignity jurisprudence. While at first glance, the deviation may seem to be simply a detour, the cases may shed light on dignity as we have to come to recognize it in the rest of the world. In particular, the U.S. Supreme Court's recent attention to the dignity of states may well be related to the notions of agency and tells us something important about the relationship between autonomy and dignity.

Once we are familiar with the case law and have come to see some of the underlying themes that permeate this body of law, we can start to see what

work dignity is doing in the cases and in modern constitutionalism generally. At the level of the individual, as Chapter 5 reveals, the judicial focus
on agency as the justification for and purpose of protecting human dignity
begins to paint a picture of the courts' perception of what it means to be
human in modern times: we see, for instance, that to constitutional courts
to be a human being is to have agency, to be able to and want to make decisions about one's own life, to own one's reproductive and private life, and to
live in community with others on a basis of equal respect. These are a few of
the values that are promoted when courts protect the right to dignity, regardless of the factual setting of the case. The question we are left with, then, is
whether any of this global juridical "infatuation" with dignity is in fact having
any effect. Is it changing society? At the societal level, one prominent effect
dignity jurisprudence might be having is its contribution to the consolidation
of democratic practices and institutions. The many ways in which human
dignity can help democracy take root in a nation are explored through the
cases in the last chapter of the book.

1

"Of All Members of the Human Family"

The term "dignity" is not new. It is referred to throughout the Corpus Juris Civilis as a synonym for rank or high office and is often qualified by "patrician," "prætorian," "consular," and so on, and so usually pertains to an office and to those who hold or are worthy of such office.[1] Even this ancient text, however, refers to the "dignity of mankind,"[2] although in the context of trying to reconcile the human with the property status of slaves.

The English Bill of Rights of 1689 recognizes only "royal dignity."[3] By the time of the Enlightenment, dignity was extended, but only to the noble class: Enlightenment-era constitutional references to dignity include the 1789 French Declaration of the Rights of Man and of the Citizen, which referred to dignity as pertaining to offices, as well as the Polish-Lithuanian Constitution of 1791, which acknowledged "the dignity of the noble estate."[4] In 1879, the Constitution of the Kingdom of Bulgaria referred to dignity only to confirm the hereditary nature of the royal line.[5] These invocations reflect the concept of *dignitas*, which confirmed social stratification, reserving the benefits of dignity to a privileged few. They describe dignity as a status, a way of being; they conjure the value of high office by suggesting the privileges that pertain to it. These privileges have always involved some obligations to which commoners were not subject, such that one could be prosecuted for violating the dignity of one's own office. But they also often involved immunities or exemptions, such that dignity meant being outside, or above, the law. Rarely was dignity used *offensively* against another, except in cases of defamation where someone would be sued for denigrating a noble's dignity (whether truthfully or not). But it was never used as a claim of rights against the state.

The modern concept of dignity departs from this model in profoundly important ways. First, it applies to *all* persons and not just an elite few.

Second, it functions as an equalizer: if everyone has dignity, then everyone is subject to the same obligations and is entitled to the same benefits under the law. Third, as rendered in constitutions and enforced by constitutional courts, it is a *right* that can be and often is asserted against the state or others and enforced by a court.

The first hints of a change came in several unrelated constitutions in the early twentieth century that acknowledged dignity either as a right or as a value. Mexico's 1917 constitution established that "[Education in each state] shall contribute to better human relationships, not only with the elements which it contributes toward strengthening and at the same time inculcating, together with respect for the dignity of the person and the integrity of the family, the conviction of the general interest of society, but also by the care which it devotes to the ideals of brotherhood and equality of rights of all men, avoiding privileges of race, creed, class, sex, or persons."[6] In 1922, Latvia's constitution affirmed that "The State shall protect human honour and dignity," further explaining in the same provision that "Torture or other cruel or degrading treatment of human beings is prohibited. No one shall be subjected to inhuman or degrading punishment."[7] Ecuador's 1929 constitution more emphatically presaged the modern understanding of dignity by confirming that "The State will protect, especially for the worker and the farmer, and will legislate so that the principles of justice will be realized in the sphere of economic life, assuring for all a minimum standard of well being, compatible with human dignity."[8] This reflects the aspect of dignity recognized in the Weimar Constitution of 1919, which also associated dignity with the right to a "decent" standard of living.[9] Ireland's constitution from 1937 likewise associated dignity not with the nobility but with the average person: "And seeking to promote the common good, with due observance of Prudence, Justice and Charity, so that the dignity and freedom of the individual may be assured, true social order attained, the unity of our country restored, and concord established with other nations."[10] Already we can see the range of understandings of dignity that will mark the contemporary paradigm. In Ireland, its importance is as an inherent attribute of the individual; in Latvia, it is a bulwark against degrading treatment. In Mexico, by contrast, its significance is not for safeguarding human freedom but for enriching personal and social relationships, while in Ecuador and Germany it is associated not with a high or noble quality of life, but with an adequate one to which everyone can reasonably aspire.

Although there are differences of opinion about the cause of the cavalcade of constitutional dignity rights after World War II, there is no denying that the phenomenon occurred. Nor is there really any question that the United Nations Charter and, especially, the 1948 Universal Declaration of Human Rights (UDHR) inspired the postwar constitution drafters. In 1945, the charter members of the United Nations declared human dignity to be an article of faith, determining "to reaffirm faith in fundamental human rights, in the dignity and worth of the human person."[11] Here, dignity stands as a synecdoche for the advancement of human rights. Following on the heels of the UN Charter, the UDHR became the first international statement of rights to recognize the "inherent dignity" of "all members of the human family."[12] The Declaration also specifically insists that certain "economic, social and cultural rights" are "indispensable" for the dignity and free development of the personality of each person[13] and that remuneration must be paid to each worker to ensure "an existence worthy of human dignity."[14] The conventional wisdom is that dignity was chosen for two somewhat conflicting reasons: although it so cogently encapsulates rejection of the inhumanity of the preceding world wars, its appeal lies in its very amorphousness. Its core meaning—we should "never again" allow the decimation of populations or treat people as the Nazis did—is tiny, but it is universally appealing. Beyond that, it seems to mean whatever its beholder would like it to see in it.

And yet, thin though it might be, the core meaning may have more significance than at first appears. Why must we not treat people as mere things? Why must we recognize each person's importance? As philosopher George Kateb has argued, human dignity connotes the fact that human beings are different from, and more special than, any other creatures in the universe: "the human species," he writes, "is indeed something special, [in] that it possesses valuable, commendable uniqueness or distinctiveness that is unlike the uniqueness of any other species. It has higher dignity than all other species, or a qualitatively different dignity from all of them. The higher dignity is theoretically founded on humanity's partial discontinuity with nature. Humanity is not only natural, whereas all other species are only natural."[15] Uniquely among species, we are part nature, and part more-than-nature, having the capacity of agency, the ability to create and control our world to a degree that far exceeds that of any other creature on earth (or elsewhere, as far as we know).

In categorically recognizing the "inherent dignity" of each member of the human family, the UDHR, too, takes this species-ist approach, which reflects the specialness of humanity and of each member of the human race just by virtue of being born human. Article 1 begins: "All human beings are born

free and equal in dignity and rights." The important point here is that not
only are humans endowed with dignity, but each is endowed with an equal
quantum of dignity, as if it were a special coin that is handed out to each
person at birth. This, of course, would constitute a dramatic departure from
the previous centuries' understanding of *dignitas*, which embodied a rigid
system of hierarchies according to which persons holding certain offices or
born into certain classes enjoyed a status that accorded them certain dignities
and immunities that the vast mass of humanity did not enjoy.[16] In the modern
conception of dignity, each baby born has the same coin, which is carried
throughout life and which can neither be traded nor lost through folly nor
compounded through wise investment. The Preamble and this part of Article
1 take humanity as a species, without differentiating among individual speci-
mens. Some of us are better reasoners than others, and some of us are more
morally sensitive than others, but the UDHR is indiscriminate: each of us,
just by virtue of having been born human, is endowed with human dignity.

George Kateb's explanation for human dignity is reflected in the UDHR in
other ways as well. Article I relies on the fact that human beings "are endowed
with reason and conscience and should act towards one another in a spirit
of brotherhood." Both parts of this phrase are illuminating. The first clause
indicates that for the drafters of the UDHR, like Kateb, human dignity is compelled by our unique capacity to reason, though the UDHR goes farther in
grounding it as well on the fact of human conscientiousness. That we have the
capacity to make decisions, and to understand the morality of our decisions,
makes us different and special. The second part of the sentence imposes a
moral obligation on each of us to recognize the dignity—the specialness—of
each other person. Human dignity is not just a descriptor; it is precatory. The
UDHR assertion that we are all "equal in dignity" simply by virtue of being
born human established a new moral paradigm, which, at a minimum, requires that each of us treats every other with a modicum of respect.

That we have the capacity to reason and the consciousness to reason
about ourselves means that we can plan and try to control our lives, that we
can and do develop hopes and aspirations for ourselves and for our progeny.
It also means that we may seek to develop our personalities and to fulfill our
potential (and those of our children), as no other animal can.

If the internationalization of the idea of dignity constitutes a dramatic
turning point in our understanding of the concept, from one that signaled
rank and confirmed social hierarchy to one that affirms the equality of
all, then the story of modern dignity begins in earnest with the Universal

Declaration.[17] Some, however, see more continuity between the older conception of dignity and the newer; these scholars argue that the modern conception of dignity simply reflects the evolution of the concept that people are important by expanding the group to which dignity applies until it includes all persons.[18] Still others argue that the ancient and modern conceptions of dignity are linked in that both treat the person as a member of group, defined by rank; the modern concept simply defines all of humanity as the relevant rank.[19] Stéphanie Hennette-Vauchez argues that "significant elements of the legal concept of dignity as rank still find their way in contemporary jurisprudence and that these account for its dignitarian trends, defined as those [that rest] on the construction of 'humanity' as a new rank."[20] Paolo Carozza provides an alternative interpretation. He suggests that the Universal Declaration's contribution was to affirm something that was there all along: people have been abused throughout history not because they did not have human dignity, but because their dignity was not acknowledged. The Universal Declaration, and the documents that followed in its wake, changed our awareness, even our knowledge, of each person's human dignity. And once we know it, we can never un-know it.[21]

Whatever the best interpretation, the UDHR's blunt affirmation of the dignity of all has had enormous cultural influence in all regions of the world, even though it did not—because it has no binding effect—transform dignity into a right. In the subsequent decades, the two International Covenants took dignity several steps closer, both by adding content and specificity to the value of dignity and by binding signatory states to its provisions. Under both the International Covenant for Civil and Political Rights (ICCPR) and the International Covenant on Economic, Social and Cultural Rights (ICESCR), the state parties, considering the above-quoted language from the Universal Declaration, recognize that "the equal and inalienable rights of all members of the human family . . . derive from the inherent dignity of the human person."[22] The ICCPR also protects the dignity of those deprived of their liberty,[23] while the ICESCR says that "education shall be directed to the full development of the human personality and the sense of its dignity, and shall strengthen the respect for human rights and fundamental freedoms."[24] Under the covenants, state parties further agree that education shall enable all persons to participate effectively in a free society, promote understanding, tolerance, and friendship among all nations and all racial, ethnic, and religious groups, and further the activities of the United Nations for the maintenance of peace. In addition, other conventions currently in effect protect the dignity of certain segments of society, and, from time to time, these have been enforced or given effect in the domestic courts of signatory countries.[25] Domestic constitutional courts regularly incorporate this international conception of dignity into their own jurisprudence, as either hard or soft law.[26]

But national constitutionalism has gone much farther in bringing the value of dignity from the international sphere (where it may or may not be enforceable or culturally relevant) to the domestic realm by referencing dignity—repeatedly and emphatically—in constitutional texts and by vigorous judicial enforcement of these provisions. Presently, more than one hundred constitutions mention dignity at least once, and most of those refer to it multiple times, sometimes as a right, sometimes as a value, sometimes in ways that make it hard to distinguish between the two.[27] One way or another, almost every constitution of the twenty-first century explicitly recognizes human dignity. This is perhaps the Universal Declaration's greatest legacy: the importation of the idea of human dignity into constitutional cultures around the world has created a legal basis for protection against discrimination and degradation and has helped to ensure that all peoples have access to adequate education, food, medical care, and other basic necessities.

What follows is a survey of some of these texts, to illustrate two perhaps competing points. First, we can say with some confidence that there is now global consensus on the importance of human dignity as it applies to *all* persons. Second, notwithstanding the international convergence on this point, there is enormous diversity in how constitutions reflect and protect dignity rights. A third point is also worth noting at the outset: while some constitutions protect dignity as a right and others as a constitutional value, the line between the two categories is often blurred both in the texts themselves and, as will be seen in later chapters, in the interpretation of the texts by the constitutional courts charged with breathing life into them.

The Value of Dignity

Some constitutions do not go much farther than international law, explicitly linking the *domestic* right to dignity to its international counterpart. The Spanish constitution, for instance, says that "The dignity of the person, the inviolable rights which are inherent, the free development of the personality, the respect for the law and for the rights of others are the foundation of political order and social peace." It goes on to say that "Provisions relating to the fundamental rights and liberties recognized by the Constitution shall be construed in conformity with the Universal Declaration of Human Rights and international treaties and agreements thereon ratified by Spain."[28]

But in most of the world, the domestic constitutional *right* to dignity has gone far beyond its international progenitor. As it has grown in importance, it has gradually become the standard against which we measure our rights in relation to each other and our governments. And its significance beyond other rights has become clear not only from the jurisprudence but from the constitutional texts themselves, as one after another charter has frankly asserted that the state was *founded* on the principle of human dignity. Brazil's 1988 constitution establishes in Article 1 that Brazil is "founded on sovereignty; citizenship; the dignity of the human person," among other things.[29] Likewise, the 1996 South African constitution establishes that the reinvented republic "is one, sovereign, democratic state founded on . . . Human dignity, the achievement of equality and the advancement of human rights and freedoms."[30] Similar language appears in the constitution of the twenty-first century nation of East Timor: "The Democratic Republic of East Timor is a democratic, sovereign, independent and unitary State based on the rule of law, the will of the people and the respect for the dignity of the human person."[31]

While not founding the state on the principle of dignity, other constitutions still make dignity the central value of a new constitutional order. Germany's 1949 constitution was one of the first to prominently feature human dignity, in Article 1 of the Basic Law: "Human dignity shall be inviolable. To respect and protect it shall be the duty of all state authority."[32] But this provision has always meant even more than meets the eye. According to Christoph Möllers, "the commitment to human dignity, to be reviewable by the Federal Constitutional Court, was uncontested. Additionally, it was clear that this guarantee was not open to any form of balancing test. It was the right that could 'trump' all other rights. Finally, the guarantee of human dignity could not be reached by any amendment procedure. Being the first and unamendable norm, human dignity was more than a norm and expressed the spirit of the whole Grundgesetz in a nutshell."[33]

The right to dignity can predominate over other constitutional rights and values when it is imbued with extra-ordinary qualities. In Germany, as elsewhere, the right to dignity is unamendable or eternal.[34] In Russia, it is non-derogable,[35] in Poland, inalienable,[36] and in many countries it is inviolable.[37] One other way to protect the inviolability of human dignity is to prohibit laws that do not respect it. So, for instance, Papua New Guinea's constitution permits derogation of other constitutional rights but only "to the extent that the law is reasonably justifiable in a democratic society having a proper respect for the rights and dignity of mankind."[38] Similar language is used in the constitutions of Tuvalu, South Africa, and elsewhere.[39]

When dignity is viewed in this way, other constitutional provisions must be read in light of it. The German constitutional court has referred to the "paramount constitutional value of human dignity," which represents "the highest legal values within the constitutional order. The state has the duty to respect and to protect the dignity of human beings."[40] In Hungary under the 1989 amendments, "It is specifically emphasized by the Constitutional Court that the right to life and human dignity—ranked at the top in the hierarchy of constitutional fundamental rights—has, from the very beginning, been emphasized in the decisions of the Constitutional Court. The right to human dignity is "another phrase for the 'general personality right,'" which itself is a "mother right."[41] Hungary's 2011 constitution permits judicial review of certain classes of cases only if the complaints expressly allege violations of the right to human dignity or life.

By contrast, Israel has rejected this view, in judicial language that is both practical and aspirational:

> The rights of a person to his dignity, his liberty and his property are not absolute rights. They are relative rights. They may be restricted in order to uphold the rights of others, or the goals of society. Indeed, human rights are not the rights of a person on a desert island. They are the rights of a person as a part of society. . . . Indeed, human rights and the restriction thereof derive from a common source, which concerns the right of a person in a democracy.[42]

This approach mandates balancing dignity against other social and political values. Similarly, Ghana's constitution not only protects the right to dignity but authorizes the Supreme Court to protect additional, nonenumerated fundamental rights that are "considered to be inherent in a democracy and intended to secure the freedom and dignity of man."[41] This construct follows the pattern of Canada's and other countries' constitutions but makes explicit that the meaning of an open and democratic society is based in part on dignity. Throughout these texts, one sees the lines that used to separate rights from constitutional values blur and dissipate. Dignity is often both a background principle that informs constitutional interpretation across the board, and a right that is judicially enforceable in a definable set of circumstances.

Even in Germany, where the commitment to the value of dignity is paramount, Christoph Möllers argues that it was not the product of the realization of a universal truth, but rather "turns out to be something quite political and particular. Even the universalism of the United Nations seems to be the result of a particular political decision in a specific international situation."[44] It is, he says (invoking Carlo Schmid), "the constitutive self-concept of a political community."[45] In Germany in particular, it was an incident of "democratic nationalism, inspired by the French republican tradition," and, as elsewhere, it "was not laid down into the German constitution because it was self-evident but because it had not been self-evident in the past."[46] While some see the modern turn to dignity as the ineluctable evolution of human progress, others see it as the result of particular political and historical contingencies. But how can it be both? If dignity signifies our essential humanity, then it seems justified that the right should take on normative value; it can truly function as a bulwark against majoritarianism in all its manifestations. However, as dignity's meaning swells, as it approaches the status of a truism, then it becomes superfluous in constitutions. Möllers quotes Peter Lerche as "defin[ing dignity] while elegantly abandoning it: As a good that is to be protected unreservedly, human dignity can only preserve its shape if it's fixed in the rather narrow area where the consent of the legal subjects arises naturally, a protected area which naturally has to be protected, which would have to be protected unreservedly even if Article 1 did not explicitly exist."[47] As more and more people agree on the meaning of dignity, it becomes less and less useful as a legal right. On the other hand, as the meaning of dignity fragments and becomes particularized, as it does in constitutions, then it no longer represents the sum of humanity but looks like any other right, to be applied as warranted by adjudicative facts and usually balanced against competing social and individual needs. That constitution drafters from all parts of the world have found it useful, but useful in different ways, and that courts in many countries find it indispensable in limiting the powers of the state but do so in different factual and legal contexts, suggest that dignity is not recognized as a universal truism, but as a concept with particular legal and political—if not also moral—ballast.

The truth is that in contemporary constitutionalism dignity is at once a universal value and a contextualized right. And this creates a tension that neither the constitutional texts nor the judicial interpretations have so far resolved. Any effort to find a single, unifying theory of dignity will ultimately be frustrated by the vast range of unconnected instances of its use, although, in the aggregate, it does appear that it has significance that is greater than the sum of its parts. The best way to harmonize the universal and the particular is to suggest that dignity is how we describe the essence of what it means to be human, but that the *right* to dignity is how we describe what legal claims people can assert to insist that their humanity be recognized. The texts and the cases use the second to elucidate the first.

Dignity's Particularities

Perhaps as evidence of human dignity's political particularism, constitutional texts are increasingly elaborating on its meaning, giving it, in each country, a unique coloring that befits the history and cultural values of each constitution's time and place. The 2010 Constitution of the Kyrgyz Republic, for instance, refers to dignity five times, in addition to mentioning the dignity of the presidency. Dignity is listed both as a responsibility of each citizen to "respect the rights, freedoms, honour and dignity of other people" and as a right of each person. It appears both as a general right ("Dignity of an individual in the Kyrgyz Republic shall be absolute and inviolable") and then in conjunction with more specific interests ("dignity, freedom of private life, personal and family secrecy," the guarantee against "infringement of one's honour and dignity," and the right to defense of "dignity and rights in trial").[48] Kenya's 2010 constitution is even more emphatic in its protection of dignity. It states that "The national values and principles of governance include" dignity, among other things.[49] But it goes on to say that "The purpose of recognising and protecting human rights and fundamental freedoms is to preserve the dignity of individuals and communities and to promote social justice and the realisation of the potential of all human beings"[50] and that "In interpreting the Bill of Rights, a court . . . shall promote the values that underlie an open and democratic society based on human dignity, equality, equity and freedom,"[51] and, finally, that rights can be limited "only to the extent that the limitation is reasonable and justifiable in an open and democratic society based on human dignity, equality and freedom."[52]

Belgium's constitution is unusual in its definition of the concept. The first section of Article 23—"Everyone has the right to lead a life in conformity with human dignity"[53]—asserts dignity as a general value, as is common in many constitutions. But the article then elucidates the term "dignity" by requiring the Regional Councils to guarantee certain rights "and determine the conditions for exercising them" (and taking into account corresponding obligations).[54] These economic, social, and cultural rights "include notably"

1) the right to employment and to the free choice of a professional activity in the framework of a general employment policy, aimed among others at ensuring a level of employment that is as stable and high as possible, the right to fair terms of employment and to fair remuneration, as well as the right to information, consultation and collective negotiation;
2) the right to social security, to health care and to social, medical, and legal aid;
3) the right to have decent accommodation;
4) the right to enjoy the protection of a healthy environment;
5) the right to enjoy cultural and social fulfillment.[55]

The Basic Law of Israel concerning liberty and human dignity takes a different approach, defining dignity largely in terms of property and privacy interests,[56] though through the recognition of the constitutional value of dignity, the Supreme Court has filled this tiny vessel with significantly more meaning.

Entitlement to dignity is also defined differently in different countries, but almost every country has absorbed the lesson of the UDHR that dignity applies to "every member of the human family." As a result, constitutions increasingly emphasize that "human dignity" is shared equally by every person,[57] and in many countries specific segments of the population are singled out as particularly deserving of dignity, contrary to historical practice. Uganda's constitution recognizes the dignity of individuals who are disabled,[58] Indonesia's that of the weak and underprivileged,[59] Sudan's that of those with special needs and the elderly.[60] In many countries' constitutions, including for instance those as diverse as Fiji and Albania, the dignity of persons who are detained is especially recognized.[61] In India, dignity is linked specifically to women and to children,[62] but it is also mentioned in the preamble of the constitution as an aspect of fraternity: "We, the People of India, having solemnly resolved to . . . secure to all its citizens . . . Fraternity assuring the dignity of the individual and the unity and integrity of the Nation."[63] Sudan, the state is also obligated to "combat harmful customs and traditions which undermine the dignity and the status of women."[64]

Other constitutions, while not explicitly defining what dignity entails, nonetheless give it content by adjoining it to other rights. Sister clauses in the same section may state or imply what aspects of human dignity are most relevant. For instance, prohibition of torture or cruel or degrading treatment is commonly linked to dignity, as in Macedonia: "The human right to physical and moral dignity is irrevocable. Any form of torture, or inhuman or humiliating conduct or punishment, is prohibited."[65] Finland's constitution goes farther and prohibits deportation or extradition of a foreigner "if in consequence he or she is in danger of a death sentence, torture or other treatment violating human dignity."[66] In Portugal, as elsewhere, dignity is linked to equality: "Every citizen shall possess the same social dignity and shall be equal before the law."[67] Many constitutions echo Thailand's protection of "family rights, dignity, reputation and the right of privacy."[68]

And in many countries the right to dignity is the benchmark for rights to basic necessities, such as food, shelter, and health care. For example, the Greek constitution encourages economic development but not "at the expense of freedom and human dignity."[69] Similarly, the Serbian constitution establishes that "Citizens and families that require welfare for the purpose of overcoming social and existential difficulties and creating conditions to provide subsistence, shall have the right to social protection the provision of which is based on social justice, humanity and respect of human dignity."[70] The Thai constitution also guarantees that any "person who is over sixty years of age and has insufficient income for . . . living shall have the right to receive such welfare and public facilities as suitable for his or her dignity as well as appropriate aids to be provided by the State."[71]

Some invocations of dignity are unusual or unique. In Jamaica, "all persons in Jamaica are entitled to preserve for themselves and future generations the fundamental rights and freedoms to which they are entitled by virtue of their inherent dignity as persons and as citizens of a free and democratic society."[72] In Tanzania, dignity is linked to work: "Work alone creates the material wealth in society, and is the source of the well-being of the people and the measure of human dignity."[73] Paraguay's constitution establishes that "Military service must be based on full respect of human dignity."[74] In the Andorran constitution, education is linked to dignity: "All persons have the right to education, which shall be oriented towards the dignity and full development of the human personality, thus strengthening the respect for freedom and the fundamental rights."[75] And in Mozambique, "Motherhood and fatherhood shall be afforded dignity and protection."[76] In addition to a general clause protecting human dignity, the Swiss constitution protects dignity in three separate provisions dealing with medical and genetic research, the use of reproductive and genetic material "from animals, plants and other organisms," and, in this last context, recognizes "the dignity of living beings" (as distinct from just human beings).[77]

Even where dignity is not defined in the constitutional texts (or where it is narrowly defined), courts have often taken it on themselves to give it meaning according to their best interpretive lights. For many courts, for instance, dignity is allied with the right to life. For example, the High Court of Hong Kong has held that "Even an offender, however reprehensible his crime, is entitled to respect for his life and dignity as a human being."[78] In India, the Court has held that the constitutional right to life and liberty enshrines the right to dignity (which would otherwise not be enforceable).[79] In Hungary, freedom of association has been allied with the constitutional right to dignity,[80] though in the 2011 constitution dignity is explicitly linked to fetal life (as well as to adequate working conditions). It is also the basis of human existence.[81]

These linkages help give content to an otherwise amorphous and potentially boundless concept.[82] In constitutional texts, dignity may appear abstract and general, referring to what is inherent in each member of the human family, regardless of nationality or ethnicity. Where it is linked in the constitutional texts to other rights or values, it is more concrete, more culturally contingent, and defined by the politics and social influences of a particular time and place. But regardless of how dignity manifests itself in the texts, courts have embraced the challenge of turning the concept of dignity into an enforceable right.

Interpretation and Enforcement

As Sam Moyne reminds us, human rights did not start out as claims against the state, but rather as a part of the very definition of a state. Human rights defined who the citizens of the state were, thereby creating the state and circumscribing its jurisdictional (not territorial) boundaries. "This profound relationship between the annunciation of rights and the fast-moving 'contagion of sovereignty' of the [nineteenth century] cannot be left out of the history of rights: indeed it is the central feature of that history until very recently." As originally conceived, human rights were what made the citizen, and citizens were what made states sovereign; the only available remedy for the violation of a right so conceived "remained democratic action up to and including another revolution."[83] This bears repeating precisely because it is so contrary to the contemporary notion of human rights, including especially the right to dignity.

When, in the postwar years, dignity found its way into so many of the world's constitutions, it did so in conjunction with the establishment of judicial review and, with that, the modern conception of rights as enforceable through the judicial machinery of the state, even—or principally—as against the state. This shift, along with dignity's contingent particularism in the constitutional texts, marks the complete transformation in our understanding of rights from one that signified citizenship for the purpose of conferring and affirming state sovereignty to its present use as a nonviolent weapon to be asserted individually or collectively to limit state sovereignty. As Chapter 6 shows, the strong bond between dignity and citizenship continues to this day, though its form has evolved as constitutional jurists have sought to reshape it.

In the hands of judges, these rights-driven limitations on state sovereignty can involve a range of enforcement mechanisms, including both positive and negative obligations on the government or on private individuals or groups. In South Africa, not only is dignity a cornerstone of the post-apartheid constitutional order, but "Everyone has . . . the right to have their dignity respected and protected."[84] Indonesia's constitution obligates the state to protect those most in need of support: "(1) Impoverished persons and abandoned children are to be taken care of by the state. (2) The state develops a social security system for everybody and empowers the weak and underprivileged in society in accordance with their dignity as human beings."[85] The Philippine constitution does much the same in these terms: "The Congress shall give highest priority to the enactment of measures that protect and enhance the right of all the people to human dignity, reduce social, economic, and political inequalities, and remove cultural inequities by equitably diffusing wealth and political power for the common good."[86] In the Maldives, the state's obligation to treat people with dignity is explicitly imposed on members of the security services, who are required to "treat all persons and groups equally without any discrimination, and with humanity and dignity in accordance with the decorous principles of Islam."[87] In Peru, perhaps most emphatically of all, protection of dignity is "the supreme purpose of society and the state."[88] This is a remarkable assertion whose significance is difficult to overstate: whereas people have throughout history been made citizens for the purpose of defining and securing state sovereignty, this new conception creates the state *for the purpose of* protecting citizens precisely because they are endowed with human dignity.

Dignity, like constitutions generally, reflects both rights and values; in any given constitution, dignity may be one or the other or both, or it may be impossible to discern which the drafters envisioned. Dignity's dual nature certainly contributes to its appeal. As a value, it may not be read narrowly or technically nor may it be ignored, and it should inform the interpretation of other incidents of constitutionalism. The value of dignity acknowledges the uniquely human qualities that distinguish us as a species from all others. It privileges our capacity to think and plan, and to care for one another. As a right, it uses these attributes to assert claims against the state. That is why it is viewed as a stand-in for all rights: whether in the context of discrimination or torture or social security, the recognition of human dignity means that the state must—in all its dealings with individuals—respect what is special about the human person. The rights may be thought of as the particular manifestations of the general principle or value. The values, conversely, can best be discerned from the cases defining the right.

Dignity is so amorphous, and potentially unbounded, and its application potentially so broad, that courts wishing to give effect to the constitutional text must work hard to find its true meaning. Nonetheless, courts have engaged in this project with enthusiasm. In thousands of cases, courts have shaped the meaning of human dignity and made it relevant to people around the globe. In the aggregate, these cases show convincingly that the idea of human dignity has, in the last sixty years, turned into a legal right—or many legal rights—that courts will enforce and that governments are bound to respect.

2

"Not . . . a Mere Plaything"

From sparse textual foundations, the constitutional courts of many countries have developed a robust jurisprudence of dignity. Dignity has become, in the words of one jurist, a "most fashionable concept."[1] The cases arise out of an astonishing range of factual settings, from abortion to name changes to housing to torture. They are so numerous and so frequent that they are impossible to keep up with and defy easy description.

The Colombian Constitutional Court has tried to schematize the concept of dignity, noting that the phrase "human dignity" can manifest itself in two ways: from the point of view of the concrete object of protection and from the point of view of its normative function, echoing dignity's dual nature as a right and as a value. With respect to the first perspective, the Court has identified three clear and distinct lines: human dignity can be understood (1) as autonomy or the possibility of designing a life plan and self-determining according to his or her own desires; (2) as entailing certain concrete material conditions of life; and (3) as the intangible value of physical and moral integrity. As shorthand, the court characterizes these three dimensions respectively as living as one wishes, living well, and living without humiliation.[2]

These correspond roughly to the categories of cases described throughout this chapter and the next. First, we consider the most conceptually intriguing cases, the related concepts of autonomy—the ability to make decisions for oneself—and what might be called the individuation principle—the idea that the unique dignity of each member of the human family must be respected. Another set of cases deals with the more mundane but jurisprudentially interesting questions of what quality of life is necessary for people to live with dignity, and how courts can define and enforce those standards. Specifically, what role do courts play in ensuring that individuals have sufficient access to water, food, shelter, medical care, education, and other basic necessities to maintain their dignity? In both these categories, dignity entails some aspect of self-sufficiency while the third group of cases addresses this conundrum: how can a person maintain his or her dignity when the state exerts some form of extraordinary control over him or her, whether as a result of custody such as incarceration, or otherwise? Or, in an alternative formulation, how far can states go in diminishing the dignity of those over whom they exercise control? We consider the first set of cases in this chapter, and the second and third sets in the next.

"To live as one wishes"

The individuation principle starts from the premise of the inherent dignity of each member of the human family, as recognized in the UDHR. The notion that this *philosophical* axiom could be appropriated in a declaration of *legal* rights was potentially revolutionary insofar as it suggested the possibility that states could be obligated to respect it. Its subsequent incorporation into legally enforceable *constitutions* across the globe added one more turn: it meant that the right had to be given some content, namely by courts. Where judicial review exists—and it does increasingly throughout the world—courts would have to decide whether a specific challenged governmental action effectuated a deprivation of an individual's dignity, in some meaningful sense of the word.

Claimants in these cases tend to allege either that the state has failed to respect their individuality or that it has failed to give them the equal treatment they are due. In approaching the question, courts have understood the philosophical ideal of human dignity to have four components, each of which is relevant in different ways to the constitutionalization of dignity. First, each individual has inherent value; second, each individual's value is unique; third, each individual's value is the same as every other person's; and fourth, each individual's equivalent but unique value entails some measure of self-control. These are distinct attributes, though they are undoubtedly related. In a German case about a national security measure, the Constitutional Court saw that human dignity requires each person "to be recognised in society as a member with equal rights and with a value of his or her own," while at the same time, it is "part of the nature of human beings to exercise self-determination in freedom and to freely develop themselves."[3] In recognizing these attributes of dignity, courts have had to wrestle with many difficult and often competing conceptual challenges, not the least of which is defining what the right to dignity actually means, as it is rendered in law.[4]

Courts have differed in their approaches. Some courts are content to give a purposive account, such as this elaboration in an Indian case about the right to travel. Speaking of the enforceable rights in the constitution, the court said: "These fundamental rights represent the basic values cherished by the people of this country since the Vedic times and they are calculated to protect the dignity of the individual and create conditions in which every human being can develop his personality to the fullest extent. They weave a 'pattern of guarantees on the basic structure of human rights' and impose negative obligations on the State not to encroach on individual liberty in its various dimensions."[5]

Others, like the Hungarian Constitutional Court under the 1989 constitution, try to define dignity through a generic understanding of personhood. That court called dignity a "general personality right" and provided these instances (among others): the right to develop one's personality freely, the right to self-determination, the general freedom of action, or the right to privacy, and the right to self-determination pertaining to information.[6] In particular, the court has held that "the right to human dignity includes both the constitutional fundamental right to freedom of self-determination and the fundamental right to one's physical integrity."[7] The location of dignity within the general personality right means that the right to dignity is a sort of catch-all; it can serve "as the constitutional basis of protecting the personality in each case when the Constitution does not provide for a specifically named right."[8] As we will see, the Hungarian court applied this principle on numerous occasions.

The German Constitutional Court has eschewed any effort to determine the content of the right "once and for all," saying that it cannot be definitely determined "in concrete terms."[9] Instead, it simply denotes that "Article 1.1 of the Basic Law protects the individual human being not only against humiliation, branding, persecution, outlawing and similar actions by third parties or by the state itself."

Most courts have declined to define dignity in its entirety; rather, they tend to focus on the particular qualities of dignity that appear most relevant for the particular case. One such quality borrows from the UDHR and addresses the immanence of dignity in each member of the human family.

Immanence and the Law

The Hungarian Constitutional Court has been most articulate about this. In one of its earliest rulings, invalidating capital punishment, the court equated human dignity with "human essence."[10] And in a case about the selection of names, the Hungarian court said that "Dignity is a quality coterminous with human existence, a quality which is indivisible and cannot be limited."[11] It is, as the Universal Declaration says, "inherent" in "all members of the human family" such that there is a "unity of human life and dignity."[12]

One justice of the Hungarian court further explained that the constitution protects dignity as a determining factor of human status because it is the individual's *subjective* experience that brings dignity to life: "Human dignity and human life are inviolable of anyone who is a human being, irrespective of physical and intellectual development and condition and irrespective of the extent of fulfillment of the human potential and the cause therefor. We cannot even talk of a human being's right to life without positing that person's individual subjective right to life and dignity."[13]

In Germany, dignity is even more basic, not attached to the fulfillment of human potential, but to the very fact of existence. "Unborn human life—and not just human life after birth or an established personality—is accorded human dignity," which the state is obligated to affirmatively protect.[14] Under German law, "Wherever human life exists, it should be accorded human dignity."[15] This is also the sense in which the 2011 Hungarian constitution protects in the same article the inviolability of human dignity and the life of a fetus from the point of conception.[16]

The German court takes pains to emphasize that this conception of human existence is secular and not religious or ideological, echoing the tone and orientation of the Universal Declaration.[17] By contrast, many of the peoples of the Caribbean have rooted their conception of dignity firmly in belief in a creator. The people of Saint Lucia, according to their constitution, "believe that all persons have been endowed equally by God with inalienable rights and dignity" and "realize that human dignity requires respect for spiritual values,"[18] while the people of Grenada "firmly believe in the dignity of human values and that all men are endowed by the Creator with equal and inalienable rights, reason, and conscience; that rights and duties are correlatives in every social and political activity of man; and that while rights exalt individual freedom, duties express the dignity of that freedom."[19] The Israeli conception of dignity is based on that nation's status as a Jewish state: As the

Israeli court has explained, "The basis for the supreme principle of human dignity is that man was created in the image of G-d, and by virtue of this perspective, *he* too is commanded to protect his dignity, since an affront to his dignity is an affront to the image of G-d, and every person is commanded *in this regard*, even a person who dishonours himself."[20]

Whether religious or secular, dignity's immanence presents a jurisprudential challenge. The more the courts emphasize the inherent nature of dignity in human beings, the more friction there can be between the idea of dignity and the idea of law. The very conception of dignity as innate and immanent in the human being appears to be antithetical to the idea of law. While dignity is ineffable, law (and especially constitutional law) needs to be articulated and defined in clear terms. Dignity is personal and subjective, whereas law is objective and the same throughout. Dignity is unique to the individual, but law regulates collectivities and treats similarly situated people similarly. Dignity is personal, but law is public. If dignity is innate in the human being, it is descriptive of what is, whereas law is normative.

If the concept of dignity is not only opposite to but *resistant* to law, then it is difficult to see how law—even constitutional law—can regulate dignity. Can there be a "right" to what is a condition of nature? Can the right be enforced or compelled? How can constitutional law enhance or diminish a person's dignity if it is inherent, equal, indivisible? If it is inviolable, as so many constitutions say, how can courts find violations? Or is dignity impervious to law, existing in the given amounts, regardless of what law does or does not do?

Some court cases ignore this tension, apparently happy to embrace dignity both as an ineffable state of being and as a positive right. Other cases have tried to reconcile the two aspects, by walling off separate spheres for dignity and law. Reminiscent of the U.S. Supreme Court's efforts to protect a "zone of privacy" from government regulation,[21] these cases delineate a realm of personal space into which the government may not intrude, relegating the remainder to the public sphere of the law. In a case about the right to choose a name, the Hungarian court found that "the natural existence of personality is independent from the State," and thus name use could not be regulated; it was impossible for the state (as an "external party") to determine "the legal enforceability and the essential content" of the right pertaining to names. (Somewhat paradoxically, the court digressed with a historical review of the evolution of the use of names from originally identifying clans and regional ancestry to indicating individuals, as a concomitant of the bourgeois state, thereby casting doubt on the claim that use of a name to identify an individual is exo-statist.) But the idea of dignity as independent of the state remains important in Hungary because it prohibits state intrusion into the "untouchable essence"—the "zone of privacy" or "basically free sphere"—of the human personality.[22] Likewise, in a case involving the right to travel, the Indian Supreme Court said that "It cannot be disputed that there must exist a basically free sphere for man, resulting from the nature and dignity of the human being as the bearer of the highest spiritual and moral values. This basic freedom of the human being is expressed at various levels and is reflected in various basic rights. Freedom to go abroad is one of such rights, for the nature of man as a free agent necessarily involves free movement on his part."[23]

Given the ubiquity in legal texts not just of the concept of dignity but of the *right to* dignity in recent years, it seems that the time when law and dignity simply ignored each other, as they had for most of human history, is over. In one way or another, most courts must confront the relationship between dignity and law. But once they begin to notice each other, what happens? Does the very notion of dignity threaten the hegemony of law? Or does the ever-expanding reach of the law threaten primordial human dignity? Or can they sit side by side, like two restless children on a park bench, enduring or provoking occasional skirmishes over the boundary lines, but basically leaving each other intact? Or, perhaps, do they have not an antagonistic relationship, but rather an interdependent obligation to nurture one another to their mutual benefit? The answers to these questions depend in large part on how courts, in the context of specific cases, characterize the multiple qualities of individual dignity, beyond its basic inherence in human existence.

At the very least, the idea of immanence may suggest limits on state power at the boundaries. The state may not injure what is so important to people—because it is the essence of our humanity—nor may it diminish its value or impose conditions on its enjoyment. The state does not grant or confer it, nor can it take it away. Moreover, just as the law can be called on to protect the environment outside human beings, it can be expected to protect and nurture what is inside. The fact that dignity is a quality that inheres in every individual does not mean that it is indifferent to or unaffected by law.

Individuation

A second attribute of dignity that many courts have recognized is that each person's dignity makes him or her unique in the world. Dignity thus serves to individuate us, entitling each of us to resist majoritarian norms. The early Hungarian court in particular dwelled on the uniqueness of each individual person that is ensured by his or her innate dignity. In one case, the court held that rights relating to names are components of the fundamental right to dignity, though it distinguished between the right to have or bear a name and the right to choose, change, or amend a name. The former is inviolable because "One's own name is one of the—fundamental—determinants of personal identity, serving the purpose of identification and distinction from others, thus it is one of the manifestations of one's individuality and unique character which cannot be substituted for."[24] Names are important because they serve to distinguish one individual from another. Hence, the state could no more require all citizens to bear the same name than they could require the use of a number or a symbol. The individuation principle thus creates a protective bubble around the individual in which the state may not regulate—may, literally, not "reg"-ulate—that is, the state may not make everyone conform to a rule.

The right to *select* or change a name, however, is normally not associated with dignity, so the state can impose reasonable restrictions on the choice of names (limiting choices to within a specified list) and on the ability to change a name. However, where the change of names is "directly related to human dignity"—such as where the name one wants to change is unworthy or obscene, or where the family name invokes "painful memories" (e.g., if the name is associated with a notorious criminal or has become "ill-famed in the course of history"), or where the family names sound "repulsive or ridiculous or . . . give ground for ambiguous or offensive puns"—the state must allow the change of names because to restrict the choice would diminish the individual's dignity vis-à-vis others (sometimes referred to as the public face of dignity).

But the individuation explanation has its limits: it is unlikely that the government could prevent the use of a name on the ground that it was already being used (the particular case of property interests in celebrity names aside). In other words, while there is a right to express one's unique personality through the use of a name, that right is not exclusive of another's right to express his or her uniqueness through the use of the same name. In this view, the autonomy aspect of dignity (i.e., the right to choose) may prevail over the uniqueness aspect (the right to have a unique name), should the two come into conflict.

In an extreme version of the uniqueness question, the German Constitutional Court has considered whether "branding"—which occurred in both senses of the word in a case about an advertisement for the clothing company Benetton—implicates dignity interests. In the ad, models appeared to have been "branded"—quite literally stamped with words in order to promote the Benetton brand name. The court acknowledged that this commodification of persons can threaten individual dignity, and allowed the government some leeway in trying to counteract desensitization concerning discrimination "against persons who are afflicted by suffering and the emergence of a mentality of 'branding' people." The court further explained that "This especially applies to younger people who look at this advertisement, as they do not necessarily draw a comparison to past manifestations of the exclusion of persons from society."[25] Ultimately, though, the court found that freedom of expression interests outweighed the putative interests in protecting against being branded.

Indeed, perhaps the greatest protections of individual uniqueness are found in constitutional provisions that protect freedom of conscience, whether in speech or religion or otherwise, as the paragon of individuality. In countless cases from around the world, courts have linked matters of conscience with human dignity whether or not their constitutions required them to do so. To provide just a very few examples, in Italy, the Constitutional Court has invalidated a civil oath that included a reference to God, on the ground that it violated the freedom of conscience that is an essential part of human dignity.[26] In Israel, the right to conscientiously object to military service has been protected as a dignity right.[27] In these cases, the individual's dignity is protected even when he or she stands alone, precisely because dignity is inherent in "each member" of the human family, regardless of how others act. One's dignity demands that his or her choice to worship God be respected while another's dignity demands that his or her choice to worship no God be protected. The quality of uniqueness, then, insists that matters relating to one's dignity can be governed only by the self and resist regulation and regularization by the state. This is the aspect of dignity that mandates recognition of same-sex marriage: part of human dignity ensures that each individual's unique personal choices are respected whether or not those choices are consistent with majoritarian values. Same-sex marriage is not appropriate for all, but must be protected for those for whom it is appropriate.

In these cases, we begin to see the conflation of dignity and equality. Dignity demands that we respect each person's individuality, but in so doing, it also requires that we treat each person the same: to recognize the dignitarian interests of some but not others denigrates both the equality and the dignity interests of the latter. This presents a paradox that is evidenced in the cases: if dignity demands that each person's uniqueness be respected, then how can all persons be equal and without distinction before the law?

Equality

It is striking how often the concepts dignity and equality are conjoined in both constitutional texts and constitutional jurisprudence.[28] Indeed, the UDHR implies a convergence of dignity and equality ("All human beings are born free and equal in dignity and rights"), and this implication seems to have resonated in constitutional law throughout the world. The Italian constitution is typical: Article 3 states that "All citizens have equal social dignity and are equal before the law, without distinction of sex, race, language, religion, political opinion, personal and social conditions."[29] The connection between dignity and equality, however, is not always obvious: sometimes dignity is held to incorporate equality, at other times equality is held to incorporate dignity.

Courts have devoted much ink to the relationship between these two concepts, which in the aggregate yields the principle that human dignity is held distinctly, yet in common, by each person on earth. Judge Hartmann, then of the Court of First Instance of the High Court of Hong Kong elaborated on the implicit presence of dignity throughout Hong Kong's Basic Law in a case concerning the criminalization of homosexual activity: "As to the Basic Law, in its protection of a wide range of rights, I see it as contemplating an open and essentially democratic society, one based on equality of all persons before the law and on the dignity of the individual, by which I mean all persons—in their sameness and difference—being worthy of respect."[30]

Somehow, the ideas of equality and dignity must embody both the sameness and the difference of members of the human family. Perhaps it is the one way in which all human beings are identical: each has the same quantum of uniqueness, deserving of equal measure of respect. Dignity simultaneously unites and individuates us.[31]

In contemporary constitutional law, equality appears in two guises: first, in the context of discrimination, when courts consider whether a particular measure unconstitutionally discriminates against a portion of the population; second, in the context of affirmative action, when courts consider whether a measure designed to remedy past discrimination nonetheless violates a constitutional equality principle. Although in both situations the government is treating people differently based on some usually immutable characteristic, most courts (outside the United States) would invalidate the first but uphold the second. What justifies the different results? The distinction between the two may be seen in a deeper investigation of the concept of dignity.

Invidious Discrimination

Equality jurisprudence implicates dignity because rank discrimination violates dignity: judging someone or conferring benefits and burdens on the basis of some general category (race, caste, religion, gender, sexual orientation) to which a person belongs both limits his or her ability to define him- or herself and constricts his or her individuation by treating him or her solely as a member of a class. At its worse, it entails humiliation and degradation, which can (as the U.S. Supreme Court said in *Brown v. Board of Education*) affect hearts and minds in a way unlikely ever to be undone. Indeed, racism, U.S. Supreme Court Justice Murphy wrote at the end of World War II, "renders impotent the ideal of the dignity of the human personality, destroying something of what is noble in our way of life."[32] For some, unconstitutional discrimination is defined by the humiliation that results from the differential treatment. Justice Dorner of the Israeli Supreme Court has been more particular in her assessment of the relationship between inequality and indignity. "The perception of inferiority, which is based on the biological or racial difference, causes discrimination, and the discrimination strengthens the deprecating stereotypes of the inferiority of the victim of discrimination. Therefore the main element in discrimination because of sex, race or the like is the degradation of the victim. My opinion is therefore that the Basic Law protects against a violation of the principle of equality when the violation causes degradation, i.e., an insult to the dignity of a human being as a human being."[33]

For others, it is not humiliation that marks a dignity-based violation of equality rights, but generalization. That is, the injury is in the failure to treat the person as an individual, particularly when combined with a burden. In Canada, the Supreme Court has held that the central concern of the equality guarantee is "combatting discrimination, defined in terms of perpetuating disadvantage and stereotyping." However, after almost a decade of experimentation, however, in which the court invalidated laws that classified on the basis of disability, handicap, citizenship, gender (with regard to identification on a birth certificate), imprisonment, the right to organize, sexual orientation, and residency,[34] the Canadian court expressly repudiated the practice of defining discrimination by way of dignity because "human dignity is an abstract and subjective notion that . . . cannot only become confusing and difficult to apply; it has also proven to be an *additional* burden on equality claimants, rather than the philosophical enhancement it was intended to be."[35] In Canada, the promotion of human dignity continues to be the "lodestar" of the protection of all rights guaranteed in the Charter of Human Rights, but it is no longer the defining test of discrimination.

The new dispensation in South Africa, Justice Albie Sachs said hopefully, is "characterised by respect for human dignity for all human beings. In this era, prejudice and stereotyping have no place."[36] For Justice Sachs, it is the very presence of the insult to dignity that renders the inequality invidious: "Differential treatment in itself does not necessarily violate the dignity of those affected. It is when separation implies repudiation, connotes distaste or inferiority and perpetuates a caste-like status that it becomes constitutionally invidious."[37] In the context of discrimination on the basis of sexual orientation, he explained the connection between equality and dignity in these terms:

> At the heart of equality jurisprudence is the rescuing of people from a caste-like status and putting an end to their being treated as lesser human beings because they belong to a particular group. The indignity and subordinate status may flow from institutionally imposed exclusion from the mainstream of society or else from powerlessness within the mainstream. . . . To penalise people for being what they are is profoundly disrespectful of the human personality and violatory of equality.[38]

Thus the South African Constitution envisions that a violation of human dignity may be actionable both under the protection of human dignity in Article 10 and under the equality guarantee insofar as both are concerned with the feeling of degradation that results from unjustified differences in treatment.

In still other cases, indignity results not from the feeling of lesser worth, but from the objective limitation on choices that is imposed on some but not others. When the Israeli government allowed Yeshiva students to defer their military service, while not giving the same opportunity to other Israeli citizens, the court found that the law violated both dignity and equality. "The violation of human dignity," the court said, "is in the deeply upsetting feeling that another person is not obliged to perform such service to the same extent."[39]

Some countries have tried to define constitutional inequality as the deprivation of dignity. In Hungary, a claimed violation of equality is actionable only if the action is unreasonable, violates a fundamental right, or violates human dignity.[40] The question in every case, then, is whether dignity demands, permits, or prohibits the government from taking a particular individual difference into account. In Colombia, the court held that service windows in public buildings that are all the same height and designed to suit most people violate the right to dignity of dwarfs, who may not be able to use them.[41] Holding that the government may vary a fine depending on the financial situation of the defendant, the Constitutional Court of the Czech Republic explained: "In the settled case law of the Constitutional Court, equality under Art. 1 of the Charter is not understood in the abstract, but in relation to the dignity and rights of an individual, that is, without privileges, and without discrimination (e.g. in property)."[42] Governments are permitted or may be required to recognize individual differences where doing so would enhance individual dignity, for instance, by assuring access to public services. On the other hand, where recognizing differences (on the basis of race, gender, etc.) would demean the individual, the government may be prohibited from doing so. The principle is not defined by a preference for equality or individuality in the abstract; it depends on whether the action is in the service of or in derogation of individual dignity.

Affirmative Action

Affirmative action adds another layer of complexity. After some years of equivocation, the U.S. Supreme Court finally concluded that affirmative action—that is, discrimination for the purpose of remedying past injustice—is no less pernicious than invidious discrimination because in both cases people are treated not as individuals but on the basis of group identity.[43] It is, perhaps, no accident that a court that declines to consider the impact of laws on human dignity and that embraces formal equality considers all classifications to be equally pernicious; abstraction has always been a hallmark of American constitutional jurisprudence. Most other modern countries, however, accept affirmative action precisely because of the net gain in human dignity. And far from dismissing affirmative action as merely reverse discrimination, many constitutions impose on the government affirmative obligations to remedy past discrimination.[44]

In India, for instance, the Supreme Court has held that affirmative action is not only permitted, but constitutionally required to promote the dignity interests of the constitution. "The aim of the Constitution is to equip each member of the weaker sections with the ability to compete with other citizens with dignity on a level playing field."[45] Thus, "Parliament is entrusted with the responsibility of improving the lot of backward classes by creating a reservation policy that is consistent with the objective of promoting fraternity among all citizens, assuring the dignity of the individual and unity of the Nation."[46] Where it is a constitutional truth that rank discrimination disparages human dignity and that remedial measures promote it, the legal questions concern only the details: exactly what percentage points should be allocated to the disadvantaged class? How should disadvantage be defined? And so on. But there is no question that distinguishing on the basis of immutable characteristics in ways that enhance rather than erode human fulfillment is a constitutional value.

Full Development of the Personality

These three attributes of human dignity that courts repeatedly recognize—that dignity is inherent or immanent in each person and in no way conditional and that dignity marks both each person's uniqueness and our common humanity—are the building blocks of an understanding of the human experience that coalesces around each person's capacity to develop his or her personality: each person has the same inherent right as every other to control the course of his or her own life. Hence, the Colombian court's shorthand for these cases as protecting the human desire "to live as one wishes." This includes some measure of control over both what a person becomes and does; although these are not the same, they are closely allied in reality and often conflated in the cases.

The Indian Supreme Court has said that the aim and objective of that nation's struggle for liberation was "to build a new social order where man will not be *a mere plaything* in the hands of the State or a few privileged persons but there will be full scope and opportunity for him to achieve the maximum development of his personality and the dignity of the individual will be fully assured."[47] This recalls U.S. Supreme Court Justice Louis Brandeis's formulation that "the final end of the state is to make men free to develop their faculties."[48] In Hungary, a purposive account of the right to dignity grounds the court's view that the two prongs of the right to dignity are the protection of physical integrity and of self-determination, which it also describes as the "freedom to make independent decisions" or the full development of the personality.[49] These cases concern all kinds of personal decisions and choices, including those relating to intimate relationships and family, choice of occupation, and how one expresses one's faith.

Many courts use the term "autonomy"—literally *self*-rule—to describe this attribute of dignity. Autonomy embraces not only the capacity to make certain decisions for oneself, but the capacity to live according to one's own dictates. Autonomy assumes that the capacity for self-regulation is inherent, since it could not logically emanate from any superior authority. And it accepts the uniqueness of each individual, in allowing each person to set the rules for him- or herself. Describing dignity in terms of these attributes of immanence, individuation, and equality, courts have buttressed people's ability to live according to their own rules, to fully develop their personalities according to their own dictates. Our human dignity entitles us to some measure of autonomy, which is necessary for the full personality development; without some degree of autonomy, our personality is developed not by our own dictates but by those of others.

In American jurisprudence, the notion of autonomy is most vivid in the Supreme Court's privacy jurisprudence, particularly in the context of abortion. As the court said in its original decision on the topic, the "right of privacy . . . is broad enough to encompass a woman's decision whether or not to terminate her pregnancy,"[50] explicitly connecting the notion of privacy to the ability to make rules for oneself. As the court's jurisprudence has matured, it has veered away from the right to "privacy" and focused more on liberty as the textual anchor for the right to make decisions relating to procreation and family. In the Supreme Court's most eloquent opinion on the subject, three justices wrote that in the context of abortion "the liberty of the woman is at stake in a sense unique to the human condition, and so, unique to the law. . . . Her suffering is too intimate and personal for the State to insist, without more, upon its own vision of the woman's role, however dominant that vision has been in the course of our history and our culture. The destiny of the woman must be shaped to a large extent on her own conception of her spiritual imperatives and her place in society."[51] This goes beyond the ability to merely make a decision for oneself; it protects the ability to determine the course of one's life. Applying this principle (rather restrictively), the only limitation the court invalidated was the requirement that the pregnant woman notify her husband of her intention to have an abortion; this was unconstitutional precisely because it would necessarily subordinate her to her husband's imperative. In remarkably similar terms, the Colombian Constitutional Court in an abortion case has invalidated "norms in which the legislature denies the minimum condition of the human being as being capable of deciding on her own course and life choice." The court explained that penalizing the decision to terminate a pregnancy is "not consistent with the doctrine of the essential nucleus of the right to the free development of the personality and autonomy as the maximum expression of human dignity."[52]

It makes more sense to rely on dignity than liberty or privacy to protect the right to choose to terminate a pregnancy. While the decision to have an abortion is very personal, it is not "private," since it is normally a commercial transaction performed in a professional office or procured in a pharmacy. It may not be done alone, nor in the privacy of one's home. Nor is "liberty" completely apposite, since abortion can in no sense be said to affect only the one person making the decision. Rather, as the South African Constitutional Court explained in the context of same-sex marriage, invoking a century-old phrase from American law, what people want is "not the right to be left alone, but the right to be acknowledged as equals and to be embraced with dignity by the law."[53] In this view, mere or formal autonomy is not enough to preserve dignity; it requires support from the state.

Indeed, outside the United States, constitutional courts that have ruled on abortion have typically contextualized it as a dignity right, as did the Hungarian court in recognizing women's "right to self-determination—as part of the right to human dignity."[54] As noted, the Colombian Constitutional Court has ruled the same way, explicitly weaving together the antiobjectification and autonomy threads: "to not be treated as an object upon which others make decisions that are transcendental in their impact on the course of a person's life, in this case the woman, is part of the right to human dignity. A decision of such high importance as whether to interrupt or continue a pregnancy, when this represents risks for the life and health of the woman, is a decision that the woman alone can make, based on her own criteria . . . since it is she who will have to live with the consequences of such a decision."[55] She must base the decision on her own "criteria," that is, according to her own rules—auto-nomy.

The Peruvian Constitutional Tribunal has been emphatic about this:

> The right to reproductive self-determination is a right implicitly contained in the more generic right to the free development of the personality. This right consists of the autonomy to decide things that pertain solely to the person. But it also is affirmed that the right to reproductive self-determination partakes of the recognition of the dignity of the human person and of the general liberty right in which it is inherent. Dignity and liberty in concrete terms start from the necessity to be able to exercise freely and without any interference the act of transcending across generations. Liberty to be able to decide rationally, with responsibility, about: 1) the appropriate moment and opportunity for reproduction; 2) the person with whom to procreate and reproduce; and 3) the form or method of reproducing or preventing it. As a result, every woman has the right to choose freely her preferred method of contraception, which is directly related to decisions relating to how many children to have, with whom, and when.[56]

The court has further held that "the right to information about contraceptive methods is one way to concretize the principle of dignity of the human person and forms part of the essential elements of a democratic society, because it enables the exercise of sexual rights in a free, conscientious, and responsible manner."[57] Nonetheless, the court found that the free distribution of the "morning after" pill to any woman who wanted it was not necessary to vindicate her very strong interest in making important decisions, and having the requisite information by which to make such decisions effectively, and insufficiently protected the life of the unborn.

Germany has likewise recognized that a woman's interest in abortion is not an aspect of her privacy, but of her self-determination, although its enthusiasm has been more temperate than that of Colombia and Peru. Following shortly on the heels of *Roe*, and presaging *Casey*, a 1975 German case held that a woman's right to terminate a pregnancy was a necessary incident of her interest in "the free development of her personality." However, a later case placed abortion not in the context of the woman's autonomy interest but in the fetal right to life, which in turn is deeply rooted in fetal dignity.[58] Thus, dignity is implicated in both decisional autonomy and the right to life. But, as one justice on the Constitutional Court pointed out, tethering the woman's right to terminate a pregnancy to self-determination while rooting "the fetal right [to life] in the dignity clause . . . predestined [the court] to give precedence to the protection of unborn life over the pregnant woman's right to self-determination."[59] Life would always win out over lifestyle. Placing the issue of abortion in the fetal right to life would also be inconsistent with the U.S. Supreme Court's formulation in *Roe* that the state's interest in protecting the unborn varies with the progression of the pregnancy. "If a human being's dignity lies in its very existence," the German court said, and if this applies to unborn life, "then we must refrain from making distinctions in the duty to protect based on age or stage of development of the unborn life or based on the willingness of the woman to allow the life to continue to live within her."[60] In Germany, where dignity is the pre-eminent right, it is immanent in human existence, and undifferentiable.

Abortion presents one of the most difficult dignity problems because the fetal interest in life can outweigh even the strong dignitary interest in self-determination and autonomy. In other cases of preeminent decisions, where there is no countervailing interest in life, courts have been sympathetic to the dignity claims of those who seek to determine their life course for themselves. The Israeli Supreme Court has held that women have a dignitary interest in maintaining a pregnancy, even over the objection of a former husband.[61] And in several countries, same-sex marriage has been protected as a fundamental incident of the right to dignity. As the South African Constitutional Court put it, "the capacity to choose to get married enhances the liberty, the autonomy and the dignity of a couple committed for life to each other."[62]

The interest in controlling one's life is also evidenced in cases that concern how one presents oneself to others. In Hungary, the right to information that was kept by the secret police during the Communist period is vindicated as a dignity interest because, again, it implicates a person's capacity to control how he or she is viewed by others.[63] This interest implicates what one commentator has called the "public face of dignity."[64] In Lithuania, public officials are discouraged from referring to a person as a criminal if he or she has not been proven guilty: "otherwise, human honour and dignity could become violated and human rights and freedoms could be undermined."[65] The Peruvian Constitutional Tribunal has recognized that "the fundamental purpose of the recognition of the right to a good reputation is the principle of human dignity," and that the "right to a good reputation . . . is in essence a right that derives from the personality and, in principle, deals with a personality right. Thus, its recognition (and the possibility of protective jurisdiction) is directly linked to the human being."[66]

The Argentine Supreme Court has weighed in more emphatically: "the right of reply is a natural fundamental right that is essential to the legitimate defense of one's dignity, honor and privacy." As the court explained, "Journalists, commentators, and newscasters should not make the life of the common man into the stuff of scandals. The individual should have control over his life, privacy, as well as honor and should have the means to maintain his reputation."[67] Likewise, there are scores of defamation cases that protect an individual's interest in his or her reputation as an aspect of human dignity.[68] Typical is the Malaysian High Court's explication: "The right to reputation is part and parcel of human dignity. And it is the fundamental right of every person within the shores of Malaysia to live with common human dignity."[69] Dignity allows us to control not only how we live, but also how we present ourselves to the world. When the state or other individuals seek to control (usually to our detriment) how we would present ourselves, they violate our human dignity. Dignity is thus both inward-looking and outward-looking: it concerns how we are and how we act, how we think of ourselves and how we present ourselves to others. It is an essential part of a person's identity from both an individual and a social standpoint. (This distinguishes dignity from liberty, which is entirely individual and indifferent to the social setting in which human beings live.)

A person's right to control how he or she lives his or her life extends to the moment of death, and in some cases, even beyond. "Death with dignity" statutes have allowed individuals to determine the circumstances under which they will die and to exert some control over their own death. In some countries, this autonomy interest is so strong that it transcends life itself and operates even *after* death. The German Constitutional Court has held that the son of a deceased man could enjoin the publication of a book about his father because publication would demean the late father's dignity. "It would be inconsistent with the constitutional mandate of the inviolability of human dignity, which underlies all basic rights, if a person could be belittled and denigrated after his death." The court concluded: "Accordingly an individual's death does not put an end to the state's duty . . . to protect him from assaults on his human dignity."[70] The Israeli Supreme Court has held that legal limitations on what can be written on a tombstone may violate the dignitary interests of both the living and the dead.[71] The obligation to recognize the dignity of people who have died is consistent with international law,[72] because one may wish to control one's public face in death, just as in life.[73]

The Canadian Supreme Court has encapsulated dignity's protection of control:

> The idea of human dignity finds expression in almost every right and freedom guaranteed in the [Canadian Charter of Rights and Freedoms]. Individuals are afforded the right to choose their own religion and their own philosophy of life, the right to choose with whom they will associate and how they will express themselves, the right to choose where they will and what occupation they will pursue. These are all examples of the basic theory underlying the *Charter*, namely that the state will respect choices made by individuals and, to the greatest extent possible, will avoid subordinating these choices to any one conception of the good life.[74]

This even includes the right to make foolish decisions: "The right knowingly to be foolish is not unimportant; the right to voluntarily assume risks is to be respected. The State has no business meddling with either. The dignity of the individual is at stake."[75] Or, as U.S. Supreme Court Justice Scalia characterized it more wispily, "the supreme human dignity of being master of one's fate."[76]

Objectification

For many courts, objectification is dignity's foil. To objectify—to use a person as an object to achieve some other purpose—denies all that is important to dignity, turning the person into a plaything. It tends to treat everyone the same: to objectify is deny a person's uniqueness. By allowing one person to exert control over another, it negates the equality principle that is at the core of the modern understanding of human dignity. And by permitting one person to impose values or decisions on another, it denies each person's ability to chart his or her own course, as it suggests that the dignity one is born with can be lost or conditioned at the election of another.

Justice England of Israel has noted that this aspect of dignity is distinctly secular, compared with traditional religious doctrines that view man's life in the service of God. "Simply put, it was a gradual transition from man as a creature to man as a person," Englard has written. As such, it is a distinctly modern concept as well, invoking Kant's categorical imperative based on the idea of human dignity: "Act in such a way that you treat humanity, both in your person and in the person of each other individual, always at the same time as an end, never as a mere means."[77] The German Constitutional Court has absorbed this Kantian maxim as a general background fact: "the obligation to respect and protect human dignity generally precludes making a human being a mere object of the state."[78] Christoph Möllers, however, has questioned the unquestioning reliance on Kant's moral philosophy, even in German constitutionalism. "It is methodically not clear," Möllers writes, "why it is Kant's and no other philosophy that is supposed to form the source of any legal doctrine of human dignity. Kant is mentioned in the Parliamentary Council, but not with greater emphasis than other authors. When interpreting a constitutional text, it is maybe best to do without a house philosopher."[79] And yet, the influence of this Kantian view is undeniable.

Though the anti-objectification principle is offered in terms of a moral aspiration, it has palpably political implications. One extreme example of the application of this principle arose when the German Constitutional Court was called on to rule on a 9/11-inspired law, the Air Transport Security Act.[80] The case concerned Section 14 of the Act which authorized the use of armed force against a passenger plane "where it must be assumed under the circumstances that the aircraft is intended to be used against human lives, and where this is the only means to avert the imminent danger." In finding that the killing of the passengers authorized by the act would violate not only their right to life, but their right to dignity as well, the court emphasized that, as victims of the hijacking, and then of the government's attempt to shoot down the plane, the passengers could "no longer influence the circumstances of their lives independently from others in a self-determined manner. . . . [They] cannot escape this state action but are helpless and defenceless in the face of it with the consequence that they are shot down in a targeted manner together with the aircraft and as result of this will be killed with near certainty." This treatment "ignores the status of the persons affected as subjects endowed with dignity and inalienable rights," and instead "By their killing being used as a means to save others, they are treated as objects." This objectification denies them "the value which is due to a human being for his or her own sake."[81] The opinion repeatedly refers to the individual's "quality" or "position" as "subject" (as distinguished from the Kantian "object"). The subject acts on the object; dignity requires that every human being with the capacity to do so is acted on only by him- or herself and not by another. As Oliver Lepsius has explained, objectification—the use of human beings for the benefit of other state objectives—"transforms persons into things and delegalizes them (*verdinglicht und zugleich entrechtlicht*)."[82]

Nor is the Kantian view of dignity limited to Germany. When the Indian Supreme Court inveighs against treating a man as a mere plaything in the hands of the state or a privileged few, it is protecting the man from objectification. In the Hungarian name change case, the court noted that "the human being remains a subject, not amenable to transformation into an instrument or object,"[83] thereby limiting the ability of the state to control the full expression of the individual personality, even for the purpose of promoting nationalism. When the courts of Latin America speak against *cosificar*—literally, "to make into a thing"—they, too, are protecting against objectification. In Colombia, the Constitutional Court held that in cases of rape, "the woman's dignity is subjugated by the force necessary to convert her into an object of he who exercises power over her. Similarly, her dignity as a human being is denied when the legislator imposes on the woman, likewise against her will, the obligation to serve as an instrument effectively to procreate by penalizing abortion without any exception. . . . In these cases, [to prohibit abortion] would be to objectify the woman as only a womb, separated from her consciousness."[84] The Malaysian High Court, too, has found that "Rape is an experience which shakes the foundations of the lives of the victims. The offence of rape must be dealt with as the gravest crime against the human dignity."[85] Perhaps emanating from the same source is the Israeli case finding that pornography violates women's dignity.[86] In none of these cases does it matter whether the objectifier (as it were) is the state or a private person; in either case, the victim's human dignity is impaired because the direction of her life is defined not by herself but by another.

The principle applies equally when there is *no* particular purpose in objectifying individuals, as is illustrated in this early case from Hungary. In 1991, the Hungarian Constitutional Court held "that the collection and processing of personal data without a specific purpose for arbitrary future use is unconstitutional" in that it offended human dignity because it subjected individuals to the control of the government. The data processor would likely "familiarize himself with the totality of, and the relationships between data pertaining to individual persons. This fact renders the persons whose data is on file entirely dependent, it permits insight into their private lives, and results in an unequal communication situation in which the affected person is unaware of what the data processor knows about him." According to the court, "All this gravely endangers the freedom to make independent decisions and constitutes a threat to human dignity. Personal numbers whose use is unrestricted may become the means for total control."[87] The problem is not only that such data mining limits individual self-determination, but that it treats people as an object in the control of another. The Hungarian cases go even farther: not only does dignity preclude the state from obtaining information about individuals; it also *requires* that individuals be able to obtain information from the state. Thus, in Hungary there is a right to information to ensure the meaningful exercise of the right to self-determination.[88] The right to information is also prevalent throughout Latin America, where many constitutions recognize a specific writ of *habeas data* to ensure that individuals' access to information is unobstructed by procedural hurdles.

But the strictness of the Kantian imperative is often softened in the context of particular factual situations that require practical solutions. Indeed, it would have to be, since every government policy objectifies people to some extent: requirements that we obtain drivers' licenses or pay taxes or send our children to school or not kill our neighbors all restrict freedom in order to achieve some social purpose. In particular, the criminal law in every country seeks to balance the nation's need to punish those who harm others against the imperative to respect each individual's human dignity. In Peru, which has explicitly adopted the Kantian imperative,[89] the principle of dignity extends to criminals; as the Constitutional Tribunal said in one case about the equality rights of prisoners, the principle of the dignity of the person, "in its negative version, insists that human beings may not be treated like things or instruments (but rather as subjects of rights and obligations) . . . since each person, including criminals, should be considered as an end in and of himself."[90] The Slovenian Constitutional Court has followed the same course, explaining that the constitutional protection of "the right to be present at his trial and to conduct his own defence or to be defended by a legal representative" exists to ensure "that the defendant is not just an object but a subject of the proceeding, that is, a person having at his disposal a wide range of possibilities for defence, which ensures full protection to his personality, his freedom and his dignity."[91] In a later case, the same court found that the constitutional guarantee of personal dignity "guarantees to every individual that in proceedings in which decisions are made concerning his or her rights, obligations, or legal interests, he or she is treated as a person and not as an object."[92]

In the context of punishment, the prohibition on objectification would preclude a state from using general deterrence as a justification for punishment; criminal punishments would have to be private to avoid using the individual's sentence as an object lesson to deter others from committing crimes. Regimes that would seem to show the least respect for human dignity—such as the United States under slavery and Jim Crow and Afghanistan under the Taliban—are those that turn punishment into public spectacle, thereby maximizing the objectification of the individual. In fact, a strong version of this argument would impugn the legitimacy of all compelled military service, in which the state puts the lives of men and women at risk, with certain death for some number, in order to pursue the political goals of the state.

At the other end of the spectrum, courts in post-apartheid South Africa and postwar Germany have taken the precept against objectification most seriously. In a landmark ruling even before the new constitution was adopted, the South African Constitutional Court invalidated the death penalty—even though neither the interim constitution nor the proposed permanent constitution explicitly did so—in large part on the basis of human dignity. The court held that the death penalty "involves, by its very nature, a denial of the executed person's humanity," which is "degrading because it strips the convicted person of all dignity and treats him or her as an object to be eliminated by the state."[93]

In Germany, the Constitutional Court has twice held that a sentence of life imprisonment with no possibility of release (parole or pardon) would implicate not only the convicted person's right to liberty, but his or her right to dignity as well: "It would be incompatible with human dignity if the convicted person, regardless of the development of his or her personality, had to abandon all hope of ever regaining liberty," explained the court in a 2005 case.[94] In both cases, the courts could have relied on more precise textual provisions (life in the death penalty case and liberty in the imprisonment case), but they chose to base their rulings on the fundamental right to dignity, as if hope were an intrinsic part of what it means to be human.

In an earlier case, from the 1970s, the German court elaborated on the importance of hope as an element of human dignity. Invoking the Kantian language against objectification, the Constitutional Court invalidated the punishment of life imprisonment without the possibility of parole. It held that "The command to respect human dignity means in particular that cruel, inhuman and degrading punishments are not permitted. The offender may not be turned into a mere object of [the state's] fight against crime under

violation of his constitutionally protected right to social worth and respect."
The court continued: "Within the community each individual must be recognized, as a matter of principle, as a member with equal rights and a value
of his own. The sentence, 'the human being must always remain an "end in
itself"' has unlimited validity in all areas of the law; for the dignity of man
as person, which can never be taken away from him, consists particularly
therein, that he remains recognized as a person who bears responsibility for
himself."[95] Insisting that man must be the "end in itself," the court braids
into its definition of human dignity the notions of equality and inalienability
drawn from the Universal Declaration—and, on the other side, of the responsibility of the individual toward the state and fellow citizens. The court
explained that "This is founded on the conception of man as a spiritual-
moral being, that has the potential to determine himself in freedom and
develop from within."[96] In the German Air Transport Security case, too, the
court noted that shooting down the hijackers would not impair their dignity, because they would have acted of their own volition, thereby subjecting
themselves to the consequences of their actions. They would have acted as
their own agents, whereas the passengers would have merely been the objects of the hijackers' plans.

Consent

This distinction raises the problem of consent that dogs the dignity cases.
If dignity protects an individual's decision regarding his or her own life
course, then what happens when he or she consents to something that would
otherwise be considered undignified, where self-fulfillment paradoxically
diminishes one's dignity? For various reasons—some honorable and under-
standable, and some less so—not all of us choose maximum dignity at all
times. When these situations arise in litigation—where courts are called on
to intervene on an individual's behalf, but somewhat against his or her will—
courts are divided precisely because the dignity needle points in opposite directions at once. Should they protect the individual's autonomy and ability
to act as a "spiritual-moral" being, or should they protect him or her against
objectification and discrimination?

Some constitutions explicitly protect autonomy, allowing citizens to consent to even some of the most extreme indignities. Armenia, for instance, prohibits subjecting any person "to medical or scientific experimentation without

his or her consent" as an incident of the right to dignity.[97] Where the constitution does not explicitly prohibit objectification, many courts have nonetheless read the right to dignity to protect against this type of infringement.

In cases involving the right to refuse medical treatment, and vaccination in particular, the Hungarian court has explained:

> the law gives a wide range of possibilities for this since it does not regulate the field and the rights to self-definition and activity . . . guarantee this possibility. The restrictive paternalism of the State is a matter of constitutional debates only in borderline cases (from the punishment of drug use to euthanasia). . . . It can be concluded on the basis of the practice of the Constitutional Court that [the right to dignity] grants a wide scale of protection for the right to self-determination of persons capable of making free, informed and responsible decisions about their own bodies and lives.[98]

Much of the current discussion in western Europe about the wearing of religious veils divides on this question: is it a woman's choice to cover her face, in which case the state should not intervene on behalf of her dignity, or is she coerced into doing so (by family or culture, which thereby objectifies her and diminishes her agency), in which case the state should intervene to protect her dignity? In a case about a woman who was not hired as a teacher because she would have worn a head scarf in class, the majority of the German Constitutional Court held that, given the woman's dignity interests in choosing how to present herself in public, the decision to suppress one alternative had to be made legislatively, and cautiously. The court considered the "image, reflected in the Basic Law, of humanity that is marked by the dignity of humans and the free development of personality in self-determination and personal responsibility." Her free choice needed to be respected, even though the choice was to cover herself. The dissent did not see how the woman's choice implicated her constitutional right and was willing to let the school authorities make the determination that the wearing of the head scarf could lead to conflict at school, particularly as the head scarf was only one step away from full face covering, which could be seen "as incompatible with the dignity of humanity: free human beings show their faces to others."[99] Once again the veil confounds the dignity paradigms. Can a person present herself publicly by obscuring herself publicly and presenting herself only privately? What should be the state's role in protecting her dignity when her culture or her religion restricts how she presents herself, or when her male relatives do?

From a dignity standpoint, these are among the hardest cases, because they seem to pit the individual's interest in self-determination against the interest in the full development of her personality. But societal ambivalence about the veil may rest in large part on the unanswerable question of whether, in general or in a given case, the choice to cover one's face is the product of the woman's free will. If it is, then the state's intervention to "protect" her seems not only paternalistic but unjustifiably circular insofar as the state would override an autonomous decision in order to "protect" her right to make autonomous decisions. However, if the choice to cover one's face results from cultural or familial oppression, then the state may well be justified in protecting her (without the quotation marks) from these undue pressures, particularly where the empowerment of women is an important constitutional and cultural value, as it may be in France. One other interpretation is that it is a bit of both: it is a rational decision, but one that is made necessary by the indignities visited on women by men. If this is the case, the state is in a true quandary: in the name of dignity and for the public interest, the state should protect women from sexual harassment, but it should not protect them from their own rational decisions to protect themselves. These cases reveal that, far from being a universal value as the internationalists would have it, dignity, *in its instantiations*, is profoundly culturally and factually contingent.

In other contexts, the prohibition against objection often outweighs the interest in self-determination when they point in different directions. This is certainly true where the "subjects" have no particular capacity for self-determination: genes, which of course can not self-determine, are nonetheless protected against objectification and commodification. "No country . . . allows patents on the human body. . . . [T]his understanding derives from the universal principle of respect for human dignity, one element of which is that humans are not commodities."[100] Likewise, children, whose capacity for self-determination is reduced, are nonetheless fully protected against objectification, as the Hungarian court made clear in holding that children do not have to submit to compulsory vaccination. "A person is entitled to the right to physical integrity," the court said, "regardless of whether he or she has decision-making capacity and whether he or she is able to exercise the right to self-determination. A person may never be regarded as an instrument to reach a public objective," even though, in general, the state has broader authority to restrict the rights of children, "since *the subjects lack the ability to make [certain] decisions.*"[101] Likewise, the Slovenian court has recognized the developing dignity of children in a case about the legal representation of children as defendants:

> In the opinion of the Constitutional Court, only such interpretation is in agreement with the UN Convention on the Rights of the Child, which in article 40 recognized the right of every child suspected, accused or found guilty of a violation of the penal code to be treated in a special way, that is, in a way in conformity with the developing of child's sense of dignity and value which fosters the child's respect for human rights and fundamental freedoms of others and which takes into consideration his age and desirable encouragement of his reintegration into society and the assuming of an active role in it.[102]

But even where the capacity for self-determination is unquestioned, courts often override the person's choice when the choice is to be objectified. Courts have held that sex shows that objectify women constitute violations of human dignity, even where the "model" has voluntarily chosen this profession, because she is used as a means to the end for business or the patron.[103] There are cases concerning the banning of dwarf-throwing competitions as a violation of the dwarfs' human dignity, notwithstanding the dwarfs' voluntary choice (given available alternatives) to engage in this profession.[104] And even where a person consents to engaging in pornography, a court may override that decision to give greater effect to some sense of objective dignity than to her exercise of her individual autonomy. In these cases, a person's agency in a matter of importance is *not* respected precisely because it does not conform to the views of the majority. Stéphanie Hennette-Vauchez writes that the European courts have tended to privilege a universalist concept of dignity—the dignity of the human race, rather than the dignity of its individual members—when people have made choices that make the rest of us uncomfortable, such as refusing medical treatment, taking occupations that seem "undignified" (such as dwarf-throwing or sex work), or engaging in sexual practices that are generally disapproved of. In all of these cases, courts have imposed on individuals the obligation to conform, rather than vindicate their own personal (even if unpopular) choices. Some cases investigate the burdensome conditions under which some of these decisions are made, noting that coercion sufficient to diminish the meaning of consent may come from a variety of sources: sometimes an individual has pressured the consenter (as in the European Court of Human Rights case of the sado-masochistic judge whose wife was put in situations beyond what she had willingly consented to), and sometimes the pressure comes from socioeconomic circumstances beyond the control of any particular individual, as when an individual takes employment that many others would prefer not to take. As Hennette-Vauchez shows, this turns the conventional understanding of dignity on its head: it gives dignity an objective significance—it becomes a standard that everyone must meet, rather than an inherent quality of being unique. It erases individuation in favor of normalization, and it enables the majority or the state to impose on the individual obligations that limit free choice, rather than justifying the individual's claim of rights against others and the state, or vindicating the exercise of his or her own free will.[105] These are among the most challenging dignity cases because they pit two or more core attributes of dignity against each other, and nothing in the principle of dignity, from the Universal Declaration on down to modern-day constitutions, provides any guidance to courts as to how to weigh the competing dignitarian interests.

Aside from the complication of waiver, the courts are remarkably consistent across the globe in recognizing the value of individual but equal human dignity as a basis for the fulfillment of human potential. Many courts, however, have also recognized that, as a practical matter, one can develop one's personality only if one has the necessary means to do so: living in deprivation and dependence can dramatically limit, if not preclude, the choices one has in charting the course of one's life. In many constitutional systems, therefore, dignity is not just the inherent quality of being a unique and autonomous human being; dignity also has material manifestations that are equally important. This aspect of dignity is discussed in the next chapter.

3

"The Minimum Necessities of Life"

Material Dignity

Law is a practical enterprise: it deals with a real problem in real people's lives. It is not enough in law to recognize the inherent dignity of every human being. That only matters if each person is in fact living a life with dignity, where his or her individuality and autonomy are valued in conjunction with everyone else's. For most of the world's people, of course, the capacity to chart one's own life course is limited by circumstances. People who are poor, who are infirm, who are dependent on others for their well-being are restricted in how effectively they can write their own rules.

At the extreme, we might think, with Christoph Möllers, that "human dignity expresses the prohibition to reduce those who have been recognized in this way to their body."[1] To reduce one to one's body—whether by torture, extreme poverty, or other degradation—is to compel a person to focus only on fulfilling his or her bodily needs. From a dignity perspective, this has several significant implications. Because we are more similar in our bodies (all having like needs for food, water, medical care, shelter, etc.) than in our minds, reducing one to one's body erodes the value of individuation that dignity seeks to protect. Extreme deprivation can also impair a person's ability to plan his or her life course. And of course, in most societies, not *everyone* is equally deprived; there are always some who are living comfortably and in control of their destinies, usually at the expense of those who live at the margins. At a social level, Möllers argues, reducing one to one's body also diminishes the "integrity of the political community."

This realization indicates the complexity of the modern understanding of human dignity. The conception of dignity that comes from the UDHR and its progeny in national constitutions is centered on the concept of immanence: the recognition of the *inherent* dignity of each member of the human family. This suggests, too, the immutability of human dignity; it attaches simply by virtue of our humanity, and it is with us from birth (or before) until death (or after). But the course of people's lives tells a different story: although each baby may have this inherent quality, many people struggle to live in conditions of dignity, to maintain their dignity throughout life. A reversal of fortune that renders a person homeless or a refugee, an arrest or detention, or inability to find work that is not exploitative may make it difficult for a person to maintain his or her dignity. This aspect of dignity may be lost or gained, perhaps many times during the course of a person's life. It is not enough to have dignity as a birthright; it is necessary, also, to *live* in dignity. Governmental authorities, including courts, must be ever vigilant to foster and preserve the conditions in which dignity thrives. As long as people live together in society, dignity requires sustenance of the social structure.

Some constitutions explicitly protect the right to sufficient means to live in dignity. Finland's constitution provides that "Those who cannot obtain the means necessary for a life of dignity have the right to receive indispensable subsistence and care."[2] Many similar provisions are said to derive from the Weimar Constitution of 1919, which established that "The organization of economic life must conform to the principles of justice to the end that all may be guaranteed a decent standard of living" or *Menschenwürdigen*, often translated as "dignity."[3] Where the constitutions are not so explicit, many courts have nonetheless developed a jurisprudence of the social welfare of human dignity. Typical is the assertion of the Constitutional Court of Hungary that "the [constitutional] right to social security . . . entails the obligation of the State to secure a minimum livelihood through all of the welfare benefits necessary for the realisation of the right to human dignity."[4]

The Material-Autonomy Continuum

Like Germany with its abortion decisions, India has linked dignity to the constitutionally protected right to life. In India, however, the right to life is not a state of being, but an agglomeration of situations and conditions to be experienced, which collectively or separately may enhance or diminish human dignity. The Indian Supreme Court has repeatedly insisted that the right to life includes the right to live with human dignity[5] *and* "all that goes along with it namely, the bare necessaries of life such as adequate nutrition, clothing and shelter over the head and facilities for reading, writing and expressing oneself in diverse forms, freely moving about and mixing and commingling with fellow human beings."[6]

More specifically, the Indian Supreme Court has said:

> It is the fundamental right of every one in this country, assured under the interpretation given to art 21 . . . to live with human dignity, free from exploitation. This right to live with human dignity enshrined in art 21 derives its life breath from [certain] Directive Principles of State Policy . . . and at the least, therefore, it must include protection of the health and strength of workers, men and women, and of the tender age of children against abuse, opportunities and facilities for children to develop in a healthy manner and in conditions of freedom and dignity, educational facilities, just and humane conditions of work and maternity relief. These are the minimum requirements which must exist in order to enable a person to live with human dignity and no State—neither the central government nor any state government—has the right to take any action which will deprive a person of the enjoyment of these basic essentials.[7]

As such, the government has an obligation to protect not only the life but also the material dignity of every person within India, whether citizen or not.[8] Similarly, the Peruvian Constitutional Tribunal has recognized that the unjustified denial of social security benefits, including pensions, "indubitably deprives a person of his right to the minimum necessities of life for his subsistence, impeding his satisfaction of basic necessities, which is a direct threat to his dignity."[9] In another case, the court explained that in a social state, respect for dignity refers essentially to the fulfillment of a better quality of life for people.[10]

In Colombia, the right to dignity is linked to housing in the constitutional text itself: "All Colombian citizens are entitled to live in dignity. The state will determine the conditions necessary to give effect to this right and will promote plans for public housing, appropriate systems of long-term financing, and community plans for the execution of these housing programs."[11] Since the constitution also protects dignity generally ("The right to dignity is guaranteed. The law will provide the manner in which it will be upheld"[12]), the court has, in scores of cases over the last couple of decades, had to decide what accouterments of life are requisite to living a dignified life, especially since, in each instance, the constitution anticipates affirmative actions by the state to promote and protect dignity, in both its individual and collective manifestations. Many of these cases have arisen when the government health service has declined certain benefits or services, and claimants have argued—and the court has often agreed—that the denial constitutes not only a deprivation of the right to health, but also of the right to live with dignity. In one case, the Colombian court held that denying disposable diapers to a woman who had become wheelchair-bound and incontinent violated her right to a dignified life;[13] in another, the court ordered reconstructive surgery following a mastectomy "for the purpose of protecting the fundamental rights to health and to life in conditions of dignity" of the patient, whose treatment was discontinued when the government refused to cover it.[14] In a third, the court ordered the government to pay not just 90 percent but the remaining 10 percent as well of the cost of supplying a girl with durable medical goods, in order to ensure that she would live a life of dignity.[15] Moreover, in several cases, the court has explained that failure to provide a prompt, effective, and comprehensive diagnosis may violate the right to health,[16] and, furthermore, that appropriate treatment be recommended even if the patient is unable to pay,[17] and transport to the medical facility to obtain the treatment be paid for.[18]

Throughout these health-related cases, the Colombian court has explained that the right to health can be judicially enforced when it is intimately linked to the right to life, integrity, and dignity. The right to health is not a right to be healthy, per se, but neither is it merely the right to "biological existence." Rather, the right to health is defined in terms of human dignity: "A human being needs to maintain appropriate levels of health, not only to survive, but also to perform adequately, such that the presence of certain conditions, even if they are not serious illnesses, can deteriorate and can threaten dignity; it is legitimate to think, then, that the patient has a right to harbor the hope of recovery and, in effect, to seek relief for her suffering and a life according to her human condition."[19] The right to health is compromised where government action diminishes people's capacity to develop those inherent human faculties in a dignified way and determine the course of their lives.[20] Given this broad interpretation of the reach of the right to dignity, it is not surprising that the court has on numerous occasions been called on to determine whether the administrators of the national health plan violated the right to dignity in denying medical treatment.[21]

In India, "Using the notion of a right to life with dignity, judges expanded the ambit of health to include physical, social, and mental well-being and aimed at the policy goals of a healthy environment, nutrition, and socioeconomic justice."[22] In these cases, as in others, courts recognize not only the link between certain enumerated constitutional rights and dignity interests, but also the interplay between the material aspects of dignity and its autonomy and self-determination aspects. They see that self-determination is an empty promise without a certain level of material comfort: a person's ability to control the course of her life is severely compromised if she is consumed with the need to acquire the durable medical goods she needs or does not have transportation to a medical clinic. The Peruvian court has also made this connection explicit. In a case about the provision of HIV drugs, the court said that social and economic rights, such as the right to social security, public health, life, education, and other public services, represent the social purposes of the state through which the individual can develop his or her full self-determination.[23] The Colombian court has acknowledged that the state has a special obligation to protect those who are least able to protect themselves: children, people with mental and physical disabilities, poor people, and others. It is these individuals who are least able to determine the course of their own lives and who therefore are most deserving of the state's support in protecting their dignity.

Another reason why dignity requires certain material minima is suggested by the Indian court's reference to freedom from "exploitation." A person who is materially deprived is more likely to be exploited, that is, more likely to be under the control of another (or of the state) and not in control of his or her own life. Exploitation is simply another way to think about objectification. A certain level of material comfort makes one less vulnerable to the indignity of exploitation by which one can be objectified or by which one's autonomy may be reduced; material minima thus help to secure *independence*, which enhances dignity. In *Danial Latifi v. Union of India*, the Indian Supreme Court held that a Muslim woman had a right to a certain level of maintenance after a divorce to protect her against destitution. Insisting on maintenance as a constitutional mandate helps to protect divorced women from exploitation by their current or former husbands. Against the claim that the law providing for such maintenance was religious because it interpreted the Qur'an, the court insisted that the right to live in human dignity was a societal mandate, not a religious one. "Solutions to such societal problems of universal magnitude pertaining to horizons of basic human rights, culture, dignity and decency of life and dictates of necessity in the pursuit of social justice should be invariably" decided on grounds other than religion or "national, sectarian, racial or communal constraints,"[24] the court said. Avoidance of destitution was so important to the woman's dignity that the state had an obligation to intervene.

This implicates both the equality and the autonomy values of dignity. Against the background of historically entrenched and pervasive discrimination against women, the principle of dignity demands that each person be regarded not as a member of a class or caste, but as a human being in and of herself, of equal worth to everyone else. Everyone, regardless of qualities of birth, is therefore entitled to a decent life, and the state must protect against any effort to deprive anyone of that decent life. Having alimony or the resources to pay for a wheelchair means that one is not dependent for one's dignity on the state's (or a former husband's) whim regarding whether or when or what to provide. This material security promotes equality as it facilitates exercise of autonomy.

The cases regarding material well-being tap into not only the autonomy aspect of dignity, but its social aspects as well: in many countries, one measure of whether the individual is living with dignity is the degree to which he or she is integrated into and participates in the broader society. The Peruvian court has said that the liberty, dignity, and autonomy of individuals living with HIV/AIDS, particularly where they lack the resources to pay for appropriate treatment, are affected by the deterioration of their health and the risk to their lives, "turning them into social pariahs," which in no way is consistent with the constitution.[25] It is in this sense that the Indian court suggested that human development, which is protected under Indian and international law, connotes more than the elimination of poverty but also "allows individuals to lead a life with dignity with a view to participate in the Governmental process so as to enable them to preserve their identity and culture"[26]—even where, ironically, the result of such political participation is the strengthening of parochial interests. In South Africa, where the social *is* the political, the court has been explicit about the connection between material dignity and political participation. In *Grootboom*, where the question was not whether the housing provided to the plaintiffs was adequate, but what could be done to ensure that *some* housing was provided to plaintiffs within a reasonable time, the court noted that "There can be no doubt that human dignity, freedom and equality, the foundational values of our society, are denied those who have no food, clothing or shelter. Affording socio-economic rights to all people therefore enables them to enjoy the other rights enshrined in [the Constitution]."[27]

Not surprisingly, South Africa has rooted both the need for socioeconomic improvement and the constitutional aspiration of human dignity in the country's history of apartheid. "We live in a society," the court has said,

> in which there are great disparities in wealth. Millions of people are living in deplorable conditions and in great poverty. There is a high level of unemployment, inadequate social security, and many do not have access to clean water or to adequate health services. These conditions already existed when the Constitution was adopted and a commitment to address them, and to transform our society into one in which there will be human dignity, freedom and equality, lies at the heart of our new constitutional order. For as long as these conditions continue to exist that aspiration will have a hollow ring.[28]

In this view, the entire structure and fulfillment of constitutional rights rest on the implementation of the right to dignity. Indeed, not only is the enjoyment of constitutional rights at risk, but the entire democratic experiment in which many countries are engaged cannot work if the citizenry is so concerned with finding shelter and health care that it cannot effectively participate in the institutions of government. The connection between dignity and democracy is explored more fully in Chapter 6.

All these cases recognize the inextricability of dignity and material well-being. A certain level of material comfort enables a person to present herself with dignity to others, to control the course of her life, and to protect herself to some extent from exploitation by the state or another person. This permits the person to integrate herself socially, and to assert her will politically. For all these reasons, material dignity plays a central role in the struggle for social justice, and courts in countries that are concerned with social justice have often used dignity as the fulcrum of their social justice jurisprudence.

Enforcing Dignity

Reading the right to dignity so emphatically presents significant challenges. These are relevant to constitutional adjudication generally, but they have particular salience for socioeconomic (or positive) rights and especially for the right to dignity. First, what *level* of provision is necessary to ensure that dignity is protected? This definitional question slides quickly into a philosophical inquiry: what does it mean to live with dignity? But to ask this in the practical context of a legal case necessarily raises a policy question: how much money can a poor and overburdened (and often indebted) nation be expected to spend on housing, health care, education, and so on to ensure that each of its citizens lives a dignified life? And this, in turn, leads to a very practical problem for the court: should judges be the ones to decide the answers to these questions?

While not unique to dignity, these questions are more pronounced here than in other contexts. Whereas every constitutional right requires *some* definition, the contours of the right to dignity are even less defined than the right to health or to due process precisely because dignity may be implicated in every aspect of life. And whereas separation of powers necessarily renders enforcement of rights problematic, judicial orders that have significant policy and fiscal implications are far more likely to create profound institutional problems for both political and judicial branches.

Courts around the world have responded to these challenges in a variety of ways. For some—notably the U.S. Supreme Court—the institutional obstacles to judicial definition and enforcement of the right to dignity are so profound that the courts avoid the problem altogether. Other courts, such as in Peru and Colombia, have embraced the challenge and placed themselves at the forefront of the sociopolitical conversation about dignity in their countries. Most other courts—such as South Africa's and India's—are walking a tightrope, trying to provide just enough moral suasion to push the political branches toward enhancing the lives of the poor majority, without being so obtrusive that they risk their own legitimacy.

One way to think about the right to dignity in its socioeconomic or material aspect is to determine the minimum core of health, shelter, food, water, recreation, and so on that is necessary to assure a dignified life. According to the United Nations Committee on Economic, Social and Cultural Rights, which developed the concept, "A State party in which any significant number of individuals is deprived of essential foodstuffs, of essential primary health care, of basic shelter and housing, or of the most basic forms of education is, *prima facie*, failing to discharge its obligations under the Covenant."[29] But this states the problem only in the negative: we know when we have a violation of the right, but we don't know what is necessary to assure there is no violation. Indeed, to state the challenge is immediately to understand why a court cannot meet it.

If it could be defined, the definition would go something like what the

South African court wrote in *Treatment Action Campaign*, a case concerning the provision of anti-retroviral drugs for the treatment of HIV/AIDS: "This minimum core . . . includes at least the minimum decencies of life consistent with human dignity. No one should be condemned to a life below the basic level of dignified human existence. The very notion of individual rights pre-supposes that anyone in that position should be able to obtain relief from a court."[30] But this articulation is circular: the right to dignity requires the minimum necessary to live a dignified life. Moreover, it neither specifies nor quantifies the state's obligation. It doesn't describe which medicines must be provided or how many rooms subsidized housing should have or even whether it should have electricity or indoor plumbing.

In a series of cases from South Africa—it seems that it is the special burden of that constitutional court to be compelled to repeat its stance on this issue ad infinitum—the court has explained why it must reject the argument that there is a constitutional violation any time the government fails to provide the minimum core of a right, if not more. In a 2009 case on water rights, the court explained this as plainly as it could. There are two reasons, it said, why the failure to provide a minimum core cannot be the test of a constitutional right. The first is a matter of institutional competence and the vagaries of specifica-tion: "the courts are not institutionally equipped to make the wide-ranging factual and political enquiries necessary for determining what the minimum-core standards," are, the court explained in the HIV case.[31] Courts are ca-pable of review, but they are not capable of deciding in the first instance what medicines are needed or how much water a person needs. And as the court noted, a judicial attempt to fix the minimum core could be counterproductive insofar as it makes change and recontextualization more difficult. Second, as a matter of cross-institutional power, it is "institutionally inappropriate for a court to determine precisely what the achievement of any particular social and economic right entails and what steps government should take to ensure the progressive realisation of the right. . . . Indeed, it is desirable as a matter of democratic accountability that [government] should do so for it is their programmes and promises that are subjected to democratic popular choice."[32] Separation-of-powers concerns, which weigh heavily on all courts, restrain courts from making bald and far-reaching policy decisions, particularly if they have significant fiscal implications.

The South African court has said that even though it will not determine in the first instance what constitutes the minimum core of a right, it will use the concept to determine whether a challenged governmental program is reasonable. That is, if the program proffered by the government as the fulfillment of a fundamental right does not even provide the minimum core, then it may turn out to be unreasonable, in the circumstances. This means that the constitutional standard turns in large part on the resources that are available to the government: if the state has the resources to provide the minimum core, it must do so. As the court explained in the HIV case, "In order for a State party to be able to attribute its failure to meet at least its minimum core obligations to a lack of available resources it must demonstrate that every effort has been made to use all resources that are at its disposition in an effort to satisfy, as a matter of priority, those minimum obligations."[33]

But even this reasonableness standard is impossible to apply without judicial review of the state's complete budgetary priorities: should the state have allocated more to fighting HIV and less to shelter or defense? And this, in turn, exacerbates the two concerns raised above: that the court is not institutionally competent to engage in this kind of review and, in a democracy, is not constitutionally empowered to do so. And, as the economic situation in South Africa has come to seem even more intractable than it did in 2002 when *Treatment Action Campaign* was decided, the court has emphasized that the constitutional right is to be determined not by reference to whether individuals have access to the minimum core of the right, but by reference to whether the government's plan *reasonably* indicates progressive realization of the right. For many, this is insufficient to fulfill the constitution's transformative potential.

Progressive realization recognizes that (particularly poorer) states cannot instantly provide adequate housing, medical care, education, and the like, but neither should they shirk their responsibilities toward their citizens completely, pleading perennial penury.[34] In the *Grootboom* case about the right to housing, the South African court explained the concept as follows:

> The term "progressive realisation" shows that it was contemplated that the right could not be realised immediately. But the goal of the Constitution is that the basic needs of all in our society be effectively met and the requirement of progressive realisation means that the state must take steps to achieve this goal. It means that accessibility should be progressively facilitated: legal, administrative, operational and financial hurdles should be examined and, where possible, lowered over time. Housing must be made more accessible not only to a larger number of people but to a wider range of people as time progresses.[35]

In practical terms, this requires the government to do *something* though not *everything* to assure the effective enjoyment of the right. But what, exactly, the government must do is left to the discretion of the court on a case-by-case basis. Some constitutional texts make clear the distinction between a government obligation to ensure dignity and an enforceable right to dignity. In other countries, though, the courts have had to infer the distinction from more opaque language. For instance, while the Hungarian state has an obligation to provide shelter for those who are homeless, it need not provide "a place of residence" to every person. Its obligation extends only as far as the "capacity of the national economy." Consequently, the court has said, "no obligation, and hence no responsibility of the State may be established for guaranteeing the 'right to have a place of residence.'"[36] In a Colombian case about the fundamental right to water for personal use, the court confronted the dual nature of the right head-on. Finding that the right to water is essential to enjoy other rights including, notably, the right to health and the right to live with dignity, the court held that the right to water operates on two levels. The first level refers to the minimum essential components of the right to water (including availability, quality, access, and nondiscrimination); if there is an evident deprivation of these elements, "the constitutional judge must order the means that are necessary to stop the violation immediately. In executing the judgment, providers of water can not complain about the lack of resources or the absence of budgetary authority," the court said. The second level, however, operates when the efficacy of the remedy depends principally on the construction of public works, and the appropriation of funds, which, in turn depend on public debate and decionmaking and execution by politicians. While the court cautioned that this does not allow the perennial postponement of the satisfaction of the right, "the judge must adopt orders that will assure that appropriate measures are taken, in furtherance at the same time, of civic participation."[37]

The compromise is this: while the state may be under a constitutional (and international) obligation to provide shelter, medical care, education, and the like sufficient to allow people to live with dignity, the right of any particular individual to demand any particular level or type of resources is much more limited. As the Japanese Supreme Court has explained in construing the welfare rights provision of the Japanese constitution, it "merely proclaims that it is the duty of the State to administer national policy in such a manner as to enable all the people to enjoy at least the minimum standards of wholesome and cultivated living; and it does not grant the people as individuals any concrete rights."[38] In the South African *Treatment Action Campaign* case, the court put it in similar terms: while in a particular case a petitioner "may show that there is a minimum core of a particular service that should be taken into account in determining whether measures adopted by the state are reasonable, the socio-economic rights of the Constitution should not be construed as entitling everyone to demand that the minimum core be provided to them." It is thus a relevant consideration in determining whether the state has fulfilled its obligation, but it is not a "self-standing right conferred on everyone."[39]

Finding that the state *must* comply with the constitutional duties allows the courts to fulfill their obligations to give meaning to the constitution, but finding that they are not constitutionally enforceable by individuals mitigates the risk that the court will be perceived as having violated separation of powers, or that the government will ignore the court's orders. The order simply states that the government *must* provide the relevant services, to a *reasonable* extent. And what is "reasonable" is defined in the first instance by the legislature and reviewed with considerable deference by the court.[40]

Most courts are wary of treading too deeply in the waters of dignity. Courts have limited enforcement powers, and the absence of either "the sword or the purse" rests heavily on judges' minds as they fashion an order. The South African court has reconciled the practical and theoretical difficulties with these words:

> Courts are ill-suited to adjudicate upon issues where court orders could have multiple social and economic consequences for the community. The Constitution contemplates rather a restrained and focused role for the courts, namely, to require the state to take measures to meet its constitutional obligations and to subject the reasonableness of these measures to evaluation. Such determinations of reasonableness may in fact have budgetary implications, but are not in themselves directed at rearranging budgets. In this way the judicial, legislative and executive functions achieve appropriate constitutional balance.[41]

In this area of protecting the material (and therefore costly) dimension of dignity, courts walk a fine line: if they order the government to provide services that the government either does not want or cannot provide, they risk being ignored or, worse, derided, and this can have long-term consequences for judicial legitimacy. But if they proceed too meekly, they risk losing the respect of the people who look to them to protect them against majoritarian and political forces. And, as has often been noted, in a constitutional democracy, it is entirely on the respect of the people that the court's legitimacy, and therefore its effectiveness, rest. The cases investigated here show that many courts have thrown in their lot with the people, by accepting the constitutional invitation to compel governments to protect and maintain people's dignity.

Dignity and the State: "Living without humiliation"

Dignity in Custody

This section concerns a third dimension of dignity—where the state is alleged to have directly violated the individual's dignity. The most common situation is where the victim of the abuse of dignity is dependent on the state in some way, usually where he or she is in the custodial control of the state. This is simply because under most circumstances where an individual is *in*dependent, his dignity is not as much at risk: the state has little opportunity to diminish the dignity of self-sufficient and autonomous individuals. Dignity is threatened to the extent that the individual depends on others to fulfill his needs; this limits his equality and autonomy. The Constitution of the Maldives recognizes this, regardless of the reason for the detention: "Everyone deprived of liberty through arrest or detention as provided by law, pursuant to an order of the court, or being held in State care for social reasons, shall be treated with humanity and with respect for the inherent dignity of the human person."[42] However, as states expand the control they exert on ordinary citizens, dignity interests are increasingly implicated even outside the custodial context. For instance, the German Constitutional Court in 2004 allowed domestic wiretapping within housing spaces insofar as such surveillance did not violate the right to dignity, noting that, in the words of one commentator, "There exists a close connection between the inviolability of housing and the dignity of man, which establishes the state's duty to respect a purely personal sphere. . . . Regulations of acoustic surveillance have to exclude any risk of violating human dignity."[43] But in general, individuals who live independently can assure their own sphere of autonomy, whereas dependence on the state means precisely that the state, rather than the individual, is in control.

   The treatment of prisoners. The starting point, which no constitutional democracy has denied, is that all individuals—even suspects and prisoners—retain their human dignity.[44] The Yemeni Constitution of 1991 makes this clear: "Any person whose freedom is restricted in any way must have his dignity protected."[45] We are born with it, and we are not supposed to lose it. As President Aharon Barak of the Israeli Supreme Court has written, "Prison life . . . does not require someone under arrest to be denied his right to physical integrity and protection against a violation of his human dignity. A person under arrest is denied freedom; he is not deprived of his humanity."[46] In *Public Committee Against Torture v. Israel*, the court held that, absent necessity, practices that violate a person's dignity (including torture) are not a part of the general interrogation powers of the State. Invoking the theme of individuation, the court explained that the limitation on state powers is "based, on the one hand, on preserving the 'human image' of the suspect."[47] Likewise, the Peruvian Constitutional Tribunal has held that total withdrawal of prison benefits not only drains the resocialization aim of punishment of its vitality; it also drains the very dignity of the prisoners. The court said that the principle of the dignity of the person "in its negative version, insists that human beings may not be treated like things or instruments (but rather as subjects of rights and obligations) . . . since each person, including criminals, should be considered as an end in and of himself."[48]

Exigent circumstances, like perhaps the war on terror, may be said to justify techniques that would otherwise be held to violate a person's dignity, although here, too, most people would argue that dignity still has some claim. Neither is the right to dignity one-sided: torture may violate a terrorist's dignity, but a car bomb violates the dignity of the public, as courts in the United States and elsewhere have suggested. The state must balance its obligations to maintain and protect the dignity of those it holds in custody against its obligations to protect the dignity of the general public. The question is not whether the conditions of detention violate human dignity—because they almost always do—but whether such violations are unnecessary or excessive.[49]

The comforts of life. Some of the cases concerning treatment of detainees focus on the physical conditions of detention and thus recall the cases from the previous section about the minimum core of comfort that is necessary to ensure that individuals live in dignity. It has been held that prisoners must be able to eat at a table rather than on the ground, that they are entitled to a certain amount of space, and that prisoners must be allowed reading materials.[50] As the Israeli Supreme Court has said, "Prisoners should not be crammed like animals into inadequate spaces. Even those suspected of terrorist activity of the worst kind are entitled to conditions of detention which satisfy minimal standards of humane treatment and ensure basic human necessities. How could we consider ourselves civilized if we did not guarantee civilized standards to those in our custody? Such is the duty of the commander of the area under international law, and such is his duty under our administrative law."[51]

But dignity in the treatment of defendants and prisoners is not absolute, and certainly not all cases that raise questions about the treatment of prisoners are decided in favor of the prisoner.[52] Indeed, part of the purpose of incarceration is precisely to humiliate the prisoners, to demean them. In most societies, recognizing the equal dignity of prisoner and warden would undermine the purpose and the perceived effectiveness of punitive incarceration. Thus, prisoners wear uniforms—in apartheid South Africa, prisoners wore short pants, like little boys would, precisely to diminish their adulthood—and they are identified by number rather than by name, live in overcrowded conditions, and are often treated rudely by prison staff. All these are designed to diminish a person's sense of his own dignity—in all its guises: they constrain the prisoner's individuality, limit his autonomy, and eradicate his equality. And yet most of these conditions are not unconstitutional. Israel has held that if it is more effective to interrogate a suspect in an undersized chair, the state will be allowed to do so, even though this can be said to violate the suspect's dignity. High courts in both Canada and the United States have held that, as a U.S. court wrote, "The indignity of the search does not, of course, outlaw it, but it does implicate the rule of reasonableness . . . that the search as actually conducted [must be] reasonably related in scope to the circumstances which justified the interference in the first place."[53] But reasonableness is invariably measured against the punitive purposes of the practice, not against the inherent dignity of the prisoner.

The indignity of death. The most extreme form of violation of human dignity is the death penalty, where the individual is dependent on the state for his or her very life. Many constitutions that explicitly protect dignity also prohibit capital punishment. Where that has not been the case, some courts have invalidated the death penalty anyway on the ground that it is incompatible with the constitutional protection of dignity. As mentioned earlier, the constitutional courts of both South Africa and Hungary flexed their muscles early on by ruling in this way. In Hungary, notwithstanding constitutional language that prohibited only *arbitrary* capital punishment, the court found that all capital punishment necessarily infringed on the old constitution's protection of the "inherent right to life and human dignity."[54] The first landmark ruling of South Africa's Constitutional Court was *Makwanyane v. State*, where the court held that "The carrying out of the death sentence destroys life, which is protected without reservation under section 9 of our Constitution, it annihilates human dignity which is protected under section 10, elements of arbitrariness are present in its enforcement and it is irremediable."[55] Members of the Canadian Supreme Court waxed more poetically: "It is the supreme indignity to the individual, the ultimate corporal punishment, the final and complete lobotomy and the absolute and irrevocable castration. [It is] the ultimate desecration of human dignity."[56] (The U.S. Supreme Court, ever an outlier in matters of both dignity and the death penalty, raised formalism to an Olympian height in ruling, in 2008, that a state's use of pancuronium bromide as a sedative in its lethal injection "cocktail" to make the condemned person appear calm and not in pain did "not offend" the Eighth Amendment because the state "has an interest in preserving the dignity of the procedure, especially where convulsions or seizures could be misperceived as signs of consciousness or distress."[57] For this court, appearing to die with dignity has greater value than avoiding the indignity of state killing.)

Autonomy, Revisited

Some cases that raise questions about human dignity implicate the autonomy principle directly—that is, the idea that prisoners retain the right, within a limited sphere, to self-determination and to some degree of autonomous decision-making (such as the German life imprisonment case discussed in the previous chapter). In particular, the right against self-incrimination has been held to preserve human dignity. The Supreme Court of Hong Kong put it this way: "The consequences of a forced answer could be literally life-threatening. The privilege protects personal freedom and human dignity. It is 'deep rooted' in Hong Kong law. . . . It protects 'the individual against the affront to dignity and privacy inherent in a practice which enables the prosecution to force the person charged to supply the evidence out of his or her own mouth.' "[58]

Still other cases invoke the individuation aspect of dignity that would ensure that even detainees retain a limited right to control their identity for themselves and for others. In considering the constitutionality of police surveillance within prisons, the Constitutional Court of Poland wrote that "[all] constitutional rights and freedoms of the individual stem from their human dignity, protected by virtue of Article 30 of the Constitution. In the case of privacy, this relationship is of a specific nature. The protection of dignity re-quires the respect of the purely personal human sphere, where the person is not forced to 'be with others' or 'share with others' their experiences or intimate details."[59] It is not the act of sharing that, on its own, violates human dignity; it is being *forced* to share. Thus, while prison authorities obviously have some power to keep prisoners under surveillance, that power is not un-bounded and needs, at some point, to yield to the prisoner's retained interest in dignity.

Here, as elsewhere, the interests converge: interrogation, imprisonment, deprivation, and torture all demean the physical body as they diminish the psychological sense of self. Placing prisoners at the mercy of the state pre-vents them, to that extent, from being the architects of their own lives and from asserting their individual dignity.

4

"Master of One's Fate"

American constitutional jurisprudence is always something of an outlier, and no less with respect to human dignity. The Supreme Court of the United States has recognized, since the beginning, that the concept of dignity is important in the interpretation of the Constitution, although it appears nowhere in its text. And yet, uniquely in the world, the U.S. Supreme Court has always been much more comfortable attaching dignity to inanimate things, such as states and courts and contracts, than to human beings. In an extraordinary series of cases from the 1990s, when the rest of the world was discovering the boundless possibilities of human dignity, the U.S. Supreme Court was exalting the dignity of states. Nonetheless, some recent cases suggest that the court may finally be softening to the idea of human dignity, although even now the court is, typically, divided, with some members accepting a more substantive version of human dignity and others still more comfortable with dignity as a formal or existential concept. Investigating both the institutional and individual streams of American dignity jurisprudence is instructive because at the confluence of the two we can gain important insights about what dignity means in the United States and in relation to the rest of the world. The Supreme Court cases on state sovereignty—spanning more than two hundred years—cast into relief what human dignity might mean if it becomes more fully developed in the United States, and shed some light, in particular, on the meaning of autonomy and self-determination as the signature feature of human dignity. The question for the court now is whether, particularly after so much work has been done abroad to elucidate the right to human dignity, the court is ready to see the relevance of human dignity to the American constitutional order. And if so, will the constitutional right to human dignity in the American context mean something similar to what it means elsewhere in the world, or will the U.S. court put its unique stamp on the concept, incorporating the ideas it has already developed in the context of state dignity and sovereignty?

To better understand the American conception of constitutional dignity, this chapter surveys Supreme Court cases in which the concept of dignity (human or otherwise) is relevant to the court's judgment or interpretation. The first section, spanning the full history of Supreme Court jurisprudence, focuses on the cases that tend to accord dignity to inchoate things and to treat dignity as a sort of immunity from encroachment. The second section examines cases from the mid-twentieth century that, influenced by the aftermath of the Second World War, begin to recognize the implications of human dignity in a variety of different legal and factual settings. In more recent cases, the justices finally appear ready to take seriously the constitutional contours of human dignity, and their focus seems to be right on the point where human and inchoate dignity converge; this evolution is examined in the last section of the chapter.

Dignity and Immunity in Premodern Cases

The Dignity of States

The first use of the term "dignity" by the Supreme Court was in the celebrated—or notorious—case of *Chisholm v. Georgia*, dating from 1793. In that case, the court was required to determine whether the constitutional provision permitting suits "between a State and Citizens of another State" permitted only suits in which states were plaintiffs, or permitted as well suits in which citizens of one state sued another state. The majority of the court read the language plainly: as Justice Blair explained, "A dispute between A. and B. assuredly [is] a dispute between B. and A. Both cases, I have no doubt, were intended; and probably the State was first named, in respect to the dignity of a State."[1] Justice Blair rejected Georgia's contention that "that very dignity seems to have been thought a sufficient reason for confining the fence to the case where a State is plaintiff."[2] For the majority of the court, dignity evinces respect, nothing more.

We should have known then that dignity would be a difficult concept for the court, because the decision spurred not only disagreement on the court, but centuries of constitutional controversy that has still not abated.

The immediate aftermath is telling: Georgia itself passed a law that prohibited compliance with the decision on penalty of death "without the benefit of clergy," and within a few years, the constitution itself would be amended to prohibit such suits against states in the future. In fact, recent cases have insisted that *Chisholm*'s failure to recognize the dignity that was due states was met with "shock and surprise" by the nation.[3]

The reaction turned on the meaning of state dignity. While the question before the court was whether a "judgment by default, in the present stage of the business, and writ of enquiry of damages, would be too precipitate in any case, and too incompatible with the dignity of a State," the majority justices found that state dignity got the state listed first in the credits but was not so weighty as to immunize states from suit. Several justices acknowledged that not only states, but individuals, too, have dignity but, as Justice Wilson expounded, the dignity of a state is inferior to that of man: "MAN, fearfully and wonderfully made, is the workmanship of his all perfect CREATOR: A State; useful and valuable as the contrivance is, is the inferior contrivance of man; and from his native dignity derives all its acquired importance. When I speak of a State as an inferior contrivance, I mean that it is a contrivance inferior only to that, which is divine."[4] (He then explains, quoting Cicero, that of all inferior contrivances, states are the most "acceptable to that divinity.")

This religious patina over the concept of dignity may be contrasted with the adamantly civic version in the opinion of Chief Justice John Jay in the same case. Speaking of the Constitution, the chief justice said: "It is remarkable that in establishing it, the people exercised their own rights, and their own proper sovereignty, and conscious of the plenitude of it, they declared with becoming dignity, 'We the people of the United States, do ordain and establish this "Constitution."'"[5] In Jay's view, dignity is not only a secular concept, but an evolving one as well. And it is not only an individual attribute but a collective one. The American people, he seems pleased to note, are gaining a dignity that is commensurate with their maturing political self-consciousness. In light of the global turn toward dignity, we might say that the concept of dignity has evolved, and continues to evolve, not only with the political maturity of the nation, but with that of the whole world.

But for other justices, and the states—and, too, the modern court, which revived the controversy in the 1990s—dignity means much more than mere respect. It has the power to immunize the bearer—whether a sovereign or a state, or a court for that matter—from unwanted encroachments. Throughout the eighteenth and nineteenth centuries, the vast majority of Supreme Court cases that refer in any way to dignity ascribe it to inchoate things for the purpose of justifying the immunity that attaches to them.[6]

In *The Schooner Exchange v. M'Faddon*,[7] Chief Justice John Marshall held that neither France nor its emperor Napoleon, could be subjected to the jurisdiction of the United States courts while the countries were at peace; an action to recover a ship that had been taken by the French could therefore not be maintained in the courts of the United States. As Marshall explained, "A foreign sovereign is not understood as intending to subject himself to jurisdiction incompatible with his dignity, and the dignity of his nation, and it is to avoid this subjection that the license has been obtained."[8] France's sovereignty, its dignity, and its immunity from suit were inextricable.[9]

The theory is further developed in Justice Johnson's opinion in *L'Invincible*,[10] in which he holds that so long as France is neutral, U.S. courts have no jurisdiction over France or its duly commissioned privateer. Johnson explains that, as "a consequence of the equality and absolute independence of sovereign states,"[11] "every sovereign becomes the acknowledged arbiter of his own justice, and cannot, consistently with his dignity, stoop to appear at the bar of other nations to defend the acts of his commissioned agents, much less the justice and legality of those rules of conduct which he prescribes to them." Again, sovereignty confers dignity, and dignity justifies immunity from suit. But Johnson's explanation of the source or nature of sovereignty is telling: it partakes of "equality" and "absolute independence." Johnson further explains that to subject France to suit "would have violated the hospitality which nations have a right to claim from each other, and the immunity which a sovereign commission confers on the vessel which acts under it; that it would have detracted from the dignity and equality of sovereign states, by reducing one to the condition of a suitor in the courts of another."[17] The linkage between dignity and "absolute independence" on the one hand and "equality" on the other presages the modern version of dignity, which is inextricably linked with inviolability or autonomy and equality.[12]

Other nineteenth-century cases reinforce this strong bond that links dignity, sovereignty, and immunity. In *United States v. Diekelman*, the court explained that "One nation treats with the citizens of another only through their government. A sovereign cannot be sued in his own courts without his consent. His own dignity, as well as the dignity of the nation he represents, prevents his appearance to answer a suit against him in the courts of another sovereignty, except in performance of his obligations, by treaty or otherwise, voluntarily assumed."[13]

But the dignity or sovereignty of the states has never been so absolute as to lend them unqualified immunity. In *Craig v. Missouri*, the majority noted the tension resulting from the states' incomplete sovereignty. "In the argument, we have been reminded by one side of the dignity of a sovereign state; of the humiliation of her submitting herself to this tribunal; of the dangers which may result from inflicting a wound on that dignity: by the other, of the still superior dignity of the people of the United States; who have spoken their will, in terms which we cannot misunderstand."[14] Indeed, as the *Chisholm* court recognized, the language of the Constitution, in Article III and elsewhere, seems to accord states some degree of sovereignty that is less than full, and their dignity is therefore not sufficient to completely immunize them from unconsenting suits. The question is whether the quantum of dignity that sovereign entities have is sufficient to confer complete immunity.

Chief Justice Marshall expressed skepticism at the thought that it was a state's dignity that protected it against suit. In *Cohens v. Virginia*, he posits that since the Eleventh Amendment—the one that overruled the result in *Chisholm*—prohibits jurisdiction only in cases brought by *individuals* against states, and not in cases brought by other states or foreign nations, "We must ascribe the amendment, then, to some other cause than the dignity of a State." But he explains this quickly: "There is no difficulty in finding this cause. Those who were inhibited from commencing a suit against a State, or from prosecuting one which might be commenced before the adoption of the amendment, were persons who might probably be its creditors."[15] In Marshall's view, then, a state's dignity is not sufficiently talismanic to protect it from all litigious advances, only from those of individuals. Indeed, the Constitution specifically allows for suits against states to be heard in the Supreme Court's original jurisdiction.[16]

It would take until the end of the twentieth century for the court to upgrade both the dignity and the sovereignty of states to the point where immunity from suit would attach for almost all types of suits in state and federal courts and before administrative agencies. In a series of cases beginning in 1996, the court held that the Eleventh Amendment, which as we have seen bars only certain suits against states brought by individuals, is shorthand for a more general immunity for states from all suits, which is based not on the words of the Eleventh Amendment, but on the dignity of the states. In *Idaho v. Coeur D'Alene Tribe*, the court recognized "the dignity and respect afforded a State, which the immunity is designed to protect."[17] "The generation that designed and adopted our federal system," the court announced in 1999, considered immunity from private suits central to sovereign dignity."[18] A few years later, the court would extend the principle to immunize states from suits before federal administrative agencies to enforce federal law: "Simply put, if the Framers thought it an impermissible affront to a State's dignity to be required to answer the complaints of private parties in federal courts, we cannot imagine that they would have found it acceptable to compel a State to do exactly the same thing before the administrative tribunal of an agency, such as the [Federal Maritime Commission]."[19] A solid bloc of dissenting justices consistently questioned the "dignity rationale" for complete immunity, calling it "embarrassingly insufficient."[20] But the die was cast.[21] Under the court's current approach, a state cannot typically be sued even for violations of its own law or federal law, including violations of the federal constitution. People must rely on the state's good faith that it will comply with federal law. The principal justification for this impressive degree of protection is the dignity of the states.[22]

There are exceptions to the immunity, but they are rare. One is that the state can still be sued by the federal government[23] or by other states.[24] Another is that, under a legal fiction in place since the early twentieth century, state officers can be sued for violations of federal law, even if the state itself cannot; the officers do not enjoy the same dignity as the inchoate state.[25] A final exception is where the state consents to suit. While consent to violations of human dignity are problematic because of the universal norms beneath which we do not generally want to see people put themselves, consent to suit in the Eleventh Amendment context is relatively uncomplicated because it results not in degradation, but in accountability to law.

These limited exceptions do not significantly detract from the by-now entrenched principle that state dignity immunizes states from suits in almost all circumstances. And while the recent cases are emphatic in the rhetoric of state dignity, they do not provide any rationale for the need to recognize state dignity or to equate such dignity with immunity from suit. Focusing on enforcement provides at least some clues as to the court's thinking: "the rule has evolved that a suit by private parties seeking to impose a liability which must be paid from public funds in the state treasury is barred by the Eleventh Amendment," the court explained in *Edelman v. Jordan*.[26] But to understand the full implications of this, we need to go even further back. In *Great Northern Life Ins. Co. v. Read*, the court explained that allowing such suits would mean that a state was "controlled by courts in the performance of its political duties"[27] and that "Efforts to force, through suits against officials, performance of promises by a state collide directly with the necessity that a sovereign must be free from judicial compulsion in the carrying out of its policies within the limits of the Constitution."[28] Thus, the problem with suits against states is that they function as a sort of exogenous control over the state, preventing it from pursuing policies that it would otherwise choose, thereby interfering with its autonomy, or dignity.[29] The court is particularly concerned with the impact that private suits for damages have on a state's ability to set its own priorities— should it spend money on schools and roads, or on complying with federal welfare regulations? As the court said in *Edelman*, quoting *Great Northern*, "when we are dealing with the sovereign exemption from judicial interference in the vital field of financial administration a clear declaration of the state's intention to submit its fiscal problems to other courts than those of its own creation must be found."[30] A state's sovereignty—just like a foreign nation's— entitles it to choose and express its policy priorities without interference.

At root, this is the same problem underlying federal laws that "commandeer" state legislative and executive action, as the court has held in its revived Tenth Amendment jurisprudence. In both *New York v. United States* and *Printz v. United States*, the court held that "the Federal Government may not compel the States to implement, by legislation or executive action, federal regulatory programs," because doing so requires the state to follow federal policy rather than the state's own policy.[31] Though neither of these cases mentions states' dignitary interests, as do the Eleventh Amendment cases, they are temporally and conceptually linked to those cases.

The Importance of Things

In hundreds of other cases, the court has found dignity in the United States, the Congress, the presidency, and most often, courts, both state and federal, both lower and appellate.[32] Mediating the tensions between state and federal courts, particularly in the wake of the expansion of federal jurisdiction during Reconstruction, is a task almost defined by sensitivity to the dignity of each judicial system.[33] The Constitution, of course, has dignity, and all the provisions within it have been held to have equal dignity.[34] Justice Swayne wrote in dissent in *The Slaughterhouse Cases* that the Reconstruction amendments to the Constitution "may be said to rise to the dignity of a new Magna Carta."[35] The dignity of the American flag has also been recognized,[36] as has American citizenship.[37]

Not only courts but their effects and incidents have been endowed with dignity. The physical space of a courtroom may have dignity.[38] In order to get into court in the first place, a person's "interest must rise to the dignity of an interest personal to him and not possessed by the people generally."[39] And only claims of "sufficient seriousness and dignity" can trigger the Supreme Court's original jurisdiction.[40] Once the case begins, courts have held that various forms of evidence implicate dignitary interests. A public record has dignity,[41] and a patent[42] or a conveyance[43] may have the dignity of record. Testimony has dignity (but not all proofs rise to the dignity of testimony).[44] And not all testimony rises to the dignity of evidence,[45] nor do all medical certificates rise to the dignity of proof.[46] And although a party may raise any issue in a case, not all issues rise to the dignity of a question.[47] A suspicion may have dignity, but not enough to contradict a person's testimony.[48] A judicial sale can have dignity.[49] And, of course, a judgment can—and should—have dignity,[50] as do judicial orders in specific settings.[51]

As time went on, other things gained dignity. In the last decade of the nineteenth century, at the height of industrialization in America, a flurry of cases considered whether a particular object rises to the "dignity of an invention." In *Leggett v. Standard Oil*, the idea of lining oil barrels with glue did not rise to the dignity of an invention,[52] nor did loosening the lacing of silk for the purpose of dyeing in *Grant v. Walter*,[53] nor did developing lighter frames for horizontal engines in *Wright v. Yuengling*,[54] nor did an innovation in windmill design in *Mast, Foos & Co. v. Stover Mfg. Co.*,[55] among other cases.[56]

Other things, too, were held to have dignity, though often not as much as counsel would like.[57] At various times, the court has considered whether a meander line rises to the dignity of a state boundary line,[58] whether a small creek can rise to the dignity of a public river,[59] whether a security is of the same dignity as an income bond,[60] whether a revenue statute can be lifted to the dignity of a crime,[61] whether a regulation rises to the dignity of a law,[62] or a commercial agreement to the dignity of a treaty,[63] or a reciprocal treaty to the level of an interstate compact.[64] Recently, one justice wrote that congressional silence should not have the same dignity as its expression.[65] The court has had to decide whether a diminution in property value rises to the dignity of a constitutional taking,[66] and whether a rebellion can rise to the dignity of war.[67] In *Gray v. Sanders*, the court held that " 'the right to have one's vote counted' has the same dignity as 'the right to put a ballot in a box.' "[68] Justice Kennedy has recently written that, "In a society based on law, the concept of agreement and consent should be given a weight and dignity of its own."[69] Not surprisingly, many cases relied on by lawyers do "not approach the dignity of a well settled interpretation,"[70] many rights claimed by litigants do not rise to the dignity of legal rights,[71] nor do trial strategies rise to the dignity of constitutional rights,[72] and many suggestions made by counsel do not rise to the dignity of an argument[73] or of a substantial federal question.[74] Two provisions in the same statute are presumably of "equal dignity."[75] But no one should give constitutional dignity to an irrelevance.[76]

In short, the Supreme Court's cases amply show its near obsession with the idea of dignity, without even a nod to the idea that human beings might have it inherently. In all these cases, dignity is used to denote importance. Sometimes, it is in a comparative sense—that the federal government is more important than, say, the states, or the court more important than the person who would hold it in contempt. The importance that attaches to dignity is not only conceptual but has cash value, as it were. As with state dignity—the only other kind the court recognized for most of its history—the dignity of things tends to immunize them from certain encroachments: a text, an institution, or a right with dignity cannot be impugned or violated; rather, what it says, controls. It sets the rules and cannot be made to yield to the rules of another. It says, "I win," because the point at which the court recognizes the dignity of the interest involved is often the end of the argument.

In other cases, dignity is not a competitive value but an absolute one that attaches to certain institutions and offices. In this sense, it is consistent with the European attribution of dignity to men of certain rank. And yet, it may also be true that the modern sense of dignity—that dignity that attaches to every human being—also denotes importance, and regards every member of the human family as being important, though equally so. To this extent, there is no necessary contradiction between the institutional dignity recognized in the American cases and the human dignity recognized elsewhere. In both, it denotes importance, or worth, and the ability that comes with importance, that is, to exert control and make choices about oneself.

The problem arises in those few but very troublesome cases where the court has privileged the institutional dignity over—and at the expense of—human dignity. In one nineteenth-century case, an attorney had the audacity to petition the Supreme Court for a writ of mandamus to order the lower court to withdraw its order disbarring him. The case arises out of an episode in which Wall, the attorney, went to the nearby jail, kidnapped a man named "John, otherwise unknown," brought him back to the courthouse, and proceeded to hang him on the courthouse steps. This was such an insult *to the court* that the district judge—who had to witness John's "dangling corpse"—was held to have acted properly in disbarring Wall, because Wall had shown "such an utter disregard and contempt for the law and its provisions," which as an attorney he was bound to uphold.[77] No mention is made of the disregard for the dignity of John, otherwise unknown.

Even more disturbingly, if only because it is current, is the 2005 case *Deck v. Missouri*,[78] in which the majority and dissent argued about whether shackling a prisoner during the penalty phase of a trial offends the dignity, not of the prisoner, but of the court. Invalidating the practice, Justice Breyer wrote that it did: "The courtroom's formal dignity, which includes the respectful treatment of defendants, reflects the importance of the matter at issue, guilt or innocence, and the gravity with which Americans consider any deprivation of an individual's liberty through criminal punishment. And it reflects a seriousness of purpose that helps to explain the judicial system's power to inspire the confidence and to affect the behavior of a general public whose demands for justice our courts seek to serve. The routine use of shackles in the presence of juries would undermine these symbolic yet concrete objectives."[79] The dignity of the court includes but most certainly is not limited to respect for the defendant. In dissent, Justice Thomas was not so moved: "Wholly apart from the unwarranted status the Court accords 'courtroom decorum,' the Court fails to explain the affront to the dignity of the courts that the sight of physical restraints poses. . . . Our Nation's judges and juries are exposed to accounts of heinous acts daily, like the brutal murders Deck committed in this case. . . . Yet, the Court says, the appearance of a convicted criminal in a belly chain and handcuffs at a sentencing hearing offends the sensibilities of our courts. The courts of this Nation do not have such delicate constitutions."[80]

The problem is that, because he lives in a constitutional culture that still does not recognize human dignity, the only strategy available to Deck to support the truism that shackles offend human decency was to invoke judicial dignity. And while the majority allowed the idea of respect to come in as an incident of judicial dignity, the dissent would not allow this social interest to be converted into an actionable constitutional right. "No decision of this Court has ever intimated, let alone held, that the protection of the 'courtroom's formal dignity,' is an individual right enforceable by criminal defendants. . . . Far from viewing the need for decorum as a right the defendant can invoke, this Court has relied on it to *limit* the conduct of defendants, even when their constitutional rights are implicated. The concern for courtroom decorum is not a concern about defendants, let alone their right to due process. It is a concern about society's need for courts to operate effectively."[81] Somewhat shockingly—particularly against the backdrop of cases around the world—neither the majority nor the dissent attributes any value to the dignity of the shackled defendant. Indeed, throughout the American cases, invocations of judicial dignity consistently serve to limit, not empower, human rights. Contempt citations that gag or constrain parties are routinely justified on the basis of judicial dignity.[82]

The Emergence of Human Dignity

The habit of assigning dignity to incorporeal things does not begin to wane until the turn of the nineteenth century, when hints of human dignity begin to emerge. Of course, the first people to be recognized as having dignity were "dignitaries," and sovereigns and other high-born individuals.[83] An 1896 dissenting opinion by Justice Field is one of the first to suggest the sense in which we currently understand dignity. The question in *Brown v. Walker* was whether a law requiring testimony relating to violations of the Interstate Commerce Act conflicted with the Fifth Amendment right against self-incrimination on the ground that it required testimony about facts that might be detrimental to him or her, though not legally self-incriminating. Arguing against the majority for broader application of the Fifth Amendment, Justice Field explained: "both the safeguard of the Constitution and the common law rule spring alike from that sentiment of personal self-respect, liberty, independence and dignity which has inhabited the breasts of English speaking peoples for centuries, and to save which they have always been ready to sacrifice many governmental facilities and conveniences. . . . What can be more abhorrent . . . than to compel a man who has fought his way from obscurity to dignity and honor to reveal crimes of which he had repented and of which the world was ignorant?"[84] But the opinion's egalitarian intonations must be read in light of the racist politics of the day. Thirty years after the end of the Civil War, Justice Field may have been ready to acknowledge the dignity of those who had been "English speaking peoples" for centuries, but the court in the same year constitutionalized racial segregation without the slightest concern for the dignity of African American citizens.

Indeed, other than a sporadic mention here and there, most of the references to human dignity in the Supreme Court's case law accord it to men of high rank. Typical is Chief Justice Taft's citation to Blackstone, who notes that at common law the king neither paid nor received costs in litigation because "it is the King's prerogative not to pay them to a subject and is beneath his dignity to receive them."[85] It would take many decades before the court would attach dignity not only to the governors, but to the governed.[86]

Dignity Risen from War

The influence of the Second World War on dignity jurisprudence in America is visible, though less pronounced than in some other countries. The first mention of dignity in an individual rights case is a fleeting reference in Justice Jackson's concurrence in *Skinner v. Oklahoma*, which invalidated forced sterilization for certain classes of prisoners. "There are limits," he writes, "to the extent to which a legislatively represented majority may conduct biological experiments at the expense of the dignity and personality and natural powers of a minority—even those who have been guilty of what the majority define as crimes."[87] This brief reference contains several of the seeds of the court's dignity jurisprudence as it would develop over the next half century. First, Justice Jackson accords dignity to all persons, as an incident of being born human, not as a consequence of accomplishment, high birth, or status. Second, Justice Jackson recognizes that certain actions may detract from the dignity of individuals. Thus, while it may be inherent and identified with "natural powers," it is nonetheless vulnerable to degradation by majoritarian impulses. Third, the Constitution may protect against such degradation. At some point, he says, efforts to diminish the dignity of another may contravene constitutional strictures. (The point at which that happens, it should be noted, is not necessarily where most of us would place it today: although Justice Jackson would not allow the sterilization of certain classes of felons, he cites with apparent approval Justice Holmes's notorious language in *Buck v. Bell* allowing the sterilization of Carrie Bell; the difference seems to be not one of principle but one of degree of the development of the scientific basis for such sterilization.) Nevertheless, the underlying principle that inherent human dignity may have constitutional status, such that a court would be justified in intervening to protect it, was a novel proposition in American jurisprudence up to that point.[88] In the 1940s and thereafter, it would become more commonplace.[89]

Of all the justices, it is perhaps the otherwise unremarkable Justice Frank

Murphy who had the most developed theory of the dignity of man and of its constitutional implications. Many of his opinions expounding the importance of constitutional dignity were, however, written in dissent. In *Korematsu v. United States*, he excoriated his brethren who had upheld the exclusion (and by implication, internment) of more than one hundred thousand individuals solely because of their Japanese heritage by comparing it to the tactics of the enemy: the orders were based on a denial of the rule that individual guilt is the sole basis for the deprivation of rights, and to give constitutional sanction to that presumption "is to adopt one of the cruelest of the rationales used by our enemies to destroy the dignity of the individual and to encourage and open the door to discriminatory actions against other minority groups in the passions of tomorrow."[90] Like Justice Jackson, Justice Murphy recognized that, although dignity inheres in all persons, judicial protection against its destruction was especially necessary for minorities. In *Steele v. Louisville & N. R. Co.*, he wrote, in concurrence, that the "utter disregard for the dignity and the well-being of colored citizens shown by this record is so pronounced as to demand the invocation of constitutional condemnation."[91]

In the next couple of years, he would elaborate on the theory. In dissent in *United States v. Screws*, Justice Murphy wrote:

> Robert Hall, a Negro citizen, has been deprived not only of the right to be tried by a court rather than by ordeal. He has been deprived of the right to life itself. That right belonged to him not because he was a Negro or a member of any particular race or creed. That right was his because he was an American citizen, because he was a human being. As such, he was entitled to all the respect and fair treatment that befits the dignity of man, a dignity that is recognized and guaranteed by the Constitution. Yet not even the semblance of due process has been accorded him. He has been cruelly and unjustifiably beaten to death by local police officers acting under color of authority derived from the state.[92]

A month and a half after the court announced its opinion in *Screws*, the delegates to the United Nations Conference on International Organization signed the Charter of the United Nations, the Preamble of which "reaffirms faith" in "the dignity and worth of the human person."[93] In particular, the Preamble acknowledges that recognizing the dignity and worth of the human person is essential to achieving the other goals of the Charter, namely to "save succeeding generations from the scourge of war."[94]

This language, and the sentiment behind it, could not have escaped Justice Murphy's notice, who incorporated it into his extraordinary opinions in a series of cases involving military trials at the end of World War II. *In re Yamashita*[95] and *Homma v. Patterson, Secretary of War*,[96] involved the trials, convictions, and speedy executions of commanders in the Imperial Japanese Army for atrocities committed in the Philippines. Justice Murphy was even more impassioned than he had been two years earlier in *Korematsu*. The language is well worth attention. In *Yamashita*, he wrote:

> The immutable rights of the individual, including those secured by the due process clause of the Fifth Amendment, belong not alone to the members of those nations that excel on the battlefield or that subscribe to the democratic ideology. They belong to every person in the world, victor or vanquished, whatever may be his race, color or beliefs. They rise above any status of belligerency or outlawry. They survive any popular passion or frenzy of the moment. No court or legislature or executive, not even the mightiest army in the world, can ever destroy them. Such is the universal and indestructible nature of the rights which the due process clause of the Fifth Amendment recognizes and protects when life or liberty is threatened by virtue of the authority of the United States.[97]

This is an elaboration on the concise expression of the UN Charter, and an exhortation to those countries that believe in the rule of law to conform to the demands of human dignity—regardless of political exigencies. "If we are ever to develop an orderly international community based upon a recognition of human dignity it is of the utmost importance that the necessary punishment of those guilty of atrocities be as free as possible from the ugly stigma of revenge and vindictiveness," wrote Justice Murphy.[98] To Murphy, recognition of human dignity was not only a moral mandate but a political imperative. It was necessary in order for the world to move on from the savagery of war, and it was necessary for the United States to lead by example in the new world order.

In *Homma*, decided the following week, the court dismissed the petition in a single sentence, citing *Yamashita*. Again, Justice Murphy would have no part of it. His dissent bores into the issue of human dignity with single-minded tenacity. Two of the three paragraphs of his dissent are reproduced here:

This case, like *In re Yamashita*, poses a problem that cannot be lightly brushed aside or given momentary consideration. It involves something more than the guilt of a fallen enemy commander under the law of war or the jurisdiction of a military commission. This nation's very honor, as well as its hopes for the future, is at stake. Either we conduct such a trial as this in the noble spirit and atmosphere of our Constitution or we abandon all pretense to justice, let the ages slip away and descend to the level of revengeful blood purges. Apparently the die has been cast in favor of the latter course. But I, for one, shall have no part in it, not even through silent acquiescence. . . .

Today the lives of Yamashita and Homma, leaders of enemy forces vanquished in the field of battle, are taken without regard to due process of law. There will be few to protest. But tomorrow the precedent here established can be turned against others. A procession of judicial lynchings without due process of law may now follow. No one can foresee the end of this failure of objective thinking and of adherence to our high hopes of a new world. The time for effective vigilance and protest, however, is when the abandonment of legal procedure is first attempted. A nation must not perish because, in the natural frenzy of the aftermath of war, it abandoned its central theme of the dignity of the human personality and due process of law.[99]

The dissents are all the more striking when one considers the crimes of which these men were convicted. Masaharu Homma's war crimes included the atrocities of the Bataan Death March in April 1942, which killed thousands of Filipino and American soldiers. Yamashita commanded the army during the Manila Massacre, in which more than 100,000 Filipinos were killed when the Japanese retreated from the Philippines. But even against the backdrop of these horrendous crimes, Justice Murphy thought that respect for the dignity of the human personality meant that every human being deserves a fair trial.[100] This conclusion—that human dignity thus imposes on the government certain obligations—would prove to be controversial as the notion of human dignity became more fully developed in the Supreme Court's jurisprudence.

In *Duncan v. Kahanamoku*,[101] decided the same month as *Yamashita* and *Homma*, Justice Murphy continued his campaign to have the Constitution comport to the demands of human dignity. Here, he lambasted in particular the racist rationale that underlay the decision by Hawaiian authorities to use military tribunals to try civilians instead of civilian jury trials (which would have included Americans of Japanese descent in the panels). A majority of the Supreme Court agreed that the closure of the civil courts violated *Ex Parte Milligan* (among other things), but Justice Murphy made clear his reasons in a long, separate concurrence. There were no security reasons for avoiding racially mixed juries, he said, and even if there had been, eliminating all jury trials was not a reasonable response:

> Especially deplorable, however, is this use of the iniquitous doctrine of racism to justify the imposition of military trials. Racism has no place whatever in our civilization. The Constitution as well as the conscience of mankind disclaims its use for any purpose, military or otherwise. It can only result, as it does in this instance, in striking down individual rights and in aggravating rather than solving the problems toward which it is directed. It renders impotent the ideal of the dignity of the human personality, destroying something of what is noble in our way of life. We must therefore reject it completely whenever it arises in the course of a legal proceeding.[102]

Again, the Constitution and the judges who interpret it have an obligation to rout out threats to human dignity, in whatever form they may take, whether racism, wartime hysteria, or something else.[103] In *Johnson v. Eistrager*, a dissenting Justice Black assumed that "Our nation proclaims a belief in the dignity of human beings as such" that precluded the denial of habeas corpus to "enemy aliens" captured overseas.[104]

By the end of the war, the concept of human dignity was firmly entrenched in the court's constitutional jurisprudence, and it became accepted that federal, and state, governments must "observe those ultimate dignities of man which the United States Constitution assures."[105] In fact, as the controversy over incorporation raged, dignity even found a home in the Constitution, in the Fourteenth Amendment's due process clause[106] (and concomitantly in the Fifth Amendment's). But the concept was still amorphous, too ill-defined even to provide content in the search for selective incorporation.[107] While some justices would have confined due process (and the dignitary interests that it implied) to narrow limits so as to keep sight of its outer boundaries, others were more comfortable with a more free-form concept. As Justice Frankfurter wrote in dissent in *Irvine v. California*, "The cases in which coercive or physical infringements of the dignity and privacy of the individual were involved were not deemed 'sports' in our constitutional law but applications of a general principle. They are only instances of the general requirement that States in their prosecutions respect certain decencies of civilized conduct. Due process of law, as a historic and generative principle, precludes defining, and thereby confining, these standards of conduct more precisely than to say that convictions cannot be brought about by methods that offend 'a sense of justice.'"[108]

Dignity in the Police State

From mid-century on, the concept of dignity arose most clearly in the context of the police state, as defendants and inmates argued forcefully that the investigative, prosecutorial, and punitive practices of the government violated their individual dignity. In many cases, of course, where the majority ruled in the government's favor, individual dignity was raised only by the dissent. In oft-quoted language, Justice Jackson set the stage in his dissent in *Brinegar v. U.S.*[109] He wrote: "And one need only briefly to have dwelt and worked among a people possessed of many admirable qualities but deprived of these rights to know that the human personality deteriorates and dignity and self-reliance disappear where homes, persons and possessions are subject at any hour to unheralded search and seizure by the police."[110] Justice Douglas continued this thread, but again in dissent. "We in this country," he wrote in *United States v. Carignan*, "early made the choice—that the dignity and privacy of the individual were worth more to society than an all-powerful police."[111] And yet, for much of the 1950s, individual dignitary interests prevailed only when the police conduct was so brutal as to shock the conscience.[112] By the end of the decade, however, the court would be more willing to consider the constitutional significance of individual dignity—at least outside the context of the cold war.

It would not come as a surprise to anyone that the 1960s saw the first real flourishing of the concept of human dignity in Supreme Court jurisprudence, the most significant example of which is *Miranda v. Arizona*.[113] In prohibiting police from coercing confessions, the court held that incommunicado and otherwise oppressive interrogations create an "atmosphere" that "carries its own badge of intimidation. To be sure, this is not physical intimidation, but it is equally destructive of human dignity."[114] The policies enshrined in the Bill of Rights, the court said, "point to one overriding thought: the constitutional foundation underlying the privilege is the respect a government—state or federal—must accord to the dignity and integrity of its citizens."[115] Objecting to the majority's new-fangled rule, Justice White's dissent seized on just this characterization; he argued that "More than the human dignity of the accused is involved; the human personality of others in the society must also be preserved."[116] If the new rule was going to result in the release of criminals on technicalities, the dignity of all members of the public was at risk. The consequence of increased crime rates would, according to Justice White, "not be a gain, but a loss, in human dignity."[117] But *Miranda* was an extraordinary case, even in the 1960s, and many cases involving police practices and the rights of the accused came down squarely on the side of the state.[118] Again, individual dignity has been kept largely to the confines of dissenting opinions; in a 2012 case, the majority upheld strip searches as an incident to a traffic stop, but only Justice Breyer in dissent recognized this as a "serious affront to human dignity."[119]

Nor has the concept of dignity been limited to Fourth Amendment searches and seizures. The court has applied it to cases raising Fifth, Sixth,[120] and Seventh[121] Amendment claims and, most prominently, to Eighth Amendment claims, as the concept of dignity extended beyond defendants, to convicted inmates.[122] In one of the most important cases, the court in *Trop v. Dulles* held that denaturalization of native-born citizens violated the Eighth Amendment, saying just that "The basic concept underlying the Eighth Amendment is nothing less than the dignity of man."[123] Soon this simple phrase would become the test by which Eighth Amendment claims were measured. In particular, the death penalty was first invalidated in 1972, then allowed in 1976, on the basis of its perceived violation of, then compliance with, human dignity, the latter decision garnering numerous dissents.[124]

In other cases, the treatment of prisoners during their period of confinement would be upheld or invalidated based on their respect for human dignity, as the court understood it. "Prisoners retain the essence of human dignity inherent in all persons. Respect for that dignity animates the Eighth Amendment prohibition against cruel and unusual punishment," the Supreme Court said in the 2011 prison overcrowding case of *Brown v. Plata*.[125] In *Estelle v. Gamble*, the court held that "deliberate indifference" by prison personnel to a prisoner's serious illness or injury may constitute cruel and unusual punishment contravening the Eighth Amendment insofar as it violates the "broad and idealistic concepts of dignity, civilized standards, humanity, and decency," which the Eighth Amendment embodies.[126] And in a series of more recent cases, the court has measured prison conditions against the demands of human dignity. In *Hope v. Pelzer*, the court held that "Hope was treated in a way antithetical to human dignity—he was hitched to a post for an extended period of time in a position that was painful, and under circumstances that were both degrading and dangerous. This wanton treatment was not done of necessity, but as punishment for prior conduct."[127] And in *Brown v. Plata* the court explained that "Just as a prisoner may starve if not fed, he or she may suffer or die if not provided adequate medical care. A prison that deprives prisoners of basic sustenance, including adequate medical care, is incompatible with the concept of human dignity and has no place in civilized society."[128] As the court explained *Roper v. Simmons*, "By protecting even those convicted of heinous crimes, the Eighth Amendment reaffirms the duty of the government to respect the dignity of all persons."[129]

Roper v. Simmons required the court to revisit capital punishment, though with exclusive attention to those who were under eighteen when the capital crime was committed. In *Roper*, the court held that such executions did violate the Eighth Amendment. There is nothing particularly new in the court's interpretation of that guarantee, and nothing new even in recognizing that "The basic concept underlying the Eighth Amendment is nothing less than the dignity of man."[130] But *Roper* is significant because it raises the concept of dignity to the level of an intrinsic constitutional value. "The document sets forth, and rests upon, innovative principles original to the American experience, such as federalism; a proven balance in political mechanisms through separation of powers; specific guarantees for the accused in criminal cases; and broad provisions to secure individual freedom and preserve human dignity. These doctrines and guarantees are central to the American experience and remain essential to our present-day self-definition and national identity. Not the least of the reasons we honor the Constitution, then, is because we know it to be our own." Apart from criminal procedural guarantees, the only general constitutional rights for individuals that the court mentions are those securing freedom and human dignity. All other constitutional rights seem to be subsumed thereunder.[131]

In far more cases, however, the court has held that the challenged conditions did not violate individual dignity, often over the strong objection of the dissenters. For instance, in *Hewitt v. Helms*, the court held that process accorded for administrative detention satisfied procedural due process.[132] Justice Stevens agreed that due process applied to administrative detention, but disagreed that the prison had provided due process. He wrote at length about the implications of dignity. Stevens argued that even in the context of imprisonment, an inmate "has a protected right to pursue his limited rehabilitative goals, or at the minimum, to maintain whatever attributes of dignity are associated with his status in a tightly controlled society."[133] Justice Scalia (along with Justice Stevens) echoed this idea in *Nat'l Treasury Employees Union v. Von Raab*, where he argued that excretory searches of customs employees were "obvious[ly] a type of search particularly destructive of privacy and offensive to personal dignity."[134]

Eventually, the concept of dignity would outgrow the confines of criminal law and attach itself to various other societal interests. In *Goldberg v. Kelly*, the court extended procedural due process to the civil context of welfare termination hearings, recognizing the dignitary interests of poor people.[135] In *Wiseman v. Massachusetts*, Justice Harlan acknowledged the dignitary interests of individuals who lived at Bridgewater State Hospital for the criminally insane, the subjects of the film *Titicut Follies*. While appreciating the societal interest in the documentary about conditions in the hospital, Justice Harlan wrote that, at the same time, "it must be recognized that the individual's concern with privacy is the key to the dignity which is the promise of civilized society."[136] In the early 1960s, Justice Douglas would explicitly expand his conception of the constitutional right of dignity to apply to "suspect minorities."[137] And in the 1970s, dignity would be explicitly extended to aliens,[138] and in the 1980s, to women,[139] older Americans,[140] and people with disabilities.[141] Indeed, as the court accepted that the principle of human dignity applies to all people, Justice Jackson's dissent in *Brinegar* would come to represent the standard: "So a search against Brinegar's car must be regarded as a search of the car of Everyman."[142]

Dignity and Discrimination

Whereas in the context of the police state, dignity was most often associated with the Universal Declaration idea of immanence—that dignity is inherent in every member of the human family—the Civil Rights period of American history underscored the necessary corollary of immanence—that each person's dignity is equal to every other person's. As the court began to focus on race discrimination, it would see Jim Crow as a "political and economic system that had denied [African Americans] the basic rights of dignity and equality that this country had fought a Civil War to secure,"[143] and the Civil Rights Act of 1964 as "the vindication of human dignity and not mere economics."[144] Likewise, gender discrimination deprives persons of their individual dignity because it is "based on archaic and overbroad assumptions about the relative needs and capacities of the sexes and forces individuals to labor under stereotypical notions that often bear no relationship to their actual abilities."[145] Thus, in a series of cases beginning with *Batson v. Kentucky* in 1986,[146] the court invalidated gender- and race-based peremptory challenges in both criminal[147] and civil[148] cases on the ground that assumptions about people because of their gender or race violate principles of human dignity. This implicates not only the principle of equality, but also that of individuation, and the ability of all persons to define themselves, by and for themselves. To discriminate is to treat the individual not as a unique being but solely as a member of a collectivity.

Unlike in many other countries, the American courts do not distinguish between race- or gender-based decisions made for the purpose of exclusion and oppression and for the purpose of remedying prior discrimination,[149] highlighting the importance of individuation to American constitutional sensibilities. Denying a person's individuality violates dignity whether or not the agglomeration is intended to burden or ameliorate. In a case involving the allocation of land to ancestral Hawaiians, the court explained: "The ancestral inquiry mandated by the State implicates the same grave concerns as a classification specifying a particular race by name. One of the principal reasons race is treated as a forbidden classification is that it demeans the dignity and worth of a person to be judged by ancestry instead of by his or her own merit and essential qualities. An inquiry into ancestral lines is not consistent with respect based on the unique personality each of us possesses, a respect the Constitution itself secures in its concern for persons and citizens."[150] Thus, in the 1990s when the court began earnestly invalidating affirmative action provisions, it did so repeatedly on the ground that *any* race-based decision-making violated the dignitary interest in being dealt with as an individual.

Dignity and Privacy

Justice Douglas's understanding of the intertwining nature of dignity, privacy, and liberty would culminate in his famous opinion in *Griswold v. Connecticut*. But in several cases in the preceding years he had suggested that these connections were constitutionally significant. In a case involving a man's refusal to let the city health inspectors into his apartment (to check for rats), Justice Douglas wrote in dissent that "The commands of our First Amendment (as well as the prohibitions of the Fourth and the Fifth) . . . are indeed closely related, safeguarding not only privacy and protection against self-incrimination but conscience and human dignity and freedom of expression as well."[151] He relied on his dissent in *Ullman v. United States*, where the court had upheld the Immunity Act, which required a witness to testify even if it would subject him to severe penalties (such as loss of employment and citizenship), so long as it did not subject him to criminal prosecution. Linking dignity and conscience, Justice Douglas had dissented: "the Fifth Amendment was written in part to prevent any Congress, any court, and any prosecutor from prying open the lips of an accused to make incriminating statements against his will. The Fifth Amendment protects the conscience and the dignity of the individual, as well as his safety and security, against the compulsion of government."[152] And yet, his opinion in *Griswold v. Connecticut* does not mention human dignity at all; the right to privacy expounded on in all the opinions in *Griswold* is significantly narrower than Douglas's conception of dignity, limited as it may be to marital relations and the "sacred precincts of marital bedrooms," and grounded in the emanations of the first ten amendments.

But just as Justice Douglas's focus on privacy would bear fruit in the later abortion cases, so, too, would his recognition that state intrusion into the private sphere of the individual might threaten his or her dignity.[153] In *Thornburgh v. American College of Obstetricians & Gynecologists*, the court wrote that "Few decisions are more personal and intimate, more properly private, or more basic to individual dignity and autonomy, than a woman's decision—with the guidance of her physician and within the limits specified in *Roe*—whether to end her pregnancy."[154]

This would find fuller expression in the court's landmark 1992 decision in *Planned Parenthood v. Casey*.[155] In *Casey*, a plurality (written jointly by Justices O'Connor, Kennedy, and Souter) reaffirmed the principle that a woman's right to terminate a pregnancy receives some degree of constitutional protection. As in many other cases since *Griswold*, the plurality grouped abortion with other decisions dealing with family, procreation, marriage, and raising children. In explaining this taxonomy of substantive due process, the plurality wrote: "These matters, involving the most intimate and personal choices a person may make in a lifetime, choices central to personal dignity and autonomy, are central to the liberty protected by the Fourteenth Amendment. At the heart of liberty is the right to define one's own concept of existence, of meaning, of the universe, and of the mystery of human life. Beliefs about these matters could not define the attributes of personhood were they formed under compulsion of the State."[156]

This language recalls several of the prominent themes in global dignity jurisprudence (although the court did not cite foreign cases). First, it highlights the individuation principle by linking dignity to decisions that are at the core of who we are and how we each want to live our lives. Relatedly, linking dignity to autonomy, it denies the authority of the majority to impose its views on the individual, by reserving to her the right to make such decisions "without compulsion of the state." But the unique American signature is evident here, too, as the court defines dignity almost exclusively in terms of being able to make decisions about oneself. The important point in American jurisprudence is that an individual who cedes control of the decision to another has lost his or her dignity to that extent. As Justice Stevens wrote in his separate opinion, "The authority to make such traumatic and yet empowering decisions is an element of basic human dignity"; Stevens called the decision to terminate a pregnancy "nothing less than a matter of conscience."[157]

Eleven years after *Casey*, the court would again find dignity relevant to constitutional rights previously associated with privacy. In *Lawrence v. Texas*, the court reconsidered the constitutionality of laws prohibiting sexual intimacy between people of the same sex. As is well known, the court had earlier upheld such laws in 1986 in *Bowers v. Hardwick*, but by 2003, the court changed its mind. "It suffices for us to acknowledge that adults may choose to enter upon this relationship in the confines of their homes and their own private lives and still retain their dignity as free persons," the court explained.[158] In describing the changes that had occurred since *Bowers* was decided, the court mentioned two cases, of which *Casey* was one. (The other was *Romer v. Evans*, which was directly on point, as it concerned discrimination on the basis of sexual orientation.) In explaining why *Casey*'s reasoning in the abortion context had cast *Bowers*'s "holding into even more doubt," the *Lawrence* court cited the above-quoted language in *Casey* about dignity and autonomy. This, it said, explained the "respect the Constitution demands for the autonomy of the person in making" personal choices dealing with family and intimate relationships.[159] Here, dignity is so closely associated with autonomy that it is entirely subsumed by it.

Dignity and Speech

The U.S. Supreme Court did not take First Amendment rights seriously until after World War I, but since then it has consistently recognized that freedom of speech enhances dignity in both its individuation and its autonomy dimensions. However, in the American cases, unlike in many of their foreign counterparts, the link between dignity and speech is not often explicit, nor is the theoretical basis for protecting the dignitary interests relating to speech well developed. But the seeds are definitely there.

One of the most thoughtful examinations of how free speech promotes human dignity came in the Vietnam era case *Cohen v. California*, in which Justice Harlan upheld Cohen's right to wear a jacket embroidered with the words "Fuck the Draft" on the ground that he had a right not only to express the idea, but to choose how to express it. Justice Harlan's reasons for protecting this untoward expression braided together ideas of political discourse, individual autonomy, and human dignity: "The constitutional right of free expression is powerful medicine in a society as diverse and populous as ours. It is designed and intended to remove governmental restraints from the arena of public discussion, putting the decision as to what views shall be voiced largely into the hands of each of us, in the hope that use of such freedom will ultimately produce a more capable citizenry and more perfect polity and in the belief that no other approach would comport with the premise of individual dignity and choice upon which our political system rests."[160]

Then, in *Beard v. Banks*, Justice Stevens in dissent argued that a prison ban on photographs and books (with very limited exceptions) did not comport with "the sovereign's duty to treat prisoners in accordance with 'the ethical tradition that accords respect to the dignity and worth of every individual.'"[161] Justice Stevens was most troubled because "the rule comes perilously close to a state-sponsored effort at mind control." Quoting *Wooley v. Maynard* (the case invalidating the requirement that all New Hampshire drivers adopt the slogan "Live Free or Die"), Justice Stevens wrote that the state may not "invade the sphere of intellect and spirit which it is the purpose of the First Amendment of our Constitution to reserve from all official control."[162] In *Beard v. Banks*, he wrote, the near-complete prohibition of secular reading material "prevents prisoners from 'receiving suitable access to social, political, esthetic, moral, and other ideas,' which are central to the development and preservation of individual identity, and are clearly protected by the First Amendment."[163] Dignity here invokes important values that stem from individuation: the human desire and capacity to learn, think, and develop one's personality. Inside the confines of prison, this is largely a mental experience that is necessary for self-preservation; outside, as described in *Cohen*, this conception of dignity also recognizes that we live together in social and political community, while still privileging the value of autonomy.

In *Citizens United v. Federal Election Commission*, the court upheld the First Amendment rights of corporations, allowing unlimited campaign contributions. Justice Stevens argued in dissent that there is no basis for extending free speech rights to corporations, because of the dignity interests free speech entails: "Freedom of speech helps 'make men free to develop their faculties,' it respects their 'dignity and choice,' and it facilitates the value of 'individual self-realization.' Corporate speech, however, is derivative speech, speech by proxy.... Take away the ability to use general treasury funds for some of those ads, and no one's autonomy, dignity, or political equality has been impinged upon in the least."[164] Justice Stevens's argument was that dignity is so closely linked to self-realization and "choice" or autonomy that it has no application to corporations. Dignity is inherent in every member of the human family but does not extend beyond the human family.

In the First Amendment area, dignity operates both as a sword (insisting on the right to express oneself freely and the right to information to make such expression meaningful) and as a shield (protecting against defamatory and other harmful speech). Thus, the court has recognized that dignity may also limit speech rights, because of the assault on dignity that some speech may produce. If speech harms reputation, diminishes self-esteem, or threatens the peace of a community, the dignity of the audience (or target) may lead to limitations on free speech. Thus defamation laws, as well as laws suppressing hate speech, fighting words, and other speech "which by its very utterance inflicts injury"[165] might in fact *promote* individual dignity. The court has accepted this argument in the context of defamation, but less frequently in the context of these other forms of speech. In *Gertz v. Robert G. Welch, Inc.*, Justice White (in dissent) captured the tension: "Freedom and human dignity and decency ... Both exist side-by-side in precarious balance, one always threatening to overwhelm the other. Our experience as a Nation testifies to the ability of our democratic institutions to harness this dynamic tension."[166] He went on to identify the civil law of libel as one mechanism that accommodates these competing forces.[167] As noted previously, at roughly the same time, Justice White was also recognizing that dignity cuts both ways in the context of criminal law: if suspects, defendants, and prisoners have dignitary interests that the Constitution must recognize, so too should the public's interest in dignity protect it from assault. In both situations, dignity justifies *limiting* individual freedom. In other cases, the court has been even more explicit in noting that defamation laws are "directed to the worthy objective of ensuring the 'essential dignity and worth of every human being.' "[168] *Estes v. Texas*, where the court held that televising a defendant's trial would impair his dignity, furnishes another example of the tension between First Amendment values and dignitary interests.[169]

Dignity in the Modern Court:
The Confluence of Institutional and Individual Dignity

Notwithstanding these myriad invocations of human dignity throughout the Supreme Court's individual rights jurisprudence, it cannot be denied that the Supreme Court has so far declined to embrace human dignity with the ardor of its global peers. In fact, perhaps more interesting than the cases in which dignity has been invoked are the cases that involve questions of human dignity where the court did not even mention it, including *Brown v. Board of Education* (invalidating racial segregation in schools),[170] *Roe v. Wade* (upholding a privacy-based right to abortion),[171] *Griswold v. Connecticut* (invalidating a ban on contraceptives),[172] *Virginia v. Black* (upholding limitations on racist speech),[173] and *Atkins v. Virginia* (invalidating the death penalty for people who are mentally retarded).[174] And the current court, since 2005 under the leadership of John Roberts, has been no more enthusiastic about human dignity than its predecessors. Dignity is not even mentioned in 95 percent of this court's cases, and in half the cases where it is mentioned it is associated with inchoate ideas[175] or institutions, such as courts and judicial proceedings[176] or states, Indian tribes, and foreign nations in their claims of immunity.[177] Of the remaining cases since 2005 that even mention *human* dignity, most refer to it somewhat inattentively as if by rote[178] and often in dissent.[179]

And yet, the cases do reiterate the principle, evident since the 1790s, that dignity is in some ways relevant to constitutional interpretation, though it is nowhere explicit. But they exemplify the protean character of constitutional dignity: it can be attributed to states, courts, statutes, and people—both in its dignitarian sense and in its "everyman" sense. And while various justices have invoked the concept in one context or another, there is no area in which the court as a whole has used individual dignity as the measure of the constitutional right. (The only possible exception to this rule is the Eighth Amendment jurisprudence, although there the Supreme Court is an outlier among the world's constitutional democracies in holding that capital punishment does not violate human dignity.) There continues to be no unifying theme—no "central meaning"—that explains the true significance of dignity. And while the justices of the court, individually and collectively, do recognize the relevance of dignity to constitutional interpretation, they do not seem particularly interested in defining it.[180] Indeed, in some instances, the court has explicitly rejected a "dignity standard."[181] This contrasts markedly with the court's eagerness to give constitutional stature to state dignity, as evidenced in the Rehnquist court's state sovereignty cases.

There has been only one exception to this inattention to human dignity in the Supreme Court's recent jurisprudence. In *Indiana v. Edwards*, the court held, over the dissents of Justices Scalia and Thomas, that "a right of self-representation at trial will not 'affirm the dignity' of a defendant who lacks the mental capacity to conduct his defense without the assistance of counsel."[182] This sparked a debate about the meaning of human dignity that is illuminating, though pithy. While Justice Breyer, speaking for the court, was concerned that "the spectacle that could well result from [self-representation at trial by a person with mental disabilities] is at least as likely to prove humiliating as ennobling," the dissent argued that this ignored the true reason why human dignity is constitutionally protected. It is not to avoid "the defendant's making a fool of himself by presenting an amateurish or even incoherent defense." "Rather," Justice Scalia wrote, "the dignity at issue is the supreme human dignity of being master of one's fate rather than a ward of the State--the dignity of individual choice." And this, in his view, ought to apply equally to those whose mental competence is beyond question and to those whose competence is in doubt. In sum, Scalia wrote, "if the Court is to honor the particular conception of 'dignity' that underlies the self-representation right, it should respect the autonomy of the individual by honoring his choices knowingly and voluntarily made."[183] This is the clearest statement to be found in any recent case about the values undergirding the fledgling conception of human dignity in American constitutional cases.

This brief colloquy also reflects the different ways courts around the world are thinking about human dignity. Breyer's opinion illustrates the universalist impulse that takes human dignity to inhere in humanity itself; it thus becomes an objective standard to which everyone must adhere. This can convert a right into an obligation if an individual does not meet the general standard, as where a person consents to work or other activity that is not dignified. Like some of the European jurists, Breyer holds that the state can *limit a person's choice* in order to enhance his or her personal dignity. For Scalia, on the other hand, dignity is defined by a person's ability to make choices for herself, to be autonomous, to be master of her fate. Human dignity is the dignity of individual choice. A state's imposition of its own definition of dignity destroys the individual's ability to decide for herself the course of her life.

But the colloquy cuts across global dignity jurisprudence in another sense as well: the two sides of the debate disagree as to the state's role in supporting dignity. For Justice Breyer, an individual can not lose his or her dignity, but the state can play an important role in supporting it: if the person's condition or decisions might compromise his dignity, the state can—and may even have an obligation to—scaffold it by providing assistance as needed, whether in the form of welfare benefits, medical care, legal counsel, or otherwise. For Justice Scalia, such support limits the person's autonomy; any effort by the state to help the person make his own rules is oxymoronic.

The association of dignity with autonomy and choice joins neatly with the court's understanding of institutional dignity as developed in the state sovereignty cases discussed earlier. From the 1790s through the present, the court has demonstrated that it is most comfortable with the dignity that attaches to inchoate constructs and that this form of dignity confers a certain level of protection or immunity on the bearer. In most of the cases, dignity attaches to states and the specific form of immunity is immunity from suit. As noted, the court's 1990s Eleventh Amendment jurisprudence specifically identifies the *indignity* to the state as the justification for immunizing states from all litigious attacks unless they consent.[184]

Viewed in this way, the already-developed case law of institutional dignity gives some definition to the still fledgling concept of individual dignity.[185] Dignity, in both senses, keeps the authority to choose with the bearer of dignity and protects against the forced surrender of control by one to another. A person who is forced into a particular sexual orientation or forced to carry a pregnancy to term can no more control her destiny or express her identity than can a state forced by court order to implement federal policy. Both the institutional and the individual dignity cases evince a deep connection between dignity and autonomy in the sense of freedom of choice, making one's own rules. From the early twentieth century on, the Supreme Court's privacy jurisprudence has always circled around this idea, as is most evident in the abortion cases, which have always been about the "right to choose." The court's focus on the language of choice was, politically, an unfortunate detour, particular in the post-Warren days when choice implied lack of responsibility. By the time *Casey* was decided, though, it was becoming clear that what it had meant (or should have meant)[186] all along was that what was at stake was not the right to choose to end a pregnancy but the right to choose how one ought to live, and that these decisions must be made by the individual. This is the "core of autonomy and self-determination" of which the critical opinions in *Casey* and *Lawrence* speak. At the other end of the spectrum are the "death with dignity" cases, which, fundamentally, are about the right to choose how to die.[187] (This may be why, even though dignity is most accepted as a bulwark against cruel and unusual punishment, the court has never seriously engaged with the dignity of inmates or even defendants: they have chosen their course and, to that extent, have surrendered their claim to dignity, even if they have not entirely surrendered their dignity. This recalls the German court's lack of concern about the dignity of a plane's hijackers: unlike the passengers, the hijackers chose their course.)

Understanding dignity in this way also ensures that the link between equality and dignity will not be broken, since each person has the same freedom of choice as any other, whether the exogenous agent would be the state or another person. As the cases suggest, dignity lies at the junction of equal protection and due process: I must have dignity to control my own life, and I must have no less dignity than any other person. All people must have their dignity respected on equal terms, just as all states come to the Union on equal footing. This conception of dignity also links to equality in another way, by prohibiting state action that classifies on the basis of criteria over which the person has no control. In American jurisprudence, classifications based on "immutable characteristics" are often suspect simply because the individual has no control over these traits and so bears no responsibility for them and should not be burdened because of them.[188] Such a law might be said to offend a person's dignity because it impinges on his power to choose his course.

But equality's coattails come with their own complications: just as the court can eviscerate the right to equality by treating it as a purely formal legal concept, it can do the same with dignity, as the Scalia-Breyer exchange in *Edwards* makes clear. Justice Scalia's notion of dignity is consistent with his formal understanding of the right to equality. In both situations, he will invalidate laws that *interfere* with what he views as the normal private ordering, but will not use the law to promote dignity or equality as a factual matter. Thus the equal protection clause prohibits any race-based discrimination, but the court will not allow it to promote equality among all citizens; that is the job of the private sector. Likewise, Scalia's conception of dignity as briefly articulated in *Edwards* is that the law should not interfere with Edwards's decision to be "master of his fate," but there is no room for state action that seeks to enhance Edwards's capacity to do so. In Justice Breyer's hands the law is relevant not only to avoiding de jure violations, but also to promoting the constitutional value of dignity: the law must not only avoid interfering with a person's right to control his or her destiny, it should also help to ensure that individuals can make meaningful choices about their lives.[189]

Understood this way, it also becomes clear that dignity has both a private face and a public face; that is, dignity may describe one who in fact is in control of one's destiny and may also describe one who *appears* to be in such control. It therefore has both subjective and objective aspects. There is a dignity interest in being able to say what we want, how we want to say it, as well as a (sometimes competing) dignity interest in protecting our reputation to ensure that others think well of us. To demean someone is to insult their dignity by lowering them in the eyes of others.[190] Dignity is not only what we choose to do, but how we choose to present ourselves to others. Peggy Cooper Davis suggests that this "is what we mean when we say that human life is valued for its expressive, as well as its natural, qualities. We respect human dignity in order to give rein to human expressive capacities and desires."[191]

Dignity in this way is linked to the old-fashioned notion of dignity as a badge of honor[192] or nobility. Those who have political and social power are more likely to have control over their own destiny. By contrast, guaranteeing the right to human dignity is more problematic in situations of dependency, whether material, brought on by abject poverty or lack of education, or physical, due to incarceration or other forms of custody, or to bodily attributes such as age (young or old) or disability (as in the *Edwards* case). In these situations, there has already been some limitation on free choice, some inability to control one's own "policies," and the question in such cases is how much more can be asked of the person. To say that such conditions do not violate human dignity is to accept uncritically the idea of the neutrality of the state and the dissociation between public power and private power.[193] It is, in this sense, a distinctly American conception of dignity.

5

"What Respect Is Due"

Dignity is important. Countries are increasingly including references to dignity in their constitutions; few recent constitutions have been adopted without mentioning human dignity, regardless of region, culture, or history.[1] And within constitutional texts themselves, dignity is being described in increasingly elaborate and detailed terms.[2] More and more, litigants are arguing their cases from the standpoint of dignity instead of or in addition to asserting other rights, and courts are responding in surprising ways. The dignity cases are unique in constitutional law for several reasons. First, dignity is becoming a universally recognized constitutional value, transcending geographic, cultural, and political boundaries. Second, dignity is undeniably broader and more amorphous and appears in a wider variety of factual settings than any other constitutional right. Third, jurists are increasingly embracing the opportunity to give meaning to dignity, even in cases where it is not necessary for the resolution of the case; that is, they are *choosing* to discuss what human dignity means in their particular constitutional culture. In these cases, we are seeing not only the development of a right, as we would see what the right to food or the right to vote means in various countries. These cases take us beyond where ordinary jurisprudence goes, and tell us something profoundly important about the relationship between the individual and the state in modern times.

For both constitution drafters and constitution interpreters, dignity's appeal is unassailable—who can be against dignity? Indeed, dignity is more appealing than some other constitutional values whose meanings have in part already been defined, if not despoiled, by their troublesome jurisprudential pasts. Unlike equality (whose meaning is routinely contested by formalists and pragmatists alike) or liberty (which is seen as too western or northern, too individualistic, and too limited for robust constitutions), dignity has not yet been deployed in domestic or international culture wars, so its invocation is not yet marred by past battles. Quite the opposite. Dignity comes to constitutional law already credentialed by the international community. With roots in both the French Revolution and the humanistic response to the Holocaust, its endorsement by Eleanor Roosevelt and other idealists from around the globe, and its subsequent inclusion in both international human rights covenants, dignity has an impressive pedigree. For anyone seeking to legitimate constitutional culture, dignity can be a profoundly attractive rhetorical device. It holds all the promise and little of the responsibility.

Its attractiveness also surely lies in part in its very vacuousness. Like other capacious terms, dignity is amorphous enough to mirror whatever the beholder puts up to it; everyone likes dignity because dignity means what each of us wants. This is why both wings of the U.S. Supreme Court can agree that the Eighth Amendment is founded on the principle of human dignity, though they disagree as to what that means in a given case. And this may explain the readiness with which constitutionalists embrace dignity. In Israel, it has been described as "the source of all human rights. . . . Indeed, it is human dignity that makes a person worthy of rights."[3] Under the 2010 Kenyan constitution, the purpose of protecting all human rights "is to preserve the dignity of individuals."[4] In Peru, promoting dignity is the very purpose of the state. It is the alpha and the omega.

For some, dignity's protean nature is its fatal flaw: dignity is so pervasive that it has lost its value. If dignity can be all things to all people, then it means nothing at all; it is a slovenly way to discuss rights, an empty signifier. Some courts worry that dignity is so broad and so fundamental that if left unattended it will swallow up all other rights. As one Israeli Supreme Court justice has written, "Some see in human dignity the principle of equality, some see in it the freedom of speech, and some see in it other basic rights that are not mentioned in the Basic Law. Someone compiling these statements could receive the impression that human dignity is, seemingly, the whole law in a nutshell, and that it is possible to apply to it the saying of the Rabbis: 'Study it from every aspect, for everything is in it.'"[5] If everything is in dignity, then it renders enumeration of all other rights superfluous: who needs equality guarantees or a prohibition against torture if we have a right to dignity? Moreover, if dignity is absolute and inviolable, it renders government nearly impotent: no balancing or inquiry into proportionality is required to determine that the government can do nothing that impinges on any right, and no ends will ever justify the means of infringing on any right that comes within dignity's embrace. One scholar has written: "Where human dignity begins, democratic self-determination ends, and whatever touches human dignity in the hands of the [court] turns to stone."[6]

Dignity cases suggest a third alternative, which places dignity somewhere on the continuum between nothing and everything. In these cases, dignity is capacious enough to be singularly important, but not so broad as to mean everything and therefore nothing at all.

But exactly what work is dignity doing in the evolution of the world's constitutional cultures?

In the aggregate, the cases suggest that the work dignity is doing can be described in two distinct but complementary ways. The cases certainly reflect the courts' efforts to define a right that is important in their society. But they are doing much more than just saying what rights people have. The idea or principle of dignity is being used to undergird other rights and interests that people have in society, from limits on interrogation techniques to when an abortion is permissible to what name to choose to the proper level of pensions. So when we read these cases, we see not only the jurisprudential development of a right—or many rights—but the development of a constitutional value, an idea that permeates throughout the constitutional culture in each country and influences, in some way, what constitutionalism becomes in each culture. This undergirding value—simply stated—is that human beings matter; they matter in and of themselves, just because they are human, and they matter to the state; they are not fungible or dispensable, and they are all fundamentally equal. These cases describe human beings in a particular way, focusing primarily on the human capacity to reason, but also recognizing other qualities of being human, such as the need to hope and plan for the future, the need to live in society with others, and the equal worth of each person. But these are not exercises in abstract philosophy, although they get closer to that than cases in any other area of the law. They are constitutional cases, which means that they are ultimately cases about the rights of individuals and the limits of state power. Through these cases, we see what human beings are, and what—as beings who matter—they are entitled to; we see what claims people can make against the state and against others to assert their worth.

The relationship between who we are and what claims we can make or what rights we have is important though often implicit. As Peggy Cooper Davis has written, "understandings about what it means to be human are central to our sense of what respect is due."[7] What we are determines what we are entitled to. And when this is understood in a legal or constitutional framework, what we are determines what we have a right to. This is reflected, for instance, in the U.S. Supreme Court's determination that one's reasonable expectation of privacy determines, to a large extent, the scope of the right to privacy. Or, as Cooper Davis explains, "When we contemplate coercion or constraint . . . we test the coercion or constraint in terms of our understandings of human capacity and human desire. How, we ask, is it right to treat a reasoning being who has self-awareness, moral consciousness, and ambitions about the construction of a life?"[8] What rights or guarantees or protections or respect does human dignity demand that we accord to our fellow human beings? And, given those rights, what can we learn about who we are, about the essential attributes of being human? About the worth of the human person?

So the second aspect of the work that dignity is doing in the cases is to define the outer limits of public power. If, as the 2010 Constitution of the Kyrgyz Republic says, dignity "shall be absolute and inviolable," then the state is limited by the extent of individual dignity; it cannot act beyond the inviolable boundary of individual dignity. Consequently, courts engaging in and developing a jurisprudence of dignity are demarcating the boundary between the individual and the state, between public and private.

These two questions—what the dignity cases tell us about what it is to be human, and what they tell us about the limits of state power—are explored in turn in this chapter.

Judicial Construction of What It Means to Be a Person

What do the cases about dignity tell us about what it means to be human in the twenty-first century? Since humans are the subject and object of most constitutional litigation, the courts do not usually deal with the primordial question about why humans are special or whether they are more special than other living things. But they do get on the train at the very next station, asking what defines being human. Courts vary in how explicitly they engage with the question and whether they approach it inductively or deductively, but, collectively, the dignity cases present a comprehensive and coherent picture of what it means to be human in the modern world.

Despite the wide range of factual situations and the diverse cultures and histories of the nations whose interpretations contribute to this composite, the picture that emerges is surprisingly simple and clear. The picture of humanity that is drawn by the cases emphasizes four distinct though overlapping features.

First, human beings are described as rational or thinking, and so dignity protects people's capacity for reason. Government action that limits choice may thereby violate the right to human dignity, whether by physical coercion (as with torture), by limiting options (as with discriminatory exclusions or burdens, or compelling certain lifestyle choices), or by duress (as with self-incrimination). In a Slovenian case about forced medication to people with mental illnesses, the court acknowledged that such coercion constituted "a most humiliating act and a degradation of the human being as a person, as it constitutes a deprivation of liberty or a deprivation of the right to decide about oneself."[9] The principal injury, it appears, is the impairment of the individual's capacity to make decisions for him- or herself.

If human beings can reason, they can reason about themselves; they can plan their own life courses and hope for the future. This may be thought of as dignity's aspirational aspect. The cases that emphasize this feature are skeptical of government action that limits a person's ability to plan that life course. This is distinct from the rationality aspect: in some ways it is more precise, inasmuch as it protects a particular type of planning; in other ways it goes beyond rationality, because people plan their futures not only on the basis of rational thought but on the basis of emotion, desire, need, morality, and many other factors and because developing one's life course is as much a matter of self-definition as it is of planning for the future. This aspect of dignity is evident when the German Constitutional Court protects a prisoner's need to hope he or she will be released. Or when the U.S. Supreme Court says that abortion cannot be absolutely restricted because "At the heart of liberty is the right to define one's own concept of existence, of meaning, of the universe, and of the mystery of human life. Beliefs about these matters could not define the attributes of personhood were they formed under compulsion of the State."[10] The Colombian cases on the right to health offer another example: that "the patient has a right to harbor the hope of recovery and, in effect, to seek relief for her suffering and a life according to her human condition."[11]

The cases from outside the United States underscore that the human condition is a communal experience. Although dignity is inherent in each of us individually, its import is also felt when we are in community with others. In some cases, this communal or outward-looking aspect of dignity is manifested in the judicial protection of relationships, such as in cases regarding marriage and family life. In the United States, these cases focus on the right to *choose* whom to marry or when to have children, though in most other countries they emphasize the emotive importance of the relationship to the individuals, as in the Israeli case allowing Israeli and Palestinian spouses to live together.

Everyone—every "member of the human family"—is deemed by law to have these capacities to reason, to plan, to hope, in equal measure. No one has more or less dignity than anyone else, no one has a greater right to have rights than anyone else; every person is equal in this fundamental regard. George Kateb has written that "the notion of equal status deepens the idea of human dignity. It carries through on the attempt to establish the value of humanity by insisting on the value of every human individual."[12] This idea overlaps with the rationality attribute in that it prevents any one person from degrading or humiliating another by limiting his or her choice of action. But it goes beyond rationality in that it also protects against degradation or humiliation that does not limit freedom of choice. Prisoners are still entitled to raise claims that their treatment violates their equal dignity rights, even though better treatment will not enhance their freedom of choice. Placing windows of public service agencies high enough so that people who are unusually short cannot easily reach them does not necessarily restrict freedom of choice, but it violates human dignity because it treats some people as less worthy of respect than others. The notion that all human beings are fundamentally equal, radical though it is, underlies all of the dignity jurisprudence; to deny equality of worth is to deny human dignity.

By describing the human condition in these ways, the cases adumbrate the rights to dignity; by describing dignity in these ways, the cases tell us what it means to be human. But few cases pay attention to the line between the right and the deeper values of human dignity.

Dignity and Rationality

That the starting point for many courts is the principle that humans are rational beings is evidenced by the plethora of cases in which individual choice and autonomy are privileged. This is exemplified in the Hungarian principle of self-determination, the German, Kantian protection against objectification and commodification, the Colombian principle of the right to "design a life-plan" or "live as one wishes," the Israeli emphasis on free will, as well as the American abortion jurisprudence that defines abortion in terms of the right to *choose* to terminate a pregnancy. As President Aharon Barak of the Israeli Supreme Court has explained, "At the foundation of the right to human dignity lies the recognition that man is a free creation that develops his body and spirit according to his desire in the society in which he lives; in the center of human dignity lies the sanctity of his life and of his liberty. At the foundation of human dignity lies the autonomy of individual desire, freedom to choose and freedom of action of man as a free creation."[13] The rationality that is recognized in these cases refers not to an economic theory about optimizing expected utilities or even to a philosophical stance about practical reasoning—judges are neither economists nor philosophers, as a rule. The sense in which it is used here refers instead to a broader notion about the capacity to make decisions, whether good or bad, whether self-interested or not, including decisions for oneself. As the Canadian Supreme Court has pointed out, "The right knowingly to be foolish is not unimportant; the right to voluntarily assume risks is to be respected. The State has no business meddling with either. The dignity of the individual is at stake."[14] In this sense, dignity partakes of autonomy in the sense that the person decides and chooses to act for him- or herself. It might be equated with the idea of agency—acting on behalf of oneself—although the cases are more comfortable with the non-philosophical notion of rationality.

The rationality principle is reflected not only in dignity jurisprudence but throughout the law. As a matter of private law, it is exemplified in the premises of tort law. It assumes that each person has willingly chosen his actions and can therefore be held to account for his choices. But this responsibility is limited in ways that are defined by the premise of rationality. The negligence standard, for example, holds each person responsible only for those consequences of his actions that a *reasonable* person could have foreseen; if a person, applying reason, would not have seen the result coming, then the defendant cannot normally be held responsible. Nor can a person be held responsible if he is deemed incapable, by reason of age, mental capacity, or otherwise, of making a free choice. Contract law is likewise imbued with assumptions about human rationality. People choose with whom they contract, and arms-length negotiations are typically enforced by a legal system that privileges the (rational) intent of the contracting parties for the purpose of creating stable conditions in which more contracts can be consented to: contract law assumes a rational actor and is designed to protect the actor's rational choices. Again, it does not matter whether the person acts in his economic best interest; contracts entered into for the silliest reasons or entirely thoughtlessly are nonetheless enforced. It only matters that the parties' ability to think was not compromised. Likewise, a testator's decision to leave his estate to his cats is not questioned as long as his capacity to act rationally can have been presumed.

As a matter of public law, the contract becomes social. This is evidenced in two ways. First, through participation in governance: individuals can rationally choose policies and representatives that conform to their rational choices, and they can run for office to pursue their own rationally chosen policies. Elected officials are held accountable by the voters; voters are responsible for the decisions that they collectively make; if they choose a bad official, the voters have only themselves to blame. In this way, rational individuals are held accountable for the political choices they make. Robert Post describes "public discourse" as the realm in which this dialectic takes place, but insists that discourse be characterized by rationality. For Post, "public discourse can perform the function that it does for democracy, which is to forge a link between the individual wills of citizens and the general will of the nation, only if public discourse is perceived as a process of rational dialogue."[15] For Christoph Möllers, too, "human dignity implies . . . *the capacity to act on the basis of reasons,* which is a prerequisite for every democratic order. Furthermore, human dignity may also allow a right to be confronted only with reasoned decisions by the democratic community, a right to reasons against the state."[16] The basis of individual and collective action, in this view, is the capacity to reason, whether or not one does a good job of it in any given instance.

Public law also represents the rationality model in the criminal law. As Justice Gonthier of the Canadian Supreme Court has written, "it could be said that the notion of punishment is predicated on the dignity of the individual: it recognizes serious criminals as rational, autonomous individuals who have made choices. When these citizens exercise their freedom in a criminal manner, society imposes a concomitant responsibility for that choice."[17] Similarly, it has been noted in Germany that "the guilt principle (nulle poena sine culpa) is deduced from" the right to dignity in Article 1 of the Basic Law.[18] In contract law and in electoral politics, just as in the criminal law, ignorance of the law is no excuse: there is an almost irrebuttable presumption that everyone is knowledgeable or capable of knowledge. Constructive responsibility and constructive consent are founded on constructive rationality, which, in turn, is founded on the attribution of dignity to every human being, regardless of actual circumstance.

In both private and public dimensions, the rationality model assumes the equal status of all parties. Enforcement of a contract assumes relative equality in bargaining power just as the social contract (particularly under the one-person-one-vote system) assumes that all voters have equal power and even that there is an identity between leaders and voters; all are equal before the law. In constitutional democracies, this formal equality entails mutual respect among the people and between the people and their temporary representatives; it therefore supersedes hierarchical feudal or clan-based systems.

This assumption of equality is so extreme that people may become fungible: each contracting party is the same as the next, just as is each voter. And yet, while the rationalist model assumes the equality of all, it also assumes the individuality of each. Exercised in one's own mind, rationality is a purely individualist attribute. One chooses one's own destiny, one plans one's own life course. Even in the public law context, the act of voting is treated as a purely individualized act. The abortion cases are the exceptions that prove the rule: while a woman's right to choose is a product of her individual rationality, the fact that her choice directly and profoundly affects another being makes abortion cases among the most contentious and problematic. Otherwise, a person's choice is accorded a strong presumption of validity as an incident of his or her dignity. The German Air Transport Security Act case, in which the court invalidated a law that would have authorized the government to shoot down a passenger plane that was hijacked and intended for use as a weapon (as in the case of the attacks on September 11, 2001) puts the issue in stark relief. Here, the court clearly distinguished between the free will of the highjackers and the lack of free will of the passengers, who had not chosen to engage in terrorist activities. (The court, however, did not consider the lack of free will of the civilians on the ground whose dignity would be sacrificed if the plane were not shot down.)

As Ngaire Naffine has shown, this model suits the state well.[19] This rational consent, implied or actual, justifies state actions because it permits any state action that is not ultra vires; war, torture, deprivation, and so on are all acceptable policy choices as long as the people have freely chosen them directly or indirectly through their representatives. In a kind of Kantian paradox, the state treats individuals as autonomous and protects them against objectification but does so *for its own ends*. The current understanding of the state, however—as well as the rationalist prohibition against objectification—requires the state to act not on people for its own benefit but for the benefit of the people; that is, it puts limits on the ends to which the state can use the people, or, in other words, limits on what the people can consent to. The role

of the state is considered more fully below, but for now it suffices to note that
the rationalist model does not do justice to a constitutionalist conception of
the state or to a state that operates under an international human rights regime, where choices are, by definition, limited.

In most accounts, the rationalist-individualist description of human nature is taken to be a western (or northern) construct, or at least the product
of western values and western thinkers from Locke to Rousseau to Kant, with
support in the legal arena from Blackstone and then Madison.[20] For all these
men, man's inherent rationality actuated his autonomy—or what John Stuart
Mill called his "sovereignty"[21]—which allowed him to determine the course
of his life and protected him against objectification or control by others; that
is, a man has the ability and therefore the exclusive power to decide his own
life course. This man has been freed from the ties of feudalism in which the
circumstances of his birth (place, class, father's occupation, gender, even birth
order) determined the course of his life; he can now determine his life's plan
(repeatedly if he wants) according to his own choices, untethered by his community of origin.[22] Susanne Baer has remarked that "Up to the present day,
many endorse a notion of autonomy that is based on a certain concept of
rationality and on a distinction between culture and nature, as well as on
a notion of independence and a property-like concept of self-realization."[23]
On the other hand, countries that are clearly outside the American/western
sphere of influence have also adopted constitutions similar to those used in
the west and that refer explicitly to human dignity, just as those in the west
do. Cuba's socialist constitution emphatically recognizes the inherent dignity
of man: "The State organizes, directs, and controls economic national activity,
in conformity with a plan that guarantees the programmatic development of
the nation, in order to strengthen the socialist system, improve the satisfaction of the material and cultural needs of society and of citizens, promote the
development of the human being and his dignity, [and] the advancement and
the security of the nation."[24] The constitution of China recognizes that "The
personal dignity of citizens of the People's Republic of China is inviolable."[25]
The 1979 Constitution of the Islamic Republic of Iran proclaims the inviolability of the "dignity, life, property, rights, residence, and occupation of the
individual,"[26] and the constitutions of the Republic of Maldives and of Alge-
ria, among others, also read human dignity as consistent with the principles
of Islam.

By and large, however, this is the story of the modern person in a postin-
dustrial and globalized society in which the individual is the foundational

unit. As the American jurisprudence makes clear, through the course of modern history, the attribute of dignity has extended to those who are not highborn, to women, to the disabled, to the "feeble-minded," and even to those whose choices have landed them in the dock or in jail. And the Kantian cases demonstrate that the attribute of dignity being equally distributed now has leveled out society, replacing the hierarchies of feudal times. But again, the linkage of dignity to rationality and autonomy represents a western-cosmopolitan perspective that may or may not be reflected in all of the world's societies. Outside the west, it is argued, the community or the family or clan or tribe are the foundational units of society, and people are defined not by the contracts they make as adults but by the circumstances of their birth and the communities in which they live. In the African traditions of *ubuntu*, for instance, people are defined *by other people.* In many constitutions, both human dignity and family are protected values.[27] It is social relations that give one dignity, not the accident of birth. For cultures that have a strong social basis, the shift from community to individuality is not a sign of progress but a questionable departure from a preferred norm.

For some, dignity's enshrinement in the Universal Declaration of Human Rights confirms this western, post-industrial bias, while for others the UDHR universalizes the value of dignity, even if its roots are in the west. And the importation of dignity into domestic constitutions may or may not perpetuate the problem: on one account, the protection of dignity in constitutions in Africa, Asia, and even the still-Soviet-influenced republics of eastern Europe and central Asia demonstrates dignity's universality, while others complain that it merely shows western influence on the constitution drafting processes in those countries.On the other hand, the 2011 uprisings throughout the Arab world may quell any skepticism about the western bias of the concept of human dignity. What have been referred to as the dignity revolutions in Tunisia, Egypt, Libya, and elsewhere are as emphatically centered on the call to respect human dignity as they are stridently homegrown.

While they illustrate currents in the thinking about the right to dignity, these conflicts—between east and west, between individuality and community—do not need to be resolved here. The importation of the international norm into domestic constitutional jurisprudence permits each nation to put its own cultural imprint on the idea of dignity. Moreover, whatever its roots and its ideological origins, the UDHR and the cases decided pursuant to domestic constitutional provisions go far beyond the rationalistic account of dignity. Rationality may be the conceptual seed of human dignity, but as dignity has branched out throughout the world it has grown into a robust, living tree.

Cracks in the Rationality Construct

One problem with the rationalist model is that it faces challenges at the boundary. While most people could be characterized as "rational," there are many whose more limited rationality does not enable them to make the kinds of decisions that are envisioned by the model. This might include those whose rationality is not fully developed (the mentally disabled) or is not *yet* fully developed (children), as well as those whose rationality is diminished by illness, age, or trauma. At the extreme, dignity protection for the unborn and the deceased challenges the idea that we protect human dignity because humans can act rationally. Can the deceased act rationally? As a factual matter, we might think not, but there are times when the law does protect the (constructively rational) decisions of the deceased, such as when it enforces a will. The Slovenian Constitutional Court suggested as much when it held that the right to reverence protects both the mourner and the mourned, and attempted to provide ongoing protection for the decisions the deceased made while alive: "The purpose of the right to reverence is also the posthumous protection of the personality of the deceased, their dignity, and the wish that the decisions they took during their lifetime will be respected also after their death."[28] The court here does not seem to distinguish between respect for the wishes of the living and that for those of the dead, suggesting that the erstwhile rationality of the deceased person survives his or her bodily death or transfers to the next of kin.

On the other hand, there are nonhumans who may exhibit some form of rationality that under some circumstances may rival or even exceed that of humans. Certain animals, for instance, have been shown to have the capacity to act in ways that can be characterized as rational.[29] (Indeed, the Swiss constitution protects the dignity of "living beings," referring to "animals, plants and other organisms."[30]) And supercomputers or even smartphones, although lacking other attributes of humanity, may well outperform humans in contests of pure rationality. Even if rationality is understood as not just mere knowledge but as partaking of will as well, corporations may also be said to act rationally, as, for instance, when they make profit-maximizing decisions; indeed, corporations can be held civilly and criminally liable for their decisions, and in the United States they even have the right to free speech on par with human beings.[31] So the rationality account does not completely explain how dignity appertains to all humans and only to humans.

The UDHR's approach is to attribute dignity to "all members of the human family," so that it is enough to be a member of the family to have dignity, whether or not in the circumstances of the individual case the person has the capacity for rational choice and whether or not that capacity is retained throughout life. And it does not admit of the possibility that other rational actors might have dignity; animals, corporations, and other entities may have some ability to self-determine, but they are not imbued with the kind of dignity that is protected by the Universal Declaration. By attributing dignity to some nonrational actors within the human family and denying it to all nonhuman rational actors, the UDHR suggests that something other than rationality is at play here.

Another problem with the rationalist model is its individualist bent, which seems to exalt the individual who lives by his or her own (auto-) laws (nomos). Taken literally, the word "autonomy" is oxymoronic, since laws by definition regulate a group, not a single person. One may live by one's own mores or principles or values (all of which are held individually), but *law* entails regularity, which requires application to more than one. And of course the purpose of laws is to regulate communities, because people live in community. Their self-determination necessarily implicates others: if they choose to work, it is with others and for others; if they choose to farm, they need seeds and tools from others, and they sell their goods to others; if they choose to marry or have children or be educated, it is necessarily in community with others. Even actions that we often consider to be solitary—such as reading a book—are in fact engaged in community, in this case between the reader and the author; and the law regulates some aspects of even these most isolated of acts, such as when a sales tax is levied on the purchase of a book and limitations are imposed on the use the reader can make of the author's work. These regulate not one person's choice of action, but the terms of the relationship between at least two people—the reader and the author, the parent and the child, the worker and the customer. Most rights of conscience such as religious rights, and cultural rights such as those pertaining to language and history, are exercised and made meaningful in community with others. So, for instance, when the Slovenian Constitutional Court protects the right of reverence as an incident of dignity, it is protecting the right of a person to revere the memory of a deceased person.[32] It is protecting not the individual's private act of grieving, but, again, the relationship—here, between the mourner and the mourned. Moreover, the particular context of constitutional governance also necessarily entails collective action: civil and political rights such as the right to vote, the right to express one's opinions, and the right to run for office may be chosen individually, but they have significance only when exercised in community with others. Indeed, many would argue that there is no individual without the community,as is suggested by the African concept of *ubuntu*. To the extent that rationality entails autonomy, then, it does not paint a comprehensive picture of the human experience.[33]

A related problem with the rationalist model is that it does not sufficiently account for the role of the state in fostering rationality, particularly in terms of providing adequate education. Even beyond education, as some constitutions and constitutional courts have recognized (along with many economists), the state may need to provide a modicum of material well-being such as housing, access to water and food, and medical care in order for people to be able to use their rationality to in fact determine their life course: most of the world's people simply do not have the wherewithal to control where they live, with whom they enter into contractual relations, and the circumstances under which they choose to marry and have children. Thus, dignity cases have imposed on the government the positive obligation to ensure that citizens live in dignity. Colombian courts have used the concept of the *mínimo vital* to identify the level of benefits to which Colombians must have access.[34] For instance, the court has voided a plan for financing public housing that would have "made dignified housing unavailable."[35] These cases follow the German concept of the *Existenzminimum* as exemplified in the *Hartz IV* case, where the court read the dignity clause in Article 1 of the Basic Law in conjunction with "social state" requirement of Article 20.1 to find that social security benefits must be sufficient to permit a person to live in a social state with dignity.[36] In these and the many cases like them, courts recognize that while dignity is "inherent" in each member of the human family, it must be nurtured and protected by the others, including the state.

There is a critical role for the state when it protects the dignity of one or a few at the possible expense of the many, as is the case in any situation that raises concerns about public security, as in the German Air Transport Security case. Likewise, in the Israeli case dealing with the blanket exclusion of Palestinians from Israel even if they were married to Israelis, Justice Barak argued that the dignity of the Israeli spouses included the right to live together as a family, although his colleagues on the court would have taken into account the dignity and life interests of the Israeli population who would thereby (potentially) be made less safe by the possibility of increased numbers of terrorists in their midst.[37] This was also an obstacle to the recognition of the dignity of defendants by some members of the U.S. Supreme Court, who found that respecting their dignity to the point of acquittal might threaten the dignity of the public.

One final problem with the rationality model is its flawed descriptive account, particularly as regards those populations who have been disempowered throughout history. Women, for instance, have been treated as having diminished rationality for most of human history in most cultures where rationality is prized, and there is certainly a broad criticism due to the rationalist account of dignity on the basis of feminist concerns. As Susanne Baer has written, "it is women, among others, who have suffered from the interpretation of dignity as prohibiting only extreme cases, just as the fillings of abstract notions of dignity allow for the imposition of not only very particular but also very heavily gendered, and thus discriminatory, concepts on people."[38] In most of these cultures, decisions have been made and life courses have been dictated heteronomously by men *for* women on the assumption that women cannot make decisions for themselves. On this account, women's experience has been one of denial of dignity, both through affirmative public law (married women's acts, inheritance laws, disenfranchisement, etc.) and through public tolerance of private acts of violence against the bodies, lives, and dignity of women. This is also true of poor and enslaved peoples, across the globe and throughout history. The rationality model, then, which assumes the instantiation of autonomy for all people is inconsistent with the actual experience of most of the world's population throughout history. And while the post-World War II turn to dignity in international law, and the constitutional dignity cascade of the 1990s and the dignity revolutions of 2011, have heightened global awareness of the value of human dignity, none of these has dramatically altered the experience of the world's historically disempowered groups.

If the rationality understanding of dignity is built on the conception of people as individualistic and autonomous, then it at once describes too much and too little. Perhaps a better way to articulate this attribute is to emphasize not rationality, as the cases suggest, but the capacity to reason, which does, of course, set humans apart from other animals. George Kateb emphasizes this aspect of humanity when he notes that "Humanity is not only natural, whereas all other species are only natural."[39] The capacity to reason finds resonance in the equality and individuation principles described in the cases because it reflects each person's ability to reason in a subjectively unique way, while reinforcing the aspirational attribute of humanity discussed further below. Even so, courts have been quick to recognize that dignity involves more than just protection of man's ability to reason, that it values other attributes of personhood as well.

Beyond Rationality

In addition to the capacity for reason, some courts protect human beings' capacity for emotion in cases dealing with intimacy, such as the Canadian and South African courts' treatment of the dignity interest in choosing a partner of one's choice, or even the U.S. Supreme Court's assertion that the criminalization of same-sex intimacy violates the right to liberty in its "transcendent" sense. Other cases protect human beings' spirituality when they limit the government's ability to coerce religion or to prohibit the exercise of religion of one's choice. The Peruvian court has been explicit about this dimension of dignity. In a case about the designation of bullfighting as a cultural experience, the court recognized the constitutional protection for cultural and ethnic identity, along with the state obligation to respect, reaffirm, and promote such customs and cultural manifestations that form this diverse and pluralistic culture.[40] But the court went on to explain the rationale for this protection of cultural diversity by reference to the twin aspects of the constitutional recognition of the human person: "This social perspective that the Constitution attributes to the human being allows, on the other hand, one to affirm that the Constitution is not only *ratio*, but also *emotio*. This means that, while democratic constitutions presuppose that people are rational and disposed to harmonize their legitimate interests with those of others, we cannot deny the emotional or 'irrational' dimension that is also inherent in human nature. It is precisely attention to this emotional dimension where the Constitution recognizes the diverse cultural manifestations that people engage in either individually or as members of a rich and diverse cultural community."[41]

Cases also acknowledge that human beings are aspirational creatures as well and limit government's ability to encroach on the right to hope (as in the German cases involving imprisonment without the possibility of parole) or to seek "beneficial innovation" for one or one's descendants. The Constitution of the Republic of (South) Korea makes this explicit: "All citizens are assured of human worth and dignity and have the right to pursue happiness."[42] Dignity cases dealing with education and employment, and even cases dealing with environmental rights, recognize this aspect of personhood—that these things are necessary for the growth and enrichment of human beings as individuals and as a species.

Finally, the cases recognize and respect that the material life is important to human beings as well, not only because material comfort conduces to greater autonomy but because it is valuable per se. It just makes people feel better, and that is important. These cases recognize that governments have an obligation to ensure that people live with a modicum of comfort, be it with regard to the minimum wage, adequate housing, working conditions, or treatment while in custody. For instance, when the Bangladesh Supreme Court held that the forced eviction of sex workers and their children violated their dignity, it insisted the rehabilitative measures must be "designed to uplift personal morals and family life and provision for jobs giving them option to be rehabilitated or to be with their relations and providing facilities for better education, family connection and economic opportunities."[43] These benefits are for both the present and the future, and they are aimed at helping the women in both intrinsic and instrumental ways. These features are all blended together because the human being does not necessarily distinguish among them but seeks betterment in all these ways at once.

Special protections for children may also reflect a constitutional commitment to the ability of children to plan for their futures. Guyana's constitution is explicit on this point, stating in its preamble that the purpose of the constitution is to "Acknowledge the aspirations of our young people who, in their own words, have declared that the future of Guyana belongs to its young people, who aspire to live in a safe society which respects their dignity, protects their rights, recognises their potential, listens to their voices, provides opportunities, ensures a healthy environment and encourages people of all races to live in harmony and peace."[44] India's constitution provides another example, stating that "children are given opportunities and facilities to develop in a healthy manner and in conditions of freedom and dignity and that childhood and youth are protected against exploitation and against moral and material abandonment."[45]

One more aspect of being human that the dignity cases recognize is that all of these interests are held by the individual, but in community with others.[46] In much of the dignity jurisprudence, courts define humans as both individual and communal creatures interconnected with others. Some of the cases, such as the right to marry cases and cases concerning culture, explicitly concern associational interests. In the Israeli case about the rights of spouses to live in Israel when one is an Israeli citizen and one is Palestinian, Justice Barak wrote about the autonomous and the relational aspects of dignity as though they were intertwined and inextricable: "Indeed, the right to live together as a family unit is a part of the right to human dignity. It falls within the scope of the essence of the right to dignity. One of the most basic elements of human dignity is the ability of a person to shape his family life in accordance with the autonomy of his free will, and to raise his children within that framework, with the constituents of the family unit living together. The family unit is a clear expression of a person's self-realization."[47]

As the South African Constitutional Court explained in the context of same-sex relationships,

> The sting of past and continuing discrimination against both gays and lesbians was the clear message that it conveyed, namely, that they, whether viewed as individuals or in their same-sex relationships, did not have the inherent dignity and were not worthy of the human respect possessed by and accorded to heterosexuals and their relationships. This discrimination occurred at a deeply intimate level of human existence and relationality. . . . The denial of equal dignity and worth all too quickly and insidiously degenerated into a denial of humanity and led to inhuman treatment by the rest of society in many other ways.[48]

This passage highlights some of the ways individual dignity must be understood in communal terms. A burden on one's relationship may constitute an infringement of one's dignity. The infringement of dignity is exacerbated when the burden is imposed on some relationships (same sex marriages) but not others (heterosexual relationships), and when the burden occurs "at a deeply intimate level of human existence and relationality." And it is further exacerbated insofar as it encourages additional private or public acts of inhumanity. In these cases, it is the harm to the relationship that constitutes the violation of the right to dignity, recognizing that relationships are fundamental to the preservation of dignity.

This trend is particularly strong in Latin America, where the courts recognize the individual as operating within society. Here the courts tend to rely on how people function in relation to one another—what the Colombian cases refer to as "convivencia ciudadana."[49] In one Colombian case about the right to water, the court said that "the water that people use is indispensable to guarantee physical life and human dignity, understood as the ability to enjoy the material conditions of life that permit the development of an active role in society."[50] Similarly, in the Mexican case allowing adoption by same-sex couples, it is not the right to be a person, per se, but the right to be *considered* (by others) *as a person* ("se trata del derecho a ser considerado como ser humano, como persona, es decir, como ser de eminente dignidad").[51] In a Brazilian case allowing stem cell research despite claims that such research violates human dignity, the court emphasized the positive effect on human dignity that such research might produce: the possibility of cure, the court said, signifies a "celebração solidária"—not just the ability of a person to chart his own life course independently but to experience the society of others.[52]

In other cases, because people live only in community, the pith of the dignity injury is when one's ability to live in community with others is hampered. Cases about the minimum social assistance required to assure that a person can live in dignity may also be thought of not only as cases about one's level of comfort but about one's ability to live in society. The Supreme Court of Israel has said that "Human dignity is violated if a person wishes to maintain his life as a human being within the society to which he belongs, but finds that his means are poor and his strength is too weak to do so."[53] Likewise, the German Constitutional Court has explained: "The fundamental right to guarantee a subsistence minimum that is in line with human dignity . . . ensures every needy person the material conditions that are indispensable for his or her physical existence and for a minimum participation in social, cultural and political life."[54] Dignified existence entails at least minimum participation in one's community. Likewise, in the Slovenian case about involuntary commitment to a mental institution, the harm was felt not as much in the deprivation of liberty as in the humiliation in the eyes of others: "The petitioner believes that an individual who has been involuntarily committed to a mental institution is not conferred any dignity by society today and has little chance of living a dignified life."[55] This suggests that human dignity may also be impinged when one is diminished in the eyes of others, as is evidenced in cases that protect a person's reputation against defamation.

Many cases recognize this principle that dignity is important insofar as it reflects how we are seen in relation to others: judicial protection of an individual's reputation or the ability to choose one's name reflect this social interest, as do cases involving the problem of data mining. Likewise, cases that prohibit various forms of humiliation—whether by torture, employment exploitation, rape, or otherwise—recognize that one's dignity depends in part on the ability to control one's public face, one's outward identity. A 2010 case from the South African Commission on Human Rights regarding the failure to enclose toilets reflects this aspect of dignity. The interests protected in these cases would be meaningless if people lived alone, without society.

Jeremy Waldron has written about this in the context of hate speech, which, he argues, is problematic not because it is offensive or hurtful, but because it violates the victims' civic dignity; that is, it violates the dignity-based assurances that people in a well-ordered society give to one another. The actionable harm, he says, is not to the individual's feelings but to his or her standing in the community. "A motivation oriented purely to protect people's feelings against offense is one thing," he writes. "But a restriction on hate speech oriented to protecting the basic social standing—the elementary dignity, as I have put it—of members of vulnerable groups, and to maintaining the assurance they need in order to go about their lives in a secure and dignified manner, may seem like a much more compelling objective."[56] This view was reflected in the landmark *Ellwanger* case in Brazil, which illustrated the collective aspect of the right to control one's reputation. In *Ellwanger*, a convicted Holocaust denier petitioned for a writ of habeas corpus, but the Brazilian Federal High Court found that the dignity interests of the Jewish population outweighed Ellwanger's free speech interests. The crime of racism, the tribunal said, offended "the principles upon which we build and organize human society, based on the respect and dignity of the human being and of his peaceful co-existence in the social environment."[57] Again, the court emphasized that the indignity harmed not so much the individual's autonomy but his or her ability to live in society with others. A harm to the dignity of one segment of the population therefore tears at the whole fabric of society.

Other cases make sense only because people are part of communities: in the equality cases, claimants are discriminated against because of a trait held in common with others (race, gender, etc.), not because of a trait that they hold uniquely; they want to be treated similarly to those in a different community (the community of students who were admitted or employees who were hired). "The violation of human dignity is in the deeply upsetting feeling that another person is" exempted from an obligation or receives a benefit, said the Israeli Supreme Court in a case involving exemptions from performing military service.[58] Indeed, the idea that each person is equal in dignity assumes that the collective is central to the idea of dignity—that an equal measure of dignity is what we all have in common. Still other cases concern rights that we hold in community with others, such as cultural and language rights; environmental rights are held by communities defined by both space and time, as many courts have begun to recognize the intergenerational interests in "environmental dignity."[59] Likewise, the concept of "civic dignity" is increasingly gaining adherents, particularly in South African courts and in other courts concerned with the interplay of individual dignity and the body politic.

One final aspect of the communal dimension of dignity is evidenced in some of the Israeli cases, where the individual aspect is multiplied throughout society. Justice Barak has written: "The presence of the accused at his trial is not only an expression of the autonomy of his personal will. The presence of the accused at his trial is of public value."[60] The idea here is that, although dignity attaches to the individual, it radiates out to everyone in society, so that everyone benefits when anyone's dignity is respected.

Peru's court has perhaps been most assertive, in the name of dignity, in securing the individual's right to a social or economic good while at the same time insisting that these such rights are *social* and not individual. In a landmark case concerning the provision of medicine to indigent people living with HIV/AIDS, the Peruvian Constitutional Tribunal reconceptualized social, economic, and cultural rights as collective responsibilities ("deberes sociales"). It explained that "Recognizing social rights like collective obligations makes it so that, in turn, each individual focuses his maximum energies in obtaining those goods that represent social rights, superseding in this way the paternalistic vision that insists that the satisfaction of needs be concentrated in the hands of the state. For this court, ensuring well being at a level for a dignified life is a collective obligation, as much of the society as for the particular individual, and the state, but not exclusively the latter."[61] Everyone has a role to play in ensuring the collective dignity of every other.

The court views the dynamic and interdependent involvement of the public (individually and collectively), the government, and the courts as essential to realizing these social responsibilities. In this case, the court ordered that patients be provided with medical diagnostic and palliative treatments as deemed necessary by the relevant medical professionals, and that the public health service comply with the legal and policy requirements of the fight against AIDS, including considering the costs of providing treatment not as an expenditure but as a priority investment, and, significantly, that the hospital treating the applicants report back to the court every six months. The fact that vindication of dignity interests is a collective responsibility does not immunize the individual defendants from having to provide a certain level of treatment to certain individuals, but it places the responsibility to assure human dignity squarely in the public domain.

Although many cases seem to privilege the rationalistic and autonomous attributes of the human being, the totality of cases also reflects our emotive, aspirational, and collective qualities. But if dignity is founded on a conception of human beings that is more than rationalistic and more than atomistic, then the power of the state must be based on more than the social contract; it is not solely a response to the consent we constructively give to the state to exert power over us. The state must be limited, too, by these other attributes of human dignity.

The Constitutional Construction of the State

By virtue of its attention to human dignity in its many and varied manifestations, constitutional dignity jurisprudence is also suggestive of what it means to be a state in the modern world. Almost all states now have constitutions of one sort or another, and many of these constitutions look somewhat similar, with long and robust bills of rights protecting many of the same interests, some form of judicial review, and governing powers described in terms of traits associated with parliamentary or presidentialist systems or a combination of the two. And yet, there remain significant differences in how states characterize themselves within their constitutional system and even within constitutional democracy.

The paradigms can be described in any number of ways, by looking at the economic systems in place, the degree of industrial development, the extent of democratic consolidation, the strength of the commitment to the "social state," and so on. One way that might be useful for this inquiry is to consider the "animating hopes" of the constitution in a country. In one system, the animating hope of the state as envisioned in its constitution might be to secure life, liberty, and the pursuit of happiness, which Donald Lutz has encoded as self-preservation, unfettered sociability, and unfettered innovation.[62] Cindy Skach has characterized this as the Franco-American approach,[63] and it does, indeed, bear more than a passing resemblance to the principles of liberty, fraternity, and equality. The contrasting paradigm would be one where the central value of constitutional democracy is, as Walter Murphy has described it, human dignity,[64] which might characterize the constitutional cultures of postwar Germany, as well as that of postcolonial India, post-communist Hungary, post-apartheid South Africa, and post-Cold War Latin America. It may also characterize the ever-evolving constitutionalism of Israel. These "post-" prefixes suggest there might be something transformative in these dignity-based constitutional cultures that is either lacking or at least less prominent in others.

The Franco-American version reflects the rationalist approach to man, who, bursting forth fully formed, is viewed as capable of making his own decisions and charting his own life course; the state's job is to get out of the way. Thus, Article 2 of the 1789 Declaration of the Rights of Man and of the Citizen avers that "The aim of all political association is the preservation of the natural and imprescriptible rights of man. These rights are liberty, property, security, and resistance to oppression."[65] As U.S. Supreme Court Justice Brandeis wrote of privacy—a close analogue of dignity—the makers of the "American Constitution conferred, as against the Government, the right to be let alone—the most comprehensive of rights, and the right most valued by civilized men."[66] Now this might have been stated in terms of dignity, but in twentieth-century America it was conceived only as privacy, as if all that matters is keeping the government away from one's private zone. This minimal approach to the state still characterizes much of American constitutional culture, as is evidenced by the 2008 case of *Edwards v. Indiana*, in which Justice Scalia writes in dissent that when even a mentally incompetent person says he does not want a lawyer to represent him in a criminal case, the state should not provide one, lest it impair the defendant's dignity by forcing his choice. Even here, where the fiction of rationality is laid bare because the subject is not mentally competent, the state still has no power or obligation to intrude on the defendant's private choice. In this version, the constitution's "animating hope" is that the government will be prevented from judicial meddling in the choices of irrebuttably rational human beings,[67] and government power to meddle is restricted to that which is identified in the positive law. In these cultures, human dignity (mentioned explicitly neither in the U.S. Bill of Rights nor in the French constitutional texts[68]) is of marginal significance, and where it is relevant, it appears in the guise of rational individual choice, as in the *Edwards* case. (Though Scalia's view was in the minority in the case, it probably reflects a predominant view in American constitutional culture.) As Ngaire Naffine has written of this view, "Human dignity resides in human reason and the freedom to put it to use."[69] Nothing more, nothing less.

The transformative version that is evidenced in the constitutional cultures of Germany, India, South Africa, Latin America, and elsewhere is one that privileges dignity as a foundational right or value. In this view, humans still have inherent dignity, as the international documents declare, but the state has an important role in nurturing and fulfilling that dignity, and the courts' role is to make sure that the state does so. As the Slovenian court has explained, "In view of the fact that human rights that protect life, physical and psychological integrity, and the dignity of individuals are fundamental values of democratic societies, the state must protect them particularly actively and must create the means for their most effective exercise possible."[70] In these cultures, dignity is not automatically self-actualizing: the right to housing, education, social and health security, and other things must be assured by the state to ensure that dignity can flourish. In the words of the Israeli Supreme Court, "A free and enlightened society is distinguished from a savage or oppressive society by the degree of dignity extended to any person as a human being."[71]

Eschewing formalism, these courts recognize that material comforts are necessary to the individual's ability to exercise other rights and to live with dignity. In a direct refutation of the Brandeis formulation, Justice Albie Sachs of the South African Constitutional Court in recognizing same sex marriage, wrote that dignity, in South Africa, "is not the right to be left alone, but the right to be acknowledged as equals and to be embraced with dignity by the law."[72] It is not enough for the state to get out of the way (because as the marriage example indicates, it never really *is* out of the way); rather, dignity is fulfilled only if the state acts affirmatively to acknowledge and embrace—or at least to respect.

One gets to much the same place by considering competing epistemic explanations for the constitutional recognition of human dignity. In one account, dignity is and always has been immanent, and law—from the Universal Declaration to this year's constitutions—is merely affirming it, possibly for the purpose of reminding humanity of its inherent dignity and possibly to reinforce the rule of law. In the opposing account, the turn to dignity is explicable only in terms that are historically and politically contingent. The greater the precursive humanitarian tragedy, the more emphatic the commitment to human dignity as a balm. Möllers argues, as noted earlier, that Germany says it falls into the first camp, with a constitution that merely affirms human dignity that is already known to exist, but in fact the assertion of dignity was the product of democratic negotiation arising out of a particular (postwar) political context.[73]

But in this sense, Germany is no different from any other state at the moment of constitutional ordination. These two paradigms may be useful for identifying the core attributes of different kinds of constitutional systems, but the reality is that very few nations operate in these extreme ways; most constitutional cultures evince a mixture of the libertarianism of the Franco-American approach and the liberalism of the transformative approach, or of the rule-of-law and the democracy approaches. Even at their roots, the paradigms are not rigid: both the French Declaration of the Rights of Man and of the Citizen and the U.S. Constitution were postrevolutionary documents that explicitly sought to respond to the injustice of the previous regimes, so in their own way they were transformative as well. This may, in truth, be true of any new constitutional order, particularly in modern times, when constitutions tend to be taken more seriously. And both implicitly recognized the inherent dignity of man by envisioning a (hu)man-centric state based on popular sovereignty. And in both France and America, the pure libertarianism of the eighteenth century has thus given way to a more balanced view in the twentieth and twenty-first. The Preamble to France's 1946 constitution (which is incorporated into the current 1958 constitution) affirmed the fundamental rights of men and women particularly in the wake of World War II and envisioned a more robust role for the state. In the current understanding of the state's role, "the safeguarding of the dignity of the human person against all forms of subordination and degradation is a principle of constitutional value."[74] In the United States, even Justice Brandeis, who is perhaps most famous for his desire to have the state simply let him alone, also recognized a more active role for the state when he said that "the final end of the state is to make men free to develop their faculties."[75] Indeed, the context in which the "let alone" phrase appears is itself more capacious than a narrow libertarian view would suggest. In the sentences immediately preceding the "let alone" comment, he writes: "The makers of our Constitution undertook to secure conditions favorable to the pursuit of happiness. They recognized the significance of man's spiritual nature, of his feelings, and of his intellect. They knew that only a part of the pain, pleasure and satisfactions of life are to be found in material things. They sought to protect Americans in their beliefs, their thoughts, their emotions and their sensations."[76] Clearly, there was room here for the state to do some transformative, dignity-enhancing work.

Daniel Whelan has suggested a way of synthesizing the two categories, showing the correspondence between the French ideals of liberty, equality, and fraternity with the generations of rights found in many transformational constitutions. Following the work of Karel Vasak, Whelan shows that the types of rights reflected in the principle of liberty are first generation civil and political rights that are asserted primarily against the state and prioritized principally in first world or developed nations. Second-generation economic and social rights, he says, reflect the principle of equality and are primarily asserted against the market and are prioritized in what he calls the "second" world, whereas third-generation solidarity and group rights reflect the value of fraternity and are prized principally in the so-called third world, where they are primarily asserted against anticolonial interests.[77] Whether or not the match is perfect, it is valuable in showing that there may be less of a division than first appears between constitutions whose animating hope reflects the Franco-American minimal version of the state paired with a rationalist conception of dignity, and those whose principal value is the fulfillment of human dignity, and assume a broader role for the state in assuring it. Indeed, most of Europe, as well as Canada, Australia, and most of Latin America have market economies, though with significant regulation, and all have significant class differences, though they all purport to provide safety nets for the poorest class, to ensure a modicum of dignity for all. This is even true in the United States, though the market may be less regulated, and the safety net less robust. And it is also true of India and South Africa, where even though the promise of safety nets is more pronounced, the resources are more restricted. No two countries balance the competing values exactly the same way, but all are somewhere on the continuum. And the choice of where on the continuum to be—how to balance regulated markets, social security, freedom of choice, and human dignity—is for each state to decide as incident of its own sovereignty.

Constitutional democracies express these policy choices in two ways: through political decisions made either by the government through law or by the people in referenda, and through judicial pronouncements by constitutional courts. Where the constitution includes a justiciable right to dignity, courts have often used this clause broadly to demarcate the limits and obligations of the state vis-à-vis the individual. Thus, in the more minimal states, courts rely on the right to dignity primarily to assure that individuals have the right to make important private decisions, such as about family matters. In social states, the right to dignity triggers (among other things) the state's obligation to provide education, meaningful social security, almost all medical care, and other goods to ensure a decent quality of life for all. In social welfare states with greater populations of poor people, courts have demanded that, to ensure that people "live with human dignity and all that goes along with it," the government provide "the bare necessaries of life such as adequate nutrition, clothing and shelter over the head and facilities for reading, writing and expressing oneself in diverse forms, freely moving about and mixing and commingling with fellow human beings," as the Indian Supreme Court has said.[78] Thus, at its core, dignity jurisprudence is helping to define what the state is in these modern times. If the cases tell us that dignity resides in the human capacity for reason, its equality, its communal nature, and its ability to plan for the future, and if dignity is not just an idea but a right that must be protected, then the right to dignity represents an important limit on governmental power. State authority may reach to the limits of human dignity, but no further. And where human dignity *demands* action by the state, state authority must be exercised. Thus, understanding the meaning of the right to dignity tells us about the limits and obligations of state power.

At a minimum, most of these characteristics call on the state to refrain from interfering. If dignity is inherent, then the state's obligation is a negative one: to refrain from actions that would impair people's capacity for reason or distort their equality toward one another. The same is certainly true for the human inclination to aspire to improvement for oneself or for future generations. One does not need the state to help one hope or dream or plan for a better future. Likewise, people are born into community and will find others on their own. The state must refrain from interfering with those natural affinities (by segregation, restrictions on family groupings, unlawful deportations, evictions, or displacements, and the like). But there is, in most cases, little the government needs to do to nurture the ability of people to live in community, other than in particular cases where a culture has been threatened or impaired, and positive action is required to regenerate it.

On the other hand, it may also be the case that these various aspects of human dignity are consistent with a more nuanced and more robust understanding of state obligations. There may be a limited positive claim to education, to enhance people's capacity for rational decision-making, and a somewhat more robust positive claim to government actions that ensure equality or overcome difficult conditions, whatever their causes. Given the enormous *in*equalities (on the basis of race, ethnicity, gender, class, sexual orientation, etc.) that pervade every modern state, we might say that respecting human dignity demands that governments take affirmative steps to minimize inequity, and that merely avoiding discrimination does not meet the demands of each person's equal dignity. For instance, if one segment of a state's population lives in arid and infertile land, more resources may need to be directed to that area to ensure that those inhabitants live in dignity comparable to that of those who live in more fertile regions. We might also say that governments have an obligation to *promote* each person's ability to live in community with others by assuring the conditions that are necessary for a "well-ordered society," as Jeremy Waldron—following John Rawls—would say. A well-ordered society is one whose "basic structure is regulated (and known to be regulated) by principles of justice and inhabited by people with an effective sense of justice."[79] But, as is evident from the course of human history, such societies do not happen by chance; rather, they require concerted and sustained effort on the part of the state to create and perpetuate such conditions as will permit individuals to live in dignity with one another, or to live with what Waldron calls "civic dignity." "Civic dignity," he says, "is not just decoration; it is sustained and upheld for a purpose."[80] And it is sustained and upheld most effectively when it is constitutionally enshrined and judicially enforceable.

The aspirational aspects of human dignity also impose both negative and positive obligations on the state. The state must not establish rigid social stratification that would consign individuals to a particular station in life, with no hope for advancement for themselves or their children. One of the deepest injuries of apartheid in South Africa, Jim Crow in the United States, or India's caste system was that it permitted people no hope for a better future. But beyond that, the state may need to fulfill the right to dignity by ensuring the minimal levels of comfort that are necessary to allow one to think beyond satisfaction of immediate needs. One who is "reduced to one's body" is less likely to have the leisure and energy to devote to planning for a better future, so another reason to ensure that people enjoy a minimal standard of living is to ensure that they have the wherewithal to work for the future. The capacity for beneficial innovation and aspiration is meaningless if it will not be realized. Other social services may also need to be provided. For instance, the state may also have to provide meaningful education and ensure that students have access to transportation, books, a place to study, and food in their stomachs if they are going to be able to exercise their dignity rights to choose professions and lifestyles. It may have to make contraceptives available and prosecute rape if the right to control one's destiny is to be effective. The cases have recognized all of these obligations, without seriously troubling about whether they are positive or negative. They must be met regardless. Under the Interim Constitution of Sudan, the obligation to assure human dignity is embedded in the allocation of resources. Under "Guiding Principles for Equitable Sharing of Resources and Common Wealth" the first principle is that the "Resources and common wealth of the Sudan shall be shared equitably to enable each level of government to discharge its legal and constitutional responsibilities and duties and to ensure that the quality of life, dignity and living conditions of all citizens are promoted without discrimination on grounds of gender, race, religion, political affiliation, ethnicity, language or region."[81] While most countries do not have the economic resources to fulfill these obligations maximally, the critical point is that they recognize the importance of human dignity and the obligations imposed on the state to fulfill it. The dynamic processes by which dignity-bearing individuals hold their governments accountable for the constitutional promises they make is explored in the next chapter.

6

"The Beginning and the End of the State"

Demarcating the Boundary

If dignity jurisprudence is defining what it means to be human and also the ambit of the modern state, then the line in between is critical. Where do the laws of the state end and the laws of the individual begin? This might be thought of as the line of sovereignty, demarcating the reach of individual sovereignty or autonomy and the boundaries of state sovereignty. In some countries—such as, paradigmatically, the United States—dignity narrows the compass of the state to ensure greater scope for the exercise of individual liberty. In other countries, human dignity demands an expanded sphere for the state to respect what is inherent and to fulfill what is to be nurtured by providing public goods and services. In all these countries, dignity is doing the work of demarcating the line between individual and state sovereignty.

To some extent, this may be true of all constitutional rights: the language of rights is how we define the state. Rights define who is within and who is outside the state, they protect against state interference in the private realm, and they secure provision of goods or services from the state to support the exercise of rights. One could say that dignity rights are just like others, only more so: the right of free speech or freedom of religion or equality or due process is relevant in certain cases, but the right to dignity is likely to be relevant in all these cases, and more. Dignity does not replace all other rights, but it denotes them in shorthand. In this view, dignity rights do not play a distinctive role in the demarcation of the boundary between the state and the individual, but because dignity operates so broadly, we can learn more from studying it and perhaps draw more significant conclusions about the work dignity rights do than when we look at other more particular rights.

And yet, there is some support for the view that dignity is in fact different from other rights. In many cultures, it is the predominant right, the "mother right" or "general personality right," the *source* of all other rights, or the *purpose* of all other rights. The variety of factual settings in which dignity rights are relevant, the range of enumerated rights to which dignity rights are textually and conceptually allied, and the seamless blending of dignity rights and dignity values lend credence to the view that the work dignity is doing in constitutional development is different from that of any other right in the panoply of rights. Because dignity is taken so seriously by the world's major courts—because courts are willing to invest it with such important and multivalent meaning—it is appropriate to ask whether dignity is doing something *more than* what other rights can typically accomplish. Even beyond the role dignity rights play in augmentation of individual rights (and in the consequent limitations on state power), dignity rights may be altering constitutional culture and the democratic discourse of which that culture is an instrumental part.

Thus, when a modern constitutional court describes the appropriate boundaries of state power, it is likely to do so in the language of dignity. In protecting the associational rights of transsexuals and transgendered people, the Supreme Court of Argentina has done this explicitly:

> it is emphasized that the protection of a guiding value like human dignity implies that the law recognizes, as long as it does not offend order and public morals, nor injure another, an ambit of liberty that is intimate and impenetrable that can conduce to personal realization (self-fulfillment) such as is required in a healthy society. The protection of this ambit of privacy, it is concluded, turns out to be one of the major values of the respect of the dignity of the human being and a basis of the essential difference between a state of rights and authoritarian forms of government.[1]

Recognizing this "ambit of liberty" obviously creates a tension: the state wants to assert its authority to make laws for individuals, and individuals want to assert their own autonomy—the authority to make laws for themselves. If the court goes too far in asserting the dignity of the individual, it risks tilting toward anarchy; if the court does not go far enough in protecting individual dignity and overprivileges the state's authority, it risks totalitarianism and ultimately genocide, at the extreme.[2] And although the language of dignity is used around the world, the balance between individual and state sovereignty varies from country to country as a matter of each nation's distinctive constitutional values.

Dignity, Democracy, and Citizenship

Dignity and Democracy

While the cases are often explicit that there is a strong connection between dignity and democracy, they rarely explain exactly what that relationship is. Several theoretical options present themselves; all of these are possible interpretations of the cases, and because they are so intimately connected, cases often reflect several of these assumptions without distinguishing among them or evaluating the implications of the differences.

The first two ways to think about the relationship between dignity and democracy are almost definitional. One could say, as Ronald Dworkin has, that democracy can exist only where human dignity is respected.[3] In this way, dignity defines democracy and gives it legitimacy. David Bilchitz has suggested this in the context of socioeconomic rights: "in circumstances in which millions of people live in dire poverty, the exclusion of guarantees in a Constitution which address the economically depressed living conditions of so many would impact upon the very legitimacy of the system itself. This point also highlights the fact that when courts enforce such guarantees against other branches of government, they are not acting, as many would have it, in an undemocratic manner; rather they are defending the conditions for the very legitimacy of the constitutional order itself in which none are excluded."[4] The argument applies more generally, as we will see, to the recognition of dignity not only as a matter of socioeconomic rights, but in all its guises. This association between dignity and the legitimacy of the state is evidenced by the frequent alliances in constitutional texts of dignity and democracy. In Peru, where the text is not explicit on this point, the court has nonetheless found the link. The process of voting, it has said, is the act that transfers individual will to the social sphere. In the context of a law that allegedly diluted the power of minority parties, that country's court said that "democracy is founded then, on the acceptance that the human person and his or her dignity are the beginning and the end of the State (article 1 of the Constitution), such that his or her participation in the formation of the political-state will is the indispensable premise to guarantee the maximum respect for the totality of constitutional rights."[5] If the very purpose of the state is to secure dignity, the state will not be legitimate if it fails to promote dignity. This adds a substantive element to the meaning of democracy insofar as the state must work toward the actualization of the dignity of each person within the polity, and that it may be held judicially accountable in such effort. Nonetheless, no constitutions directly focus on the dignity basis of democratic legitimacy. Moreover, this probably overstates the claim insofar as there are many governments—including the United Kingdom and most of its former colonies, including the United States, Australia, and Canada—that don't formally, constitutionally, recognize human dignity as a foundational value, and those states, and their governments, unquestionably enjoy political and legal legitimacy. One might say, however, that dignity is still respected in those states, even though not by juris-constitutional mandate.

Alternatively, one could say that democracy is what defines dignity. There are several strands to this argument. One follows Hannah Arendt in her assertion that to have dignity is to participate in a political community. For Arendt, to be without dignity is to languish outside of any political community.[6] In this view, dignity's very definition is to engage in democratic activity. This approach is reflected in some of the cases, as when courts explicitly vindicate dignity rights that are associated with democratic participation such as the right to vote, to associate, to speak. But this, too, may overstate the link, as we would like nonetheless to recognize the inherent and still vital dignity of those members of the human family who are stateless or otherwise alien-ated. But perhaps these are the exceptions that prove the rule. Indeed, the protest movements of the "Arab Spring" of 2011 were seen by many as efforts on behalf of the people of Arab world to assert their dignity precisely by recreating their political spaces to nurture democratic and participatory activity.

Against this, Christoph Möllers argues that dignity is more than simply the right to have rights; instead, he focuses on human dignity's implication of the "capacity to act on the basis of reasons," which, he says, "is a prerequisite for every democratic order." In particular, he argues that "human dignity may also allow a right to be confronted only with reasoned decisions by the democratic community, a right to reasons against the state."[7] In this construct, the relationship between dignity and democracy is a procedural one (and one that follows from George Kateb's view of the uniqueness of human beings within nature): it describes democracy as a system in which authority is exerted only on the basis of sound reasons and demands that those reasons be provided to individuals who are distinctive in their propensity to reason. This may suggest a dialogic approach to constitutional politics.

The weak argument for the relationship between dignity and democracy is that they are simply reflections of one another but on a different scale. Democracy is dignity writ large. Robert Post has written, "What is this value of democracy? I believe it lies in the good of collective self-determination" in which "we exercise our own collective autonomy." Here, democracy *is* dignity on a collective scale. But to make the equation between individual self-determination in the sense of dignity and collective self-determination in the sense of democracy, there must be "a link between the individual self-determination of the citizen and the communal decisionmaking of the society"—otherwise, the imposition of the collective will on the individual in the minority is a violation, rather than an assertion, of the individual's dignity.[8] Unlike a body politic, a body does not have to deal with minority views, internal inequalities, pluralism, and other attributes of community that make the "self" in collective self-determination sometimes problematic and difficult to ascertain. And yet, both courts and constitutions are often drawn to the parallels between the two scales of self-determination. The Constitution of Andorra, for instance, "recognises human dignity to be inalienable and therefore guarantees the inviolable and imprescriptible rights of the individual, which constitute the foundation of political order."[9] Bulgaria's constitution also makes the linkage clear, stating in its foundational provisions that "The Republic of Bulgaria shall guarantee the life, dignity and rights of the individual and shall create conditions conducive to the free development of the individual and of civil society."[10]

A final way to think about dignity and democracy is that they have an ontological relationship to one another: the recognition of human dignity enhances democratic praxis, and democratic consolidation results in a more robust sense of human dignity. This is where much of the jurisprudence has settled, and it explains the work that dignity does not only in terms of defining the human being but in the broader sociopolitical terms of the project of state building. The court's authority is limited to enforcing the constitutional rights—here, to dignity—but the result of valuing that right is a more secure democracy.[11]

Conversely, participatory democracy can further human dignity. Democratic discourse helps to ensure that the policies and practices adopted by the state are respectful of each human being, individually and collectively, and particularly of those who have been marginalized in the past. Participating in democratic activity is a, or maybe *the*, principal way to express one's dignity. This argument circles back to Hannah Arendt, who posits that participation in a political community is what makes human dignity meaningful: where people are members of a political community, they have the "right to have rights,"[12] that is, to voice their opinions and assert their rights through action in the public square.[13] On the other hand, the dignity of those who are outside of any political community, who are stateless, is nothing more than the "abstract nakedness" that renders them vulnerable to tyranny (as is exemplified by the Holocaust: having mere dignity did not protect people once they were alienated from their communities).[14] If, as Arendt says, dignity is the capacity to act within a political community,[15] the jurisprudence of dignity fosters that capacity.

This understanding of the relationship between dignity and democracy reflects a dynamic approach, one in which courts can and do play a vital role. As constitutional interpreters, they can and do vindicate the right to dignity, but they often do so for the purpose or with the effect of strengthening the basis of citizenship, which is the means by which democracy is practiced. To understand this dynamic more fully, we need to explore the meaning of citizenship in the context of the dignity jurisprudence.

The Feeling of Citizenship

One way to understand the dynamics of the relationship between dignity and democracy is through the lens of citizenship. Citizenship is what does the work of democracy, and yet it overlaps significantly with the principle of human dignity. The Polish constitution makes this explicit: "The inherent and inalienable dignity of the person shall constitute a source of freedoms and rights of persons and citizens."[16] Or, working backward: democracy depends on citizenship, which depends, in turn, on the recognition of human dignity. The interconnection between individual dignity and democratic governance should come as no surprise: as constitutionalism has evolved over the last century to recognize increasingly the significance of the individual, dignity and democracy are the two fundamental elements that have developed to express, respectively, the modern turn toward individual rights and the importance of structural limits on state power.

Citizenship may be thought of in various ways, but here it refers to those activities and states of mind associated with participating in civic governance.

It is not limited to the formal rules governing citizenship in a given country but extends to all those who *would* participate in the political community, whether as actual or putative citizens. So it may include children, transients, prisoners, and others who may be excluded by formal rules from exercising the incidents of citizenship. As such, the *feeling* of citizenship means more than the formal incidents of democratic participation, such as the right to vote and run for office, and the right to have one's vote counted. Just as elections do not make a democracy,[17] citizenship can mean much more than mere participation in the formal incidents of electoral politics. And indeed it must. Citizenship in a democracy requires people to be informed about the issues, which in turn may entail not only a modicum of formal education, but also an inclination and the opportunity to become informed about the issues of the day and to engage in the free exchange of ideas. Citizens may be thought of as those who are parties to the social contract and who in fact exercise their rights under the contract; they are those who, collectively, constitute "the people" that constitutional preambles are disposed to invoke.[18]

The focus here and throughout dignity rights discourse is not on the minima of belonging or formal citizenship but on what it should entail as a robust and meaningful concept. It is not enough for individuals to be citizens, legally—that is, entitled to exercise the rights associated with citizenship—because many people may not be aware of their rights or may not have the opportunity or inclination to exercise them. In countries where voting is not compulsory, enfranchisement is typically significantly lower than is legally permitted, and discussion of public issues is lower still. A more robust understanding of citizenship "refers to a class of persons who are part of a national community or who have otherwise developed sufficient connection with [the] country to be considered part of that community,"[19] as Linda Bosniak puts it. The gap between those who are legally a part of the national community and those who have otherwise developed a connection with the country qua citizen may be attributable to what Donald Lutz has called the need of the population to "feel their citizenship."[20] It is that *feeling* of belonging and participation that courts may be fostering when they develop a jurisprudence of dignity.[21]

Citizenship and dignity have much in common. Both may be felt and exercised individually, but they are given meaning only in community. The right to vote, like the right to control one's reputation or to determine the course of one's life, only makes sense when we consider individuals as members of a community.[22]

There are other common threads between citizenship and dignity.

Citizenship in a democracy, like dignity (within the human family), is held by each person individually, but in equal amounts; it therefore demands the equal respect of each person. No one's dignity, or citizenship, can be more valuable than anyone else's. Moreover, the erasure of citizenship can result in "unpersoning," with the resultant diminution of the person's dignity, such as happens when persons become "stateless."

Dignity is both a state of mind and an opportunity to take action: it is found both in the status of *being* religious and in the *action* of wearing a veil, in being rational and in obtaining an education, in the fact of being part of the human family and in the enjoyment of the company of others. Again, citizenship presents an analogue: it is found both in the psychological state and self-awareness of being a member of the community and in the overt acts of voting, discussing, and running for office, among other things.

In Bangladesh, this has implications for the judicial interpretation of the constitution. Article 11 of the Constitution of the Republic of Bangladesh ("Democracy and Human Rights") makes the link between dignity and democracy explicit: "The Republic shall be a democracy in which fundamental human rights and freedoms and respect for the dignity and worth of the human person shall be guaranteed."[23] But while the Supreme Court acknowledges that this article is not judicially enforceable, it recognizes that individuals "as citizens" (who "are enrolled as voters and do exercise the right of the franchise") are nonetheless entitled to enforce their rights to life and to the protection of the law.[24] The fact of human dignity gives people certain rights "as citizens."

The Judicial Construction of Citizenship

In the cases, the concepts of dignity and democratic citizenship fuse in several different ways. Even where the constitution does not textually demand linking dignity and democracy, many courts have done so on their own. In South Africa, the Constitutional Court has taken as its mandate the twin obligations of rectifying the most searing wounds from the apartheid era and of building up democratic culture. In *August and Another v. Electoral Commission and Others*,[25] the Constitutional Court held that the right of prisoners to vote should ordinarily not be denied and that the government has an obligation to facilitate their ability to vote. Justice Albie Sachs wrote against the ever-present backdrop of the struggle against apartheid: "The universality of the franchise is important not only for nationhood and democracy. The vote of each and every citizen is a badge of dignity and of personhood," he said plainly. His elaboration on the significance of the franchise reinforces the interconnectedness of citizenship and dignity: "In a country of great disparities of wealth and power [the franchise] declares that whoever we are, whether rich or poor, exalted or disgraced, we all belong to the same democratic South African nation; that our destinies are intertwined in a single interactive polity."[26] Like dignity, the right to vote is the same for everyone, and it therefore equalizes people notwithstanding other distinctions. Also like dignity, since the individual right to vote is made meaningful only in aggregation with others, it defines us individually while enhancing our sense of belonging to an "interactive" community. It is the fact that each person's dignity, and vote, are equal to every other person's that demands that each person respect each other's vote, and, in the aggregate, demands that each person respects the outcome of elections produced by equal voting.[27]

In *Doctors for Life*, the South African Constitutional Court went farther both in adumbrating the meaning of citizenship and in rooting it in human dignity. The court held that the right of the public to participate in the legislative process had been violated when one house of Parliament had failed to invite submissions from the public on some health legislation. Finding that democratic rights depended on more than simply the right to vote in regular elections, the court explained that "participation by the public on a continuous basis provides vitality to the functioning of representative democracy" because, among other things, it "enhances the civic dignity of those who participate by enabling their voices to be heard and taken account of."[28] The term "civic dignity" here means more than in Jeremy Waldron's invocation of a well-ordered society. Its use by Justices Ngcobo and Sachs is more active, more engaged. It makes explicit that one dimension of human dignity is the ability to participate in democratic governance: in the South African view, participation in an active and ongoing way entails more than just voting and "may well go beyond any formulaic requirement of notice or hearing."[29] Civic dignity is justified not only because South Africa's constitutional democracy is expressly founded on the value of human dignity (among other values), but also because it serves individual and collective values: "Consistent with our constitutional commitment to human dignity and self-respect, section 118(1) (a) [of the Constitution, referring to "Public access to and involvement in provincial legislatures"] contemplates that members of the public will often be given an opportunity to participate in the making of laws that affect them.

As has been observed, a 'commitment to a right to . . . public participation in governmental decision-making' is derived not only from the belief that we improve the accuracy of decisions when we allow people to present their side of the story, but also from our sense that participation is necessary to preserve human dignity and self respect.' "[30] This conception of dignity defines the very meaning of citizenship.

Similarly, the German court has said, in the course of evaluating the European Constitution, that "The citizens' right to determine in respect of persons and subjects, in freedom and equality by means of elections and other votes, public authority is the fundamental element of the principle of democracy. The right to free and equal participation in public authority is enshrined in human dignity."[31] Dignity demands a free and equal vote; and a free and equal vote recognizes and instantiates human dignity.

The Constitutional Court of Bulgaria addressed the issue in the context of the right to information. In an extended disquisition on the nature of freedom of information and expression, the court held that the relevant constitutional provisions "protect the individual's right to free performance as an equal member of the social community. These functions of the rights under [the constitution] define them as essential for individual and social development. They underlie the democratic process and enable it to function."[32]

Cases that are not specifically about citizenship rights still may promote the "feeling" of citizenship when courts—governmental authorities still—recognize the dignity in the claims of ordinary people to ordinary things. In Peru, this was made explicit in the case involving information about birth control: "The right to information about contraceptive methods," the court said, "is one way to concretize the principle of dignity of the human person and forms part of the essential elements of a democratic society, because it enables the exercise of sexual rights in a free, conscientious, and responsible manner."[33] In this way, the court places the most intimate and private decisions in the broader context of the democratic community. The U.S. Supreme Court did the same thing in *Planned Parenthood v. Casey* when, recognizing the personal dignity basis of both economic and political citizenship, it acknowledged that a woman's right to choose to terminate a pregnancy affects her ability to participate "in the social and economic life of the nation."[34]

But the dignity-citizenship link is equally clear when it is not explicit. When a court in Colombia requires the government to pay for durable medical goods or protects a woman against rape or requires the windows in government offices to be placed so as to avoid demeaning shorter members of the public, it is saying that each of these individuals—by virtue of their inherent dignity—is important to society, and equally so. Courts ensuring that individuals can marry the person of their choice or have access to fresh water are doing the same thing, as are courts recognizing that the state may not subjugate anyone, even those who have committed heinous crimes. In Canada, the Supreme Court has liberally protected language rights for this reason: "The importance of language rights is grounded in the essential role that language plays in human existence, development and dignity. It is through language that we are able to form concepts; to structure and order the world around us. Language bridges the gap between isolation and community, allowing humans to delineate the rights and duties they hold in respect of one another, and thus to live in society."[35] These cases confirm that what is important to the individual is also important to the society at large and therefore has legal and political implications. By vindicating dignity claims, the courts reinforce the connection between people and government, creating the basis for dialogue, in a mutually intelligible language. This marks a radical shift from most governments' treatment of most people over most of history.

Even where courts rule against the petitioners, they may nonetheless be promoting the "feeling" of citizenship simply by hearing—and listening to— the cases people bring. The Colombian court has done this by recognizing that dignity lies in the ability to exercise procedural rights (in particular, but by no means exclusively, with respect to health): "With the fundamental right to health, the Constitutional Court has recognized that life includes respect for human dignity and, thus, health condition that alters the dignified conditions of life must be protected by the constitutional mechanisms available for the protection of fundamental rights. This way, through the action of *tutela*, it is possible to protect the constitutional right to health when compromises and threats to it affect the dignified life of people."[36] Thus, in countries where standing to bring suit is broad, people are more likely to feel the possibility of participating in public affairs, as compared with those countries where only an ombudsman or members of parliament or other elites are permitted to make constitutional challenges. Slightly more open is the United States, where individuals are permitted to ask a court to review the constitutionality of a legislative or executive (or judicial) act, although the Supreme Court has developed an elaborate series of hurdles to ensure that only those who have a strong personal stake in the matter are permitted to litigate constitutional issues, which often operates to the detriment of plaintiffs who assert environmental, civil rights, and other public interest claims.[37]

But there are many countries where standing to bring a constitutional claim is deliberately open, and the processes for pursuing the claim are designed to encourage people to assert their rights in a judicial forum. Since the Mexican Constitution of 1857 (and even before then in the Constitution of the State of Yucatan), individuals have been authorized to petition for *amparo* to seek the court's protection against government violations of individual rights. The writ has since spread to almost all Latin American countries, and similar provisions have been adopted in Spain and the Philippines.[38] In addition, a number of countries in the region have developed a process for an *acción de inconstitucionalidad* and other processes to invite constitutional challenges. Along with greatly expanded enumerations of constitutional rights, including especially the right to dignity, the availability of *amparo* proceedings encourages individuals to seek judicial protection from the violation of constitutional rights. Many of the cases discussed in this book are examples of *amparo* proceedings.

In other countries, where the constitution did not explicitly authorize simple proceedings for constitutional challenges, courts have developed these practices through judicial loosening of standing requirements. In India, in the 1970s, the Supreme Court famously pioneered public interest litigation (PIL), which relaxed the rules of standing. The court has explained that the device was developed so that procedural hurdles "should not stand in the way of access to justice to the weaker sections of Indian humanity and therefore where the poor and the disadvantaged are concerned who are barely eking out a miserable existence with their sweat and toil and who are victims of an exploited society without any access to justice, this Court will not insist on a regular writ petition and even a letter addressed by a public spirited individual or a social action group acting probono publico would suffice to ignite the jurisdiction of this Court."[39]

Amparo and PIL cases and other cases like them in other countries have enormous expressive significance in that they signal the importance of the individual to the political community. They recognize the individual as a participant in the ongoing discussion about political rights and responsibilities, and this affirms people's dignity. This is also self-perpetuating: the more people invoke the courts' jurisdiction, the more people's dignity is affirmed, the more people are able to engage as citizens, and the more the conversation expands, in both judicial and political realms. These cases are not recalibrating the relationship among the actors—court, political authorities, and members of the public—but rather reconceptualizing the field on which political action takes place. Rather than supporting a hierarchical or confrontational relationship, or one defined by legislative grace, the courts are leveling the field, so that members of the public may approach the government as bearers of dignity that warrants respect. Thus the dialogue that is envisioned is not solely between the people and the courts—though it is there, too—but also engages the political authorities.

Encouraging people to come forth to a court to state a claim recognizes the right of each person to engage in dialogue with the government on matters of public importance. This is especially important in countries where people do not otherwise have the habit of participatory democracy: in Europe, judicial recognition of civic dignity may not be as essential as it is in South Africa or India, where building up the feeling of citizenship is absolutely essential for democracy to take root and thrive. This is also true in Latin America, where constitutional democracy, though entrenched, has nonetheless proven to be fragile: the greatest bulwark against a coup d'état is of course an engaged citizenry. It should not surprise us that it is throughout the regions with the strongest constitutional commitment to *participatory* democracy that we see the strongest judicial commitment to human dignity. Moreover, as regional or supranational courts expand their jurisdiction and increase their relevance, people are increasingly engaging in public debate across national lines, and citizenship in this sense is transcending national boundaries. Whether at the local, national, or regional level, respect for human dignity predicates engagement in public affairs.

The mutually reinforcing and interdependent relationship between dignity and citizenship, embodied in the broad term "civic dignity," reinforces the multiple dimensions of dignity. For prisoners, it means protection against exile or transportation to another country so that they remain physically a part of the polity;[40] a concern about solitary confinement so that they remain a part of some human community; and protection of the right to vote[41] and to read and even write to newspapers so that they remain civically included and engaged. In language that joins the private and public nature of dignity and belonging, the Israeli Supreme Court has explained, in holding that a prisoner has a right to write a weekly column: "Within the framework of freedom of speech, man realizes his desires and aspirations that are part of his nature and that reflect his intellectual freedom: to be educated and acquire knowledge, to be involved in communal life, to hear the opinions of others and express his own views."[42]

Outside prison walls, courts have also recognized that respecting each person's dignity strengthens democracy. In the Argentine case affirming the rights of transgendered and transvestite people to associate, the court recognized that "the very essence of our bill of Rights, which has been made stronger and more profound with the incorporation of international treaties regarding human rights, is the respect for human dignity and liberty," and that "the structure of a democratic style of life resides in the capacity of a society to resolve its conflicts through public debate of ideas," with the result that any association of individuals is constitutionally permissible as long as it does violence neither to public order and morals nor to a third person.[43] In this view, respect for human dignity and the demands of democratic culture jointly insist on free association of individuals, which in turn enhances both dignity and democracy.

Other courts have emphasized that for dignity to further the goals of democracy, people must have the *means* to participate in community. When the Lithuanian Supreme Court held, following principles of the European Community, that social security must be sufficient to ensure human dignity, it explained that "people with insufficient, irregular and uncertain resources are unable to play an adequate part in the economic and social life of the society in which they live and to become successfully integrated economically and socially." The member states are recommended inter alia "to recognise the basic right of a person to sufficient resources and social assistance to live in a manner compatible with human dignity as a part of a comprehensive and consistent drive to combat social exclusion."[44]

In this way, courts have recognized how poverty, like imprisonment, can lead to social isolation, which entails not only a diminution in dignity but a loss of citizenship as well. To live with dignity is to be able to participate with others in a political community. Linda Bosniak has shown this with regard to those who have been excommunicated from the citizenry by virtue of being deemed "enemy combatants," and relegated to geographic limbo in the statelessness of the prison facility at Guantánamo Bay. Exclusion from society is itself a form of impairment of dignity, as we have seen. But Bosniak's argument goes further: by naming them "enemy combatants," she argues, "in self-reinforcing fashion, the regime has ensured that those so designated are unable to contest the proceedings that define them as legal nonpersons in the first place. The individual has been reduced to 'bare life' in Giorgio Agamben's phrase, a status iconically represented in the post-9/11 public imagination by the caged and hooded prisoners at Guantánamo Bay,"—without citizenship, without belonging, and without dignity.[45] (Indeed, the indignity is exacerbated by the difficulty the United States has faced in finding countries who would accept these individuals, finding communities to which they can belong, or even—and this is an extreme form of belonginglessness—finding communities within or outside the United States in which they can even be tried.) The indignity of "bare life" accords with Christoph Möllers's view, discussed earlier, that dignity is violated when one is reduced to one's body.[46]

For the rest of the population, courts, by protecting human dignity, are ensuring that people can exercise their rights of citizenship. It is, of course, difficult to discern if (and if so, exactly how) these decisions expounding on human dignity in fact increase democratic activity, but it is no stretch at this point to suggest that they are likely to contribute in some way to the greater feeling of citizenship by individuals, and that this in turn conduces to sturdier democratic governance.

Activist Courts, Activist People

In most constitutional cultures, the courts—being the least representative and the least politically accountable—are meant to limit themselves to deciding the law without venturing too deeply into the world of policy. In the United States, one of the main (often unstated) reasons for declining to recognize a constitutional right to dignity (or other implied right) is precisely because, not being anchored to the text or the clear intent of the framers of the Constitution, such judicial creativity appears to be ultra vires and an open invitation to rule by judicial whim.[47] When a court develops a jurisprudence out of a single word in a constitution (sometimes even where it is not an explicit right), it may very well encourage accusations of judicial activism, which ultimately (it is said) destabilizes and delegitimizes the judiciary. In an extraordinary opinion, a two-judge bench of the Supreme Court of India expressed its frustration in 2007 with the failure of the courts to stay within the bounds of their legitimate authority. The appropriate response to political problems, the court said, lay with the political, not the judicial process: "If the legislature or the executive are not functioning properly it is for the people to correct the defects by exercising their franchise properly in the next elections and voting for candidates who will fulfill their expectations, or by other lawful methods e.g. peaceful demonstrations. The remedy is not in the judiciary taking over the legislative or executive functions, because that will not only violate the delicate balance of power enshrined in the Constitution, but also the judiciary has neither the expertise nor the resources to perform these functions."[48]

Ultimately, the problem with judicial activism is typically that the more the judicial branch flexes its muscle, the weaker the political arena becomes. It is usually conceptualized as a zero-sum game: the "candid citizen must confess," said Abraham Lincoln, that "if the policy of the Government upon vital questions affecting the whole people is to be irrevocably fixed by decisions of the Supreme Court, the instant they are made . . . the people will have ceased to be their own rulers, having to that extent practically resigned their Government into the hands of that eminent tribunal."[49] The concerns expressed in pre-Civil War America remain vital for most of the world today.

To many, then, the jurisprudence of dignity that has been described in these pages may seem in flagrant violation of the principles of judicial restraint: in some cases (as in India), the right to dignity is explicitly nonjusticiable and yet it has been expounded at length; in other cases, it is a vague and general proposition, and yet courts have enthusiastically invested it with extratextual meaning. In the most extreme examples, courts have given dignity a constitutional construction that it was obviously not intended to have, as when the courts of South Africa and Hungary relied on it to invalidate capital punishment, in contravention of the constitutions' seeming tolerance of it.

However, if the link between dignity and democracy is indeed a strong one, then dignity rights may perhaps be the best justification for judicial activism rather than the worst illustration of it. Process-based arguments for enhancing popular sovereignty through judicial activity are nothing new. Chief Justice John Marshall suggested as much in the early nineteenth century in *McCulloch v. Maryland*, followed by Chief Justice Stone in the 1930s and 1940s, and in turn by John Hart Ely in *Democracy and Distrust* in 1975. The difference here is that the dignity jurisprudence reflects a *rights*-based, not a process-based, argument: it depends on the acceptance and expansion of a substantive constitutional right to secure the benefits of democracy. But like those other arguments, the purpose and the effect of judicial interpolation are to enhance not the court's authority, but the people's. If nurturing individual self-determination fosters collective self-determination, then doing so may dampen rather than encourage judicial arrogance. If strengthening dignity strengthens democracy, then capacious readings of the right to dignity do not detract from but rather enhance the capacity of people to "be their own rulers" by participating in democratic governance—asking questions of

the legislative process, holding the government to account, insisting on respectful treatment. If this is true, then the charge of activism evaporates: the
end result of judicial engagement is more, not less, democratic activity.

In embracing this democracy-through-dignity project, many courts have
carved out a vital role for themselves in the development of democratic governance in their countries. And in the process, the role that courts have tradi-
tionally played in society is shifting.

The Evolution of Constitutional Adjudication

The twenty-first century is witnessing a dramatic shift in the way constitutional courts behave. In the nineteenth and twentieth centuries, there
was one, and then two, dominant paradigms for constitutional review: the
common law version that is most associated with the U.S. Supreme Court,
whereby a generalized court within a diffused judicial system rules on the
constitutionality of governmental action in the context of a concrete factual
situation; and the Kelsenian model, in which a specialized constitutional tribunal outside of the judicial and political hierarchies rules on the abstract
question of constitutionality, often before the law goes into effect. While the
models differ structurally from one another, both systems produce judicial
pronouncements that either affirm the government's action or disapprove of
it. That is, from a remedial point of view, the dominant forms of judicial review produced orders either allowing the government to pursue its chosen
course of action or forbidding the government to do so.

This construct is well suited to a traditional legal system defined by adherence to the principle of separation of powers to avoid concentration of
power within any one branch or section of government, as well as by a corollary skepticism about judicial power, particularly in countries that take their
democracy seriously, such as France and the United States, since in almost all
cases, constitutional judges are unelected, unrepresentative, and unaccount-
able. It is also consistent with a strong commitment to the idea of negative
rights—that is, where rights claims are thought of as individual assertions
of liberty that limit the power of government. The "rights revolution" in the
1960s and 1970s in the United States, for example, is exemplified by the expansion of the right to privacy, as well as the rights of criminal defendants,
as *against* government overreaching and intrusion, not *for* services or goods.

In the second half of the twentieth century, some constitutional courts began to stake out a different role for themselves—one that places the courts *within* rather than outside the framework of democratic governance, and thereby defies the traditional divide between judicial activism and judicial restraint. Whereas the traditional view has characterized the democratic conversation as involving the people and the government, with the courts refereeing from the sidelines, courts are now increasingly positioning themselves as participants in the process of democracy building. But unlike their counterparts, the courts' function in this newly triangulated dialogue is not to assert their own relevance, but to insist on the primacy of the constitution. Thus, we are not seeing the judicialization of politics, or the politicization of the courts, so much as the *constitutionalization* of politics: the courts are the constitutions' avatars, ensuring that the politics and policies of the day stay within the bounds of constitutional limits and further constitutional values. This might be thought of as the internal morality of democracy,[50] though I would argue that it is a distinctly constitutionalist morality.

This shift may be attributed to a number of factors, which may be briefly described as follows: first, the declining influence of the American model of judicial review on courts around the world; second, the increasing influence of international law on domestic courts, particularly in the area of human rights; and third, an increasingly sophisticated understanding of the demands of consolidated democracy.

American constitutionalism is characterized by an essential ambivalence toward judicial power: Americans want a check on governmental power, but they fear that the check arrogates governmental power to itself—that is, the judicial fox is watching the political henhouse. The U.S. Constitution even leaves the very power of judicial review to guesswork, unlike most modern constitutions, which explicitly authorize constitutional review, anticipating a robust role for the court in the expression of constitutional principles and the vindication of constitutional commitments.

Perhaps this is one reason the U.S. Supreme Court has the ultimate power of constitutional *interpretation* but has virtually no power over constitutional *implementation*: while Supreme Court textual analyses are comparatively long (and getting longer), remedial orders are startlingly brief, usually consisting of a mere four words: "It is so ordered."[51] In the unusual cases where the federal courts have asserted an ongoing interest in constitutional litigation, the backlash is often deafening, quite literally: *Brown v. Board of Education*, the monumental desegregation case of more than fifty years ago, was the last case in which the Supreme Court ordered continuing jurisdiction over state or federal authorities in a significant constitutional controversy, and it continues to be used as an example of why the court should *not* overstep its bounds.

Thus, to use John Marshall's deceptively simple phrase, when we say that it is the "province and duty of the judicial department to say what the law is," we mean that the courts have the power to interpret the constitution, but there their power ends. And if that is the case, it makes sense, further, to say that the judicial power to say what the law is should be exclusive: competing interpretations of a constitutional provision would diminish its significance. Even though some have questioned whether judicial exclusivity or even supremacy as to the constitution's meaning is wise or appropriate or necessary, the answer is usually that, notwithstanding judicial exclusivity's failure of democratic legitimacy, it is preferable to the anarchy that would ensue if each branch could determine for itself what the constitution means.[52] And this may be true. If we want simply an interpretation (e.g., the cruel and unusual punishment clause does not prohibit capital punishment; the due process clause does prohibit laws forbidding abortion), then it is true that multiple competing interpretations would yield to just the kind of uncertainty and unpredictability that lawyers abhor. How can the constitution guarantee abortion if the legislative branch forbids it? How can the court say that affirmative action is unconstitutional if the government engages in it? Focusing on interpretation rather than on implementation necessarily sets up a power struggle between the courts and the political branches, because only one can have a final interpretation. It reinforces the invisible boundary between the judicial and the political branches and dichotomizes constitutional discourse: judges are either activist or restrained, and if the former, politics are counter-majoritarian rather than majoritarian, and people will respond by being either judicial optimists or pessimists,[53] urging courts to be stronger or weaker.[54]

The pure question of interpretation, though paramount in American constitutional discourse, is beside the point in many other constitutional traditions (and especially emerging traditions). Courts in these cultures focus not on what the constitution *means* but on what it *does*.

And here it is worth considering other differences between modern constitutional states and the American forerunner. The American paradigm sees government as a necessary but problematic institution whose actions must be vigilantly scrutinized in order to allow maximum freedom to individuals. Many post-World War II and post-communist constitutions, however, expressly commit to the creation of a "social" state. This assumes a different role for the government than is typical of traditional liberal democracies. The social state assumes that the state is critical in ensuring the provision of certain goods and services in order to enhance the living conditions of the people. And this, in turn, assumes a departure from the traditional role of courts. In this construct, the courts must not only ensure that governments do not overreach; they must also ensure that the state meets its obligations to the people. So the court must necessarily be more concerned with implementation than with interpretation. And unlike interpretation, implementation is a multilateral process.

If a constitution is designed to foster a society in which everyone has access to education, shelter, employment, or water, then it matters more whether government policies produce those results than what the textual provision means: whether the right to education means that books must be free at the university level or whether the right to water means six liters per person or fifty liters per household. In these cultures, the judiciary's interpretive role is less prominent than its role as impeller of good policies. The meaning matters, but the implementation matters more. So what the courts can most usefully do is not simply announce the constitutional meaning of a term and "so order" that it be done, but actually ensure that government policies make education, housing, and water available to those who are entitled to it. Sometimes this shift in expectations of what the judiciary should accomplish is constitutionally mandated, as when the constitution recognizes values not as enumerated rights but as directives of state policy, as in the case of the constitutions of Ireland, India, and elsewhere.[55] This construct may require courts to engage with political branches, though it usually prohibits courts from mandating particular action. (In the American tradition, by contrast, the federal courts are by their own determination prohibited from issuing opinions that would be merely advisory.)

This different conception of the judicial function is particularly noticeable where the legitimacy of the nation, or its success—as measured by the ability to overcome political trauma, by the consolidation of democratic ideals, and by the rooting of peace, stability, and growth—depends on the implementation of the constitutional promise. Countries whose preconstitutional histories were inauspicious (such as Germany, India, and later South Africa, Colombia, and the nations of central and eastern Europe) depend more on the inculcation of constitutional values than do those whose momentum is carrying them forward. In these countries, the constitutional court has a critical role to play not just in saying what the constitution means but in ensuring that it does the work assigned to it: creating a better society. The issue here, then, is not who has the final word but whether the country functions effectively according to constitutional values—whether politics have been constitutionalized. And, as constitutional avatars, the courts have a particularly important role to play in this process. When done well, "Courts' decisions do not so much stop or hijack the policy debate as inject the language of rights into it and add another forum for debate."[56]

In these countries—certainly the majority of the world's nations engaging in constitutional jurisprudence—the limits on judicial power are defined not by some invisible fence that keeps each branch within its implicitly designated sphere, but by the limits of its efficacy. This is not to say that the boundaries between the unelected judiciary and the politically accountable branches are erased, or even eroded: courts must still tread carefully in social and economic cases. Not only do they lack the legitimacy of elected parliamentarians; they also lack the expertise of specialized cabinet members or administrators and the perspective of policy makers. Moreover, the fact-specific nature of each claim examined by a court creates "the potential precariousness of decisions based merely on formal, rights-fulfillment-oriented argument and not on a substantive appreciation of the merits of each action."[57]

As courts have turned their attention away from the American model, they have increasingly embraced international law. As the once-rigid lines between international and municipal law have begun to blur, international law has come to affect domestic law in both explicit and implicit ways. Every country (except Taiwan, Kosovo, and the Vatican) is a member of the United Nations, and most have signed and ratified the major human rights treaties, as well as regional human rights instruments, which can often exert even greater influence. In some countries, international obligations are self-executing and thus automatically require changes in policy, while in other countries changes in policy have been implemented at the national level to comport with international law. Some constitutional texts expressly incorporate international law into their domestic law, both in the substantive terms of the duties it imposes and in interpretive terms, obliging the constitutional tribunals to take international law into account. But the influence of international law has also been softer, though no less real, insofar as its values have permeated constitutional discourse, even where international law is not binding.

International law has also shifted its focus in the last sixty years, while becoming more influential in the domestic sphere. Not only has it become more centered on the concept of human rights—as is evidenced by the regional human rights charters in Europe, the Americas, and Africa—but the scope of human rights has also expanded to include not only "every member of the human family" in a generic sense, but, specifically, women, migrant workers, children, the disabled, and so on. Even the "disappeared" are now recognized under international law. And, increasingly, international law systems are opening themselves up to complaints by individuals. For instance, the First Optional Protocol to the International Covenant on Civil and Political Rights, permitting individual complaints, currently has 35 signatories and 113 parties, while the more recent Optional Protocol to the International Covenant on Economic, Social, and Cultural Rights (ICESCR), opened for signature in 2009, attracted 35 signatories and 3 parties in less than two years.[58] These developments are producing a growing body of human rights jurisprudence that is as influential in the domestic realm as it is internationally. Moreover, this process is mirroring the opening up of constitutional space for individual complaints, as more and more countries are moving away from abstract review brought by government officials.

One aspect of international law that is becoming particularly influential in modern domestic courts is particularly relevant here. As courts are increasingly vindicating positive rights, they are turning to the construct envisaged by the ICESCR that requires, in Article 2, that "Each State Party to the present Covenant undertakes to take steps, individually and through international assistance and co-operation, especially economic and technical, to the maximum of its available resources, with a view to achieving progressively the full realization of the rights recognized in the present Covenant by all appropriate means, including particularly the adoption of legislative measures."[59] This construct subtly alters the judicial role in several ways. First, it explicitly places the obligation to develop and implement programs and policies directly on the shoulders of political actors; it is, after all, the state parties that undertake to take these steps. At the same time, it imposes on the tribunals that would enforce the rights identified in the covenant (or in the constitutions, when they are incorporated at the domestic level) the obligation to maintain continuing oversight to ensure that rights are progressively realized. There are no positive or negative legislatures here: a court has many more options than simply rubber-stamping or interfering. A court can goad, encourage, or prod the other actors: it can prompt the political branches to take action, or empower the people to engage in the political process. It can say far more than "It is so ordered," which is insufficient to ensure the progressive realization of an important constitutional right. These courts can avoid the dichotomy of either being marginal and powerless and beholden to the powerful elites (as are so many constitutional courts where judicial independence is not guaranteed) or losing their legitimacy because they attempt to do too much. The protection of social and economic rights is not a power struggle between the judicial and political limbs but rather requires an enhanced role for both the political *and* the judicial branches, and one that requires ongoing interaction between the two.

A case from Colombia illustrates the process. In Colombia, the court has recognized that, in an Estado Social del Derecho and a participatory democracy, socioeconomic rights have a "programmatic" character that compels some sort of positive action on the part of the state, and not merely the negative refraining from interfering. The requirement for the progressive realization of such rights does not seem to be excessively burdensome: "when the effective enjoyment of a fundamental constitutional right depends on progressive development (i.e., progressive realization), the minimum that the responsible authorities must do . . . is, precisely, to develop a plan working toward the assurance of effective enjoyment of people's rights."[60] This plan must have three qualities: the plan must effectively exist, the plan's priority must be to guarantee the effective enjoyment of the right, and the processes for decision, elaboration, implementation, and evaluation must permit democratic participation.[61]

But implementing this general rule may involve myriad specific details. In a case brought by a group of poor people whose only means of support was recycling items found in landfills, the court ruled that the closure of the landfills discriminated against them on the basis of their poverty, thereby diminishing their dignity. The court's remedial orders were extensive and required each municipality where the petitioners lived, within a few months, to adopt necessary means to assure the effective enjoyment of the petitioners' constitutional rights to health, education, dignified living, and food, ensuring in each particular case that the means were connected to specific social programs.[62] This process shifts the ballast of litigation from the merits of the constitutional right and the existence of a constitutional violation to the question of enforcement of the constitutional remedy; as long as the petitioner community has the means not only to bring the suit in the first place but then ensure compliance with the court's order, and as long as the community's needs are not urgent, the result is likely to be realization of the right that is more widespread, more thoughtful, and more procedurally inclusive than if the court had simply ordered the government to provide a specific minimum core of a right. The policies still need to be developed and implemented politically, but the constitutional obligation to protect dignity imbues the court with significant power to galvanize political branches to action. And this is true whether the obligations are homegrown or inspired by developments in international law.

One last significant shift that has occurred in the last sixty years and is relevant to this inquiry is the increasing global commitment to democracy and self-determination and the accompanying increases in sophistication in our understanding of the demands of democracy. And as with international law generally, the shift here can be measured both by the increased commitment to these goals by nearly all countries of the world, as well as by an enriched understanding of what self-determination and especially democracy mean. No longer are democratic values satisfied merely by nonfraudulent periodic elections; now we understand democracy to require the deliberation, participation, and constant involvement of every portion of the adult population in the development of policy in their countries.

In the aggregate, these modulations in domestic and international law and politics have resulted in an evolving or altered role for the courts in constitutional democracies. Many courts throughout the world are breaking out of the straitjacket that had limited their powers to giving governmental actions a thumbs-up or thumbs-down. Rather, courts are increasingly seeing themselves as partners in the development of constitutional social policy—that is, policy kept within constitutional bounds. As Theunis Roux has argued, "The adjudication of human rights norms may be seen as a significant forum for deliberation on whether the outcomes of formal democratic processes are consistent with these norms. Within this conception, courts are significant components of deliberative democracy, instead of being perceived as 'counter-majoritarian' institutions requiring justification as exceptions to democratic institutions."[63] The turn toward progressive realization of socioeconomic rights is one important illustration of this more complex version of constitutionalism.

This role has been described as dialogic in that it engages in dialogue—sometimes ongoing—with the legislative and executive authorities with the aim of shaping the best policy for the people and the nation.[64] Justice Sachs of the South African Constitutional Court has described constitutional interpretation as "a principled judicial dialogue, in the first place between members of this Court, then between our Court and other courts, the legal profession, law schools, Parliament and indirectly with the public at large."[65] In other constitutional contexts, the role of the apex court has been described as one of mediator, negotiator, peacemaker, and facilitator as it seeks to nudge government into compliance with constitutional norms. Courts have convoked commissions, employed experts, issued interim remedial orders for the implementation of specific aspects of a case, required reporting back, and in some cases, even written legislation that would operate until the legislature passed its own.[66] Indeed, after surveying socioeconomic rights enforcement globally, Brinks and Gauri write that "Courts are more engaged and most effective when they act in dialogue with political, bureaucratic, and civil society actors."[67]

If we take this approach seriously, we can see rights not as unilateral assertions of power against another but as relationships between the government and the people. In a constitutional democracy, the relationship must be founded on the inherent and equal dignity of each person. To ensure the effective renegotiation of the relationship on an ongoing basis, either through politics or law, the government must not have the power to grant dignity or take it away, or to recognize the greater value of one person over another. The ability to assert one's dignity in negotiating with the government ensures that the government will treat each person with equal respect. As Justice Sachs wrote in another case, "The right to speak and be listened to is part of the right to be a citizen in the full sense of the word. In a constitutional democracy dialogue and the right to have a voice on public affairs is constitutive of dignity. Indeed, in a society like ours where the majority were for centuries denied the right to influence those who ruled over them, the right 'to be present' when laws are being made has deep significance."[68] Where the equal dignity of each individual is recognized and appreciated, the public can take part directly in the constitutional democratic dialogue, with the court as facilitator to ensure that all parties respect the rules of the game. The more empowered each member of the public, each participant, is—that is, the more work each person does to assure the development and implementation of policies that are consistent with constitutional democracy—the less work the court needs to do.

This is what is referred to in Brazil as *democracia humanizada* (humane democracy), which explicitly links human dignity to democracy and places the courts in the central role. Brazilian courts have "founded their decisions, inter alia, on a range of complementary arguments, such as that fundamental rights and human dignity prevail over administrative or budgetary norms, that certain fundamental social rights are an essential part of the 'humane democracy' that the constitution establishes, that fundamental social rights are both justiciable in ordinary tribunals, and their realization by means of legal action does not infringe on the separation of powers."[69]

Unlike Lincoln's dichotomized view that the people cease to be their own rulers when the Supreme Court gets involved,[70] this new version of the judicial role allows the people, and their government, and their courts to work together to develop public policy in light of constitutional values. In Brazil, it has been found that "after litigants and their public defenders apply further pressure on the state, authorities eventually do provide the large majority of drugs that patients demand; and in the right-to-food litigation in India, where though it has taken several years of civil society campaigning, most state government are now, in fact, complying with the court-ordered midday meals scheme. The full process of legalization has, by construction, more impact than courts acting alone."[71] This opens up "the adjudicatory space as a place for dialogue with parties."[72]

Two recent examples illustrate how the role of courts has evolved in the context of the right to dignity. In a 2010 case, the German Constitutional Court held that an unjustified diminution in the standard benefit paid to pensioners violated the right to dignity. For present purposes, the most interesting aspect of the opinion is how the court divvies up responsibility between the judicial and legislative branches. The dignity-based right to a moderate income, the court said, "is not subject to the legislature's disposal and must be honoured." It is, in other words, a constitutional mandate. However, this right, continued the court, must "be lent concrete shape, and be regularly updated, by the legislature. . . . As regards the types of need and the means that are necessary to meet such need, the extent of the constitutional claim to benefits cannot be directly inferred from the constitution. It is for the legislature to lend it concrete shape; it has latitude for doing so." Furthermore, the court said: "In order to lend the claim concrete shape, the legislature has to assess all expenditure that is necessary for one's existence consistently in a transparent and appropriate procedure according to the actual need, i.e. in line with reality."[73]

The court announces the constitutional requirement, of which there can be no breach: dignity means that people must have some control over their lives, must not be forced by circumstance to devote their lives to finding food or protection from the elements. This is a matter of constitutional interpretation, which is where the courts' expertise lies. What a small group of very learned people can do best is interpret the meaning of a text; there is no need for broad public input or political accountability to accomplish this task. But the court then says that it is for the political branches to balance the political, economic, and social choices to determine the precise measure of benefits owed to particular individuals. Here, we do not need legal learning, but rather a broad understanding of the implications of the competing policy choices; we want the most political accountability where there is most room for disagreement and debate. Thus, the court will insist (repeatedly if necessary) that dignity demands that people live a life with a certain amount of comfort (not subject, in this constitutional culture, to reasonable debate), but only the political branches should decide whether that should be in the form of benefits, entitlement grants, social insurance—formulas that are subject to reasonable disagreement, that require public input, and that warrant political accountability. The recognition of human dignity does not determine the outcome—it does not establish how much money should be given to each person—but it does ensure that the legislative determination respects the equal worth of each person.[74] This is the constitutionalization of politics.

The South African Constitutional Court was explicit on this point in a recent case about the right to water:

> Ordinarily it is institutionally inappropriate for a court to determine precisely what the achievement of any particular social and economic right entails and what steps government should take to ensure the progressive realisation of the right. This is a matter, in the first place, for the legislature and executive, the institutions of government best placed to investigate social conditions in the light of available budgets and to determine what targets are achievable in relation to social and economic rights. Indeed, it is desirable as a matter of democratic accountability that they should do so for it is their programmes and promises that are subjected to democratic popular choice.[75]

The court found that "the expert evidence on the record provides numerous different answers to the question of what constitutes 'sufficient water'. Courts are ill-placed to make these assessments for both institutional and democratic reasons."

In both these cases, courts that are famously engaged have clearly demarcated the limits of their authority. It is uncontestably up to them to establish the constitutional standard by which government action must be measured, but then the ball bounces to the government's court to operationalize the constitutional standard—to determine how to get how much water or benefits or any other public good to which households. The judiciary then steps back in to ensure that the government program is consistent with the constitutional requirement. Thus, the *Mazibuko* court continued, saying that the constitution "places a positive obligation upon the state to respond to the basic social and economic needs of the people by adopting reasonable legislative and other measures. By adopting such measures, the rights set out in the Constitution acquire content, and that content is subject to the constitutional standard of reasonableness." In this way, the court leaves the development of policy where it belongs, with the political branches, while remaining fully engaged in the project of constitutionalizing political action.

This reflects an appropriate role for courts enforcing SEC rights, or any rights whose vindication necessitates significant government involvement in terms of the balancing of priorities to develop an appropriate policy, as well as fiscal implications. Although these courts may (particularly to American eyes) seem more activist, more intrusive, and more involved in the development of policy, the courts do not see themselves that way. They see themselves playing an important judicial—though not political—role in the development of constitutional policies. Here we might think of *balance* of powers rather than *separation* of powers, the former sounding more cooperative and less antagonistic. The *Mazibuko* court explained it this way:

> A reasonableness challenge requires government to explain the choices it has made. To do so, it must provide the information it has considered and the process it has followed to determine its policy. This case provides an excellent example of government doing just that. Although the applicants complained about the volume of material lodged by the City and Johannesburg Water in particular, which covered all aspects of the formulation of the City's water policy, the disclosure of such information points to the substantial importance of litigation concerning social and economic rights. If the process followed by government is flawed or the information gathered is obviously inadequate or incomplete, appropriate relief may be sought. In this way, the social and economic rights entrenched in our Constitution may contribute to the deepening of democracy. They enable citizens to hold government accountable not only through the ballot box but also, in a different way, through litigation.[76]

Viewed through this lens, the tension generally perceived in the United States between constitutionalism (a stand-in for individual rights) and democracy (representing majoritarian politics) begins to melt. The assertion of constitutional rights is just one way to ensure that government policies reflect constitutional—as well as political, economic, and other—values, and "judicial intervention becomes not a substitute for, but a complement to, the democratic process of policy development and service delivery monitoring,"[77] as Brinks and Gauri have written. Wojciech Sadurski has noticed a similar shift in the courts of central and eastern Europe. In contrast to the common law courts of the United States, Canada, and Australia, which agonize about judicial activism in a bid to preserve their legitimacy, the constitutional courts of central and eastern Europe do not worry about "legislating from the bench" and so can more freely participate in the policy debate.[78] Sadurski posits several reasons for this divergence, including historical differences in levels of trust in judges compared with trust in democratic political institutions, the existence (or not) of explicit constitutional authorization for judicial review, and structural differences between the Kelsenian courts, which stand outside of the judicial hierarchy, and the American model, in which constitutional adjudication is diffused. Whatever the reasons, it is clear that most courts that have accepted the responsibility of enforcing socioeconomic rights do so in a manner that engages with, rather than standing in opposition to, the political process.[79] This is as true in the dignity cases as anywhere else.

Several mechanisms for implementing this dialogic turn have been noted: some courts have delayed issuing an order of invalidation to give the government time to change its policy to conform to the constitutional norms. A more involved variation on this is when courts issue a series of interim orders that require progressive action by the government, as when, for instance, the government is required to report back to the court within a few months to document its progress toward implementing the constitutional right.[80] Alternatively, in some cases, courts have invited subsequent challenges by the plaintiffs should the defendant fail to fulfill the right. As Malcolm Langford has observed, "Advocates have been creative in securing follow-up orders for ensuring remedies are implemented. In Argentina, India and South Africa, advocates have used criminal and contempt proceedings to ensure compliance with decisions."[81]

But effective judicial intervention depends on the initiative of litigants (and lawyers) who have the wherewithal and the inclination to assert their rights. For instance, in Brazil, one commentator reports that the "legalization of health care in Brazil has . . . resulted . . . from the accumulation of many individual actions on the part of middle and lower middle class claimants, who have been availing themselves of individual public and private lawyers in an uncoordinated, unorganized way."[82] In fact, throughout Latin America and South Asia, Langford reports, "numerous cases have been filed directly by individuals and small communities outside any legal mobilisation support structure."[83]

And this, in turn, requires that individuals in the populace view themselves as important in and of themselves and as valuable to the body politic. That is, it requires that people recognize their own human and civic dignity. As Gauri and Brinks have written, "The most important social prerequisites for the legalization of economic and social demands are the conditions that favor the mobilization of wants and desires into demands. In other words, there must have occurred that transformation of outlook in which, as Hannah Pitkin has put it, 'I want' has become 'I am entitled to.' "[84] Or, as Hannah Arendt would put it, "I have the right to have rights."

Dignity jurisprudence thus promotes democratization in multiple ways. First, these cases promote democratic ideals by emphasizing the fundamental equality of all members of the polity; where dignity is recognized, each person has this one very important, very valuable asset that is inalienable and irreducible and infinite, to be used as often as he or she wishes, in a multitude of circumstances.[85] Second, by helping to ensure adequate material comfort, the cases ensure that each person has the wherewithal to be involved and engaged in public discussion; democracy thrives in the middle classes, and judicial pressure on the political branches to protect against extreme poverty and to provide for a decent standard of living for all will produce the soil in which democracy can grow. Both of these forms of affirmation—the psychological and the material—facilitate democratic activity. But the cases go further and actually encourage participation in democratic discourse by opening their doors to people through the liberal use of *amparo* (or *tutela*), PIL, *habeas data*, and *habeas corpus* actions, by valuing each person's equal dignity, and by modeling a language of participatory democracy in the opinions that speak of dignity and that confirm that each person matters and is entitled to be respected. The jurisprudence of dignity invites people into the public square, provides them with an opportunity to engage in democratic discourse, and gives them the tools necessary to make their participation effective. Moreover, it insists repeatedly that the government has obligations to the populace to make good on the constitutional promise of equal dignity. The right to dignity therefore supports and strengthens democracy in countries throughout world, which, in turn, may conduce to greater protection for human dignity.

And so we have come full circle. As constitutions explicitly protect human dignity, and courts expound on its meaning, people around the world increasingly develop a *feeling* of dignity—an internalized awareness of their own worth and of the power it carries. And as they do, they increasingly participate in the constitutionalization of politics, through both political and judicial avenues, which, in turn, forces political and judicial actors to respect people's dignity and to fulfill its constitutional promise.

NOTES

Foreword

1. HCJ 5688/92, *Veckselbum v. The Defense Minister* [1993] IsrSC 47(2) 812, 830.
2. HCJ 6427/02, *The Movement for Quality Government in Israel v. The Knesset* [2006] IsrSC 61(1) 619, 685.

Introduction

Epigraphs: Aharon Barak, *The Judge in a Democracy* (Princeton, N.J.: Princeton University Press, 2008), 85; Supreme Court of Israel, HCJ 453/94 *Israel Women's Network v. Government of Israel* 48(5) PD 501 (1994) (Isr.), quoted in Ariel L. Bendor and Michael Sachs, "Human Dignity as a Constitutional Concept in Germany and in Israel (January 19, 2011)," *Israel Law Review* 44 (2011): 28, SSRN: http://ssrn.com/abstract=1743439; Christoph Möllers, "Democracy and Human Dignity: Limits of a Moralized Conception of Rights in German Constitutional Law," *Israel Law Review* 42 (2009): 416, 418, quoting Hans Carl Nipperdey, *Die Grundrechte: Handbuch der Theorie und Praxis der Grundrechte*, vol. 2, *Die Freiheitsrechte in Deutschland* (Berlin: Duncker un Humblot, 1954), 1; George Kateb, *Human Dignity* (Cambridge, Mass.: Belknap Press of Harvard University Press, 2011), 27.

Throughout this book, materials in Spanish, French, and Portuguese are translated by the author. Official and other creditable translations into English are used for materials originally in other languages.

1. Daniel J. Whelan, *Indivisible Human Rights: A History* (Philadelphia: University of Pennsylvania Press, 2010), 207, charting Karel Vasak's taxonomy of rights.
2. See Sandra Liebenberg, *Socio-Economic Rights: Adjudication Under a Transformative Constitution* (Claremont, S.A.: Juta, 2010), 33: "constitutional guarantees of both civil and political rights as well as economic, social, and cultural rights are consistent with the commitment of deliberative democracy to substantively equal participation in deliberation."
3. David Luban, Lecture: "Lawyers as Upholders of Human Dignity (When They Aren't Busy Assaulting It)," *University of Illinois Law Review* (2005): 815–45, 817 ("The

notion of human dignity plays something of a cameo role in discussions of legal ethics, although I shall be arguing that it is a lot more central than many writers appreciate").

4. Political Constitution of Peru, (1993), Art. 1: "The defense of the human person and respect for his dignity are the supreme purpose of society and the State."

5. Ronald Dworkin, *Justice for Hedgehogs* (Cambridge, Mass.: Belknap Press of Harvard University Press, 2011), 13.

6. Man Yee Karen Lee, "Universal Human Dignity: Some Reflections in the Asian Context," *Asian Journal of Comparative Law* 3, 1 (2008): 1–33, cited in Viviana Bohórquez Monsalve and Javier Aguirre Román, "Tensions of Human Dignity: Conceptualization and Application to International Human Rights Law," *SUR: International Journal of Human Rights* 6, 11 (2009): 39.

7. Stephanie Hennette-Vauchez, "When Ambivalent Principles Prevail: Leads for Explaining Western Legal Orders' Infatuation with the Human Dignity Principle," EUI Working Papers Law (December 2007).

8. Susanne Baer, "Dignity, Liberty, Equality: A Fundamental Rights Triangle of Constitutionalism," *University of Toronto Law Journal* 59, 4 (Fall 2009): 417, 457, citing Christopher McCrudden, "Human Dignity and Judicial Interpretation of Human Rights," *European Journal of International Law* 19 (2008): 655, 724.

9. See Miguel Schor, "Mapping Comparative Judicial Review," *Washington University Global Legal Studies Law Review* 7 (2008): 284, on lumpers and splitters who "disagree as to whether a common, global constitutional law is emerging."

10. Stu Woolman, "The Widening Gyre of Human Dignity," in Stu Woolman and Michael Bishop, eds., *Constitutional Conversations* (Pretoria: Pretoria University Law Press 2008), 193 (identifying five definitions or uses of dignity in the jurisprudence of the South African Constitutional Court).

11. Woolman, "The Widening Gyre of Human Dignity," 197.

12. McCrudden, "Human Dignity and Judicial Interpretation," 723–24 ("as the historical examination of the development of dignity indicated, there are several conceptions of dignity that one can choose from, but one cannot coherently hold all of these conceptions at the same time. . . . No one jurisdiction has a coherent judicially interpreted conception of dignity across the range of rights, and no coherent conception of dignity emerges transnationally").

Chapter 1. "Of All Members of the Human Family"

1. See, e.g., Corpus Juris Civilis (referring to the dignity and office of a person).

2. See The Digest or Pandects, Book XXI, Title I (44) ("The Ædiles, with great justice, refuse to permit a slave to be accessory to property of less value than himself, in order to avoid fraud being committed either against the Edict or against the Civil Law, and also, as Pedius says, against the dignity of mankind").

3. The Bill of Rights (Act), 1689 [1], Cap. II (36).

4. Declaration of the Rights of Man and of the Citizen (1789) ("All citizens, being

equal in the eyes of the law, are equally eligible to all dignities and to all public positions and occupations, according to their abilities, and without distinction except that of their virtues and talents"). See also Constitution of May 3, 1791, Art. II (The Landed Nobility).

5. Constitution of Bulgaria (1879), Chap. V, Art. 24.

6. Consitution of Mexico (1917), Art 3.1.

7. Constitution of Latvia (1922), Art. 95.

8. Constitution of Ecuador (1929), Título XIII, De las garantías fundamentales, Artículo 151: La Constitución garantiza a los habitantes del Ecuador, principalmente, los siguientes derechos . . . (18): "El Estado protegerá, especialmente, al obrero y al campesino, y legislará para que los principios de justicia se realicen en el orden de la vida económica, asegurado a todos un mínimum de bienestar, compatible con la dignidad humana."

9. Weimar Constitution (1919), s. 151: "The organization of economic life must conform to the principles of justice to the end that all may be guaranteed a decent standard of living." See Ariel L. Bendor and Michael Sachs," Human Dignity as a Constitutional Concept in Germany and in Israel (January 19, 2011)," *Israel Law Review* 44 (2011): 3–4.

10. See also Consitution of Ireland (1937), Preamble.

11. United Nations, Charter of the United Nations, 24 October 1945, 1 UNTS XVI, Preamble.

12. The UDHR Preamble begins: "Whereas, recognition of the inherent dignity and of the equal and inalienable rights of all members of the human family is the foundation of freedom, justice and peace in the world . . ." It continues: "Whereas the peoples of the United Nations have in the Charter reaffirmed their faith in fundamental human rights, in the dignity and worth of the human person and in the equal rights of men and women and have determined to promote social progress and better standards of life in larger freedom . . ." One jurist dates the application of dignity to the individual's moral qualities to Cicero: "Cicero was the first author who used the term "dignity" not in the traditional sense of social status, but in order to generally describe man's outstanding position in the world by virtue of his very nature—namely, his rational capacity. Man's special, inherent quality as a rational being was, evidently, recognized in antiquity long before Cicero, but he was the first to convey that idea by means of the concept of dignity." Izhak Englard, "Human Dignity: From Antiquity to Modern Israel's Constitutional Framework," *Cardozo Law Review* 21 (2000): 1903, 1904. Tracing the intellectual history of the concept of dignity, Justice Englard writes: "Later, this Renaissance notion of man led directly to the modern conception of individuality, of the autonomous and eventually sovereign self,"

13. UDHR, Art. 22.

14. UDHR, Art. 23.

15. George Kateb, *Human Dignity* (Cambridge, Mass.: Belknap Press of Harvard University Press, 2011), 5.

16. See Stéphanie Hennette-Vauchez, "Une dignitas humaine? Vieilles outres, vin

nouveau," *Droits* 48 (2009): 59, "En effet, la notion de *dignitas* renvoie en première intention à l'inegalité: elle indique forcément une hiérarchie, c'est un élément de distinction
sociale."

17. Susanne Baer, "Dignity, Liberty, Equality: A Fundamental Rights Triangle of
Constitutionalism," *University of Toronto Law Journal* 59, 4 (Fall 2009): 417–68, 461.

18. Stéphanie Hennette-Vauchez, "A Human Dignitas? Remnants of the Ancient
Legal Concept in Contemporary Dignity Jurisprudence," *International Journal of Con-
stitutional Law* 9 (2011): 32–57, citing James Q. Whitman, "On Nazi Honor and New
European Dignity," in *Darker Legacies of Law in Europe: The Shadow of National Socialism
and Fascism over Europe and Its Legal Traditions*, ed. Christian Joerges and Navraj Singh
Ghaleigh (Oxford: Hart, 2003), 243; Jeremy Waldron, "Dignity and Rank: In Memory of
Gregory Vlastos," *Archives Européennes de Sociologie* 2 (2007): 201–37; Waldron, "Dignity, Rank, and Rights," 2009 Tanner Lectures, University of California at Berkeley; Wal-
dron, "Dignity, Rights, and Responsibilities," European University Institute Max Weber
Lecture (May 2010).

19. Kateb, *Human Dignity*.

20. Hennette-Vauchez, "A Human Dignitas?" 16.

21. Paolo G. Carozza, "Human Dignity and Judicial Interpretation of Human Rights:
A Reply," *European Journal of International Law* 19, 5 (2008): 931, 937–38.

22. ICCPR, Preamble; ICESCR, Preamble.

23. ICCPR, Art. 10.

24. ICESCR, Art. 13.

25. See, e.g., *Kok Wah Kuan v. Pengarah Penjara Kajang*, Selangor Darul Ehsan,
[2004] 5 MLJ 193, High Court of Malaysia (Kuala Lumpur), referencing the Convention
on the Rights of the Child, Art. 37c, UN General Assembly Document A/RES/44/25 (12
December 1989) ("Every child deprived of liberty shall be treated with humanity and
respect for the inherent dignity of the human person, and in a manner which takes into
account the needs of persons of his or her age").

26. See, e.g., Pl. US 25/94 (Constitutional Court of the Czech Republic) (13 June
1995), II (concerning the provision of free public education and referring to "Article 28
para. 2 of the Convention on the Rights of the Child, promulgated under No. 104/1991
Sb., . . . provides that States Parties shall take all appropriate measures to ensure that
school discipline is administered in a manner consistent with the child's human dignity
and in conformity with the present Convention'"); see also Decision 42/2000 (XI. 8.) AB
(Constitutional Court of the Republic of Hungary) (considering the state's obligation to
provide a place of residence under both domestic and international law); *Kayano et al.
v. Hokkaido Expropriation Committee* [The Nibutani Dam Decision], 1598 *Hanrei jihō*
33 (Sapporo D. Ct., March 27, 1997) (Japan), trans. Mark A. Levin), reprinted in Curtis
J. Milhaupt, J. Mark Ramseyer, and Mark D. West, *The Japanese Legal System: Cases,
Codes, and Commentary* (New York: Foundation Press, 2006), 267 (applying ICCPR
provisions relating to minority cultures because "our nation has a duty [*gimu*] to faith-
fully observe this guarantee").

27. See, e.g., Constitution of India (1950), Preamble: "We, the People of India, having solemnly resolved to . . . secure to all its citizens . . . Fraternity assuring the dignity of the individual and the unity and integrity of the Nation"; Basic Law Federal Republic of Germany (1949), Art. 1: "Human dignity shall be inviolable. To respect and protect it shall be the duty of all state authority"; Basic Law Hong Kong (1990), Art. 6(1): "All persons deprived of their liberty shall be treated with humanity and with respect for the inherent dignity of the human person"; Model Constitutional Code, Art. 26: Human dignity must be "respected in any case" and "Protection of human dignity is a duty of the State."

28. Constitution of Spain (1978), Art. 10(1), (2).

29. Constitution of the Federative Republic of Brazil (1988), Art. 1.

30. Constitution of the Republic of South Africa (1996), Art. 1.

31. Constitution of the Democratic Republic of East Timor (2002), Section 1.1.

32. Basic Law for the Federal Republic of Germany, Art. 1.

33. Christoph Möllers, "Democracy and Human Dignity: Limits of a Moralized Conception of Rights in German Constitutional Law," *Israel Law Review* 42 (2009): 416, 419.

34. See, e.g., German Basic Law, Art. 79(3). Ulrich R. Haltern, "High Time for a Check-Up: Progressivism, Populism, and Constitutional Review in Germany," http://www.jeanmonnetprogram.org/papers/96/9605ind.html: "In answer to the disdain of human dignity between 1933 and 1945, this provision is unalterable due to Article 79 (3)."

35. Constitution of the Russian Federation (1993), Art. 21(1).

36. Constitution of the Republic of Poland, (1997), Art. 30. See also Procedural Decision of 24th October 2001, SK 10/01 Constitutional Complaint and the Principle of Equality (Constitutional Court of Poland): "It is worth noting that the constitutional right to protection of dignity, as enshrined in Article 30 and—similarly to the principle of equality—located amongst provisions defining the general principles of the chapter on rights and freedoms, may not be subjected to limitations allowed for by Article 31(3), since none of the values included in this provision justify limits on the constitutional guarantees of the dignity of the human being." (Dissenting opinion of Judge Marek Safjan) (holding that the constitutional guarantee of equality is not independently enforceable, but enforceable only in conjunction with other provisions.)

37. See, e.g., Constitution of Tajikistan (1994), Art. 5: "Life, honor, dignity, and other natural human rights are inviolable." Similar language is found in many constitutions of the former Soviet republics. See also Constitution of the People's Republic of China (1982), Art. 37; Constitution of Ghana (1992), Art. 15.

38. Constitution of the Independent State of Papua New Guinea (Consolidated to Amendment No. 22) (1975), s. 38.

39. Constitution of Tuvalu Ordinance (1986), s. 15: "(1) Notwithstanding anything to the contrary . . . all laws, and all acts done under a law, must be reasonably justifiable in a democratic society that has a proper respect for human rights and dignity."

Constitution of South Africa (1996), Art. 36: "The rights in the Bill of Rights may be limited only in terms of law of general application to the extent that the limitation is reasonable and justifiable in an open and democratic society based on human dignity, equality and freedom."

40. See, e.g., Head Scarf Case, BVerfG, 2 BvR 1436/02 vom 24.09.2003, para. 53, referring to the "paramount constitutional value of human dignity (Art. 1.1 of the Basic Law; cf. BVerfGE 52, 223 (247)); see also Life Imprisonment Case, 45 BverfGE 187 (1977): "The free human personality and [human] dignity represent the highest legal values within the constitutional order"; quoted Norman Dorsen, Michael Rosenfeld, András Sajó, and Susanne Baer, *Comparative Constitutionalism: Cases and Materials*, American Casebook Series (St. Paul, Minn.: Thompson-West, 2003). 515. As such, it is not subject to constitutional amendment.

41. Decision 48/1998 (XI. 23.) AB, in the Name of the Republic of Hungary (Permitting an Act of the Parliament permitting abortion in case the pregnant woman is in a situation of serious crisis). See Decision 58/2001 (III.2.) (Regarding change of names): "The Constitutional Court regards the right to human dignity as another phrase for the 'general personality right.' The general personality right is a 'mother right', i.e., a subsidiary fundamental right which may be relied upon at any time by both the Constitutional Court and other courts for the protection of an individual's autonomy when none of the concrete, named fundamental rights are applicable to a particular set of facts." Decision 8/1990 (IV. 23.) AB, ABH 1990, 42, 44, 45. Constitution of Hungary (2011) Art. 37.

42. HCJ 70 15/02, *Ajuri v. Commander of IDF Forces in the West Bank* (2002), reprinted in "Judgments of the Israel Supreme Court: Fighting Terrorism Within the Law," Israel Ministry of Foreign Affairs (2005), 157, http://www.israel-mfa.gov.il/.

43. Ghana Constitution (1992), Art. 15, Art. 33 (5).

44. Möllers, "Democracy and Human Dignity," 420.

45. Ibid., 428.

46. Ibid., 422.

47. Ibid., 459 n. 59.

48. Kyrgyzstan Constitution (2010), Arts. 13, 15, 16, 18, 88.

49. Kenya Constitution (2010), Art. 10.

50. Ibid., Art. 19.

51. Ibid., Art. 20.

52. Ibid., Art. 24.

53. Belgium Constitution, Art. 23(1).

54. Ibid., Art. 23(2).

55. Ibid., Art. 23(3).

56. Basic Law: Liberty and Human Dignity (1994). Property is protected in Section 3 and in Section 7 (b) and (c) under privacy.

57. Baer, "Dignity, Liberty, Equality," 461.

58. Constitution of the Republic of Uganda (1995), Art. 16.

59. Constitution of Indonesia (1945), Art. 34.

60. Interim National Constitution of the Republic of the Sudan (2005), Art. 45(1) and (2).

61. Constitution of Fiji (1988), Section 27: "1) Every person who is arrested or detained has the right: . . . (f) to be treated with humanity and with respect for his or her inherent dignity." Constitution of the Republic of Albania (1998), Art. 28: "5. Every person whose liberty was taken away . . . has the right to humane treatment and respect for his dignity."

62. India Constitution, Art. 51A(e): "It shall be the duty of every citizen of India . . . to promote harmony and the spirit of common brotherhood amongst all the people of India transcending religious, linguistic and regional or sectional diversities; to renounce practices derogatory to the dignity of women"; Art. 39(f): "The State shall, in particular, direct its policy towards securing . . . that children are given opportunities and facilities to develop in a healthy manner and in conditions of freedom and dignity and that childhood and youth are protected against exploitation and against moral and material abandonment." See, e.g., *Aruna Roy & Ors v. Union of India & Ors* [2002] 3 LRI 643, para. 52 ("What is sought to be imparted is incorporated in art 51(A)(e), which provides to promote harmony and the spirit of common brotherhood amongst all the people of India transcending religions, linguistic and regional or sectional diversities; to renounce practices derogatory to the dignity of women").

63. India Constitution, Preamble. If not truly enforceable, this language is at least influential to the Indian Supreme Court. *See EV Chinnaiah v. State of Andhra Pradesh & Ors* [2004] 4 LRI 705, para. 88: "The operation of reservation policy ought to be in a manner consistent with the objective of promoting fraternity among all citizens, assuring the dignity of the individual and unity of the Nation."

64. Interim National Constitution of the Republic of the Sudan (2005), Art. 32(3).

65. Macedonia Constitution (2001), Art. 11(1).

66. Constitution of Finland, (1999) (731/1999, amendments up to 802/2007 included), Section 9.

67. Portugal Constitution (2005), Art. 13.

68. Constitution of the Kingdom of Thailand B.E. 2550 (2007), Section 35.

69. Constitution of Greece (1975), Art. 106(2).

70. Constitution of the Republic of Serbia (2006), Art. 69.

71. Constitution of the Kingdom of Thailand B.E. 2550 (2007), Section 53.

72. Constitution of Jamaica (2011): "AN ACT to Amend the Constitution of Jamaica to provide for a Charter of Fundamental Rights and Freedoms and for connected matters," s. 13(b).

73. Tanzania Constitution of 1977 as amended to Act No. 1 of 2005 and GN No. 150 of 2005 18 (1977) s. 25. See also Constitution of Brazil (1988), Art. 170: "The economic order, founded on the appreciation of the value of human work and on free enterprise, is

intended to ensure everyone a life with dignity, in accordance with the dictates of social justice."

74. Constitution of the Republic of Paraguay (1992), Art. 129.

75. Constitution of the Principality of Andorra (1993), Art. 20. See also Constitution of Lesotho (1993), Art. 28.

76. Constitution of the Republic of Mozambique (2004), Art. 120.

77. Federal Constitution of the Swiss Confederation of 18 April 1999 (Status as of 7 March 2010).

78. *Sukhmander Singh v. Permanent Secretary for Security and Others*, HCAL 68/2005 (High Court of the Hong Kong Special Administrative Region—Court of First Instance), 2005 HKCU LEXIS 1195; [2005] 1242 HKCU.

79. "These fundamental rights represent the basic values cherished by the people of this country since the Vedic times and they are calculated to protect the dignity of the individual and create conditions in which every human being can develop his personality to the fullest extent. They weave a 'pattern of guarantees on the basic-structure of human rights' and impose negative obligations on the State not to encroach on individual liberty in its various dimensions." *Maneka Ghandi v. Union of India*, [1978] INSC 17; [1978] 2 SCR 621; [1978] 1 SCC 248; AIR 1978 SC 597 (25 January 1978), 667–68.

80. "The freedom of association is related to the general freedom of action and the right to free personal development that form part of the right to human dignity [Art. 54 para. (1) of the Constitution]. Every person has the right to associate with others for any freely chosen purpose, among others, for the establishment of a cultural, religious, scientific, social or leisure community, furthermore, to set up, voluntarily join or freely leave an organisation," Decision 6/2001 (III. 14.) AB, http://www.mkab.hu/en/enpage3.htm.

81. Constitution of Hungary (2011), Art. II ("Human dignity is inviolable. Everyone has the right to life and human dignity; the life of a foetus will be protected from conception"); Art. XVII ("Every employee has the right to working conditions that respect his or her health, safety and dignity"); Preamble ("We hold that human existence is based on human dignity").

82. See also Constitution of the Republic of Korea (1948, 1987), linking dignity to happiness (Art. 10), working conditions (Art. 32), and marriage and family life (Art. 36).

83. Samuel Moyne, *The Last Utopia: Human Rights in History* (Cambridge, Mass.: Belknap Press of Harvard University Press, 2010), 26–27.

84. Constitution of the Republic of South Africa (1996), Art. 10.

85. Indonesia Constitution (1945), Art. 34.

86. Philippine Constitution (1987), Art. XIII, s. 1.

87. Constitution of the Republic of Maldives (2008), Art. 246.

88. Political Constitution of Peru (1993), Art. 1.

Chapter 2. "Not . . . a Mere Plaything"

1. Izhak Englard, "Human Dignity: From Antiquity to Modern Israel's Constitutional Framework," *Cardoza Law Review* 21 (2000): 1903, 1923.

2. Sentencia T-088/08, para. 3.5.5 (Constitutional Court of Colombia): "Y es que el contenido de la expresión 'dignidad humana' puede presentarse de dos maneras: a partir de su objeto concreto de protección ya partir de su funcionalidad normativa. Al respecto, en la sentencia T-881 de 2002 esta Corporación manifestó: 'Y Al tener como punto de vista el objeto de protección del enunciado normativo "dignidad humana," ' la Sala ha identificado a lo largo de la jurisprudencia de la Corte, tres lineamientos claros y diferenciables: (i) La dignidad humana entendida como autonomía o como posibilidad de diseñar un plan vital y de determinarse según sus características (vivir como quiera). (ii) La dignidad humana entendida como ciertas condiciones materiales concretas de existencia (vivir bien). . . . (iii) la dignidad humana entendida como intangibilidad de los bienes no patrimoniales, integridad física e integridad moral (vivir sin humillaciones)." See also Sentencia T-009/09.

3. *AirTransport Security Case,* BVerfG, 1 BvR 357/05 vom 15.2.2006, Absatz-Nr. (1–154), para. 119.

4. Dignity "cannot be taken away from any human being. What can be violated, however, is the claim to respect which results from it (see BVerfGE 87, 209 (228))," Air Transport Security Case, BVerfG, 1 BvR 357/05 vom 15.2.2006 para. 117.

5. *Maneka Ghandi v. Union of India* [1978] INSC 17; [1978] 2 SCR 621; [1978] 1 SCC 248; AIR [1978] SC 597 (25 January 1978), 667–68.

6. See Decision 27/2002 (III.1.) (Hungary) (regarding screening for AIDS). On the right to information, see *Wilo Rodriguez Gutierrez v. President Alejandro Toledo Manrique,* Habeas Data on Appeal, Record No. 959 0959-2004-hd/tc, First Chamber, Constitutional Court (Peru), Nov. 19, 2004, reprinted in Angel R. Oquendo, *Latin American Law* (New York: Foundation Press, 2006), 378 ("The right to public information includes, additionally, the right to the truth, which translates into the right to obtain reliable and undisputed information from administrative agencies . . . [T]he right to truth [is] a new fundamental entitlement, which the 1993 Constitution does not mention expressly [but which] derives from the notions of human dignity, of a democratic and social state under the rule of law, as well as of a republican form of government").

7. Decision 39/2007 (VI. 20.) AB in the Name of the Republic of Hungary, para. 4.1 (vaccination case), citing Decision 75/1995 (XII. 21.) AB, ABH 1995, 376, 381.

8. Decision 8/1990 (IV. 23.) AB, ABH 1990, 42, 44–45 (Hungary), quoting Decision 35/2002 (VII. 19.) AB 2002 (finding no violation of the right to dignity in the use of cameras at sporting events).

9. Air Transport Security Case, BVerfG, 1 BvR 357/05 vom 15.2.2006, Absatz-Nr. (1-154), para. 119.

10. Decision 23/1990, 31 October 1990, on Capital Punishment (Lábady and Tersztyánszky, JJ., concurring), para. 3.

11. Decision 58/2001 (XII.7). AB (Hungary 2001) quoting Decision 64/1991 (XII. 17.) AB. available at http://www.mkab.hu/content/en/en3/00059804.htm.

12. Ibid.

13. Ibid. (Dr. András Holló, dissenting).

14. BVerfG, 2 BvF 2/90 vom 28.5.1993, paras. 145, 146. One of the dissenters in the Hungarian abortion case adopted this view: "Since in a biological sense, the foetus is a human, i.e. a genetically fully developed individual human being, and since the term 'inherent right to life' means—even in the terminology of international treaties ('droit inhérent de la vie,' 'angeboneres Recht auf Leben')—a right not gained through birth, but 'formed' together with the man, i.e. a right that originates in the existence, the humanity of the man, the lack of human dignity and having no right to life cannot be justified by the Constitution in case of a foetus not yet born." Decision 48/1998 (XI. 23.) AB (Hungary) (Dr. Tamás Lábady, dissenting).

15. BVerfG, 2 BvF 2/90 vom 28.5.1993, paras. 145, 146 (quoting BVerfGE 39, 1 [41]).

16. Constitution of Hungary (2011), Art. II: "Human dignity is inviolable. Everyone has the right to life and human dignity; the life of a foetus will be protected from conception."

17. BVerfG, 2 BvF 2/90 vom 28.5.1993, 147: "This right to life which does not depend upon acceptance by the mother for its existence, but which the unborn is entitled to simply by virtue of its existence is an elementary and inalienable right stemming from the dignity of the person. It applies irrespective of any particular religious or philosophical views, which the state is anyway not entitled to pass judgment on, because it must remain religiously and ideologically neutral." See also BVerfG, 2 BvR 1436/02 vom 24.9.2003, para. 42 (explaining that "The free state of the Basic Law is characterised by openness towards the variety of ideological and religious convictions and bases this on an image of humanity that is marked by the dignity of humans and the free development of personality in self-determination and personal responsibility").

18. Constitution of Saint Lucia (1978), Preamble.

19. Grenada Constitution Order (1973), Preamble (c). See also Constitution of Barbados (1966), Preamble: "The people of Barbados—proclaim that they are a sovereign nation founded upon principles that acknowledge the supremacy of God, the dignity of the human person, their unshakable faith in fundamental human rights and freedoms, the position of the family in a society of free men and free institutions."

20. CrimA 2145/92 *State of Israel v. Guetta* [1992] IsrSC 46(5) 704, 724–35, quoted in CA 506/88 *Yael Shefer v. State of Israel* (1993).

21. *Griswold v. Connecticut*, 381 U.S. 479, 484 (1965) (Douglas, J.).

22. A. B. 58/2001 (XII.7) (Hungary 2001). Hungarian jurists in the death penalty case maintained that to judicially define dignity is to violate its essence: "[When] the Constitution mentions the inherent rights to life and dignity—with regard to the adjectives 'inviolable and inalienable,' in Art. 8(1)—it provides for categories that are superior to legal values, and must be given the fullest possible legal protection. The standards for the protection of these values (as real legal prohibitions) are unlimited

and consequently binding upon the State." To define the contours of dignity is to "arbitrarily restructure the above values protected by the Constitution." Decision 23/1990, 31 October 1990, on Capital Punishment (Lábady and Tersztyánszky, JJ., concurring), para. 5.

23. *Maneka Ghandi v. Union of India* [1978] 2 SCR 621, 695.

24. Decision 58/2001. One of the dissenters, while agreeing in general with the protection of the right to choose a name, would have located it with family and marriage rights, noting that the right to choose a name for one's child is a family right, inhering in the parents rather than in the named child (Dr. Attila Harmathy, Judge of the Constitutional Court, dissenting).

25. BVerfG, 1 BvR 1762/95 vom 12.12.2000. The case concerned the constitutionality of sanctions against United Colors of Benetton for an advertising campaign that showed a "photograph of naked human buttocks with the words 'H.I.V. POSITIVE' stamped on them." The Constitutional Court found that the government could, in principle, protect against harms to dignity in commercial advertising, but that this ad was constitutionally protected.

26. Sent. 334/96, (Italy 1996).

27. See *Zonenstein v. Military Advocate* (High Court of Justice, Israel, 2005) ISR-2002-3-005 HC 7622/02.

28. See, e.g., Constitución Política reformada por Acuerdo Legislativo No. 18–93 del 17 de Noviembre de 1993, Art. 4: "In Guatemala, all human beings are free and equal in dignity and rights." (En Guatemala todos los seres humanos son libres e iguales en dignidad y derechos); see also Representatives of the Federal District Legislative Assembly V, Article 334 (iii), Penal Code; Article 131b, Code of Criminal Procedure; Unconstitutionality Action 10/2000 XV GSJF 415 (Ninth Epoch) Plenum, Supreme Court (Mexico) Feb. 14, 2002: "Article 1 enunciates the principle of equality among all individuals on our national territory. It entitles them to exercise the rights established in the Constitution regardless of their nationality, race, religion, sex, etc. The right to equality thus applies to all human beings. This constitutional provision also forbids slavery, as well as all discrimination that undermines human dignity or personal rights and liberties. In sum, it grants all citizens the right to equality."

29. Constitution of Italy (1947), Art. 3.

30. *Leung TC William Roy v. Secretary for Justice* [2005] 3 HKC 77, 104 (CFI).

31. Susanne Baer views liberty, equality, and dignity as an integrated triangle. "Because of equality and liberty, dignity is not a status such as *dignitas* or a moralistic vision of dignified behaviour. Because of dignity, equality is not symmetry but the right to be different, free from subordination; and because of liberty, equality is the claim to make different uses of one's liberties and not suffer from that." Susanne Baer, "Dignity, Liberty, Equality: A Fundamental Rights Triangle of Constitutionalism," *University of Toronto Law Journal* 59, 4 (2009): 417–68.

32. *Duncan v. Kahanamoku*, 327 U.S. 304, 334 (1946) (Murphy, J., concurring).

33. HCJ 4541/94, 49(4) PD 94 [1995] (Isr.)., cited in Ariel L. Bendor and Michael

Sachs, "Human Dignity as a Constitutional Concept in Germany and in Israel," *Israel Law Review* 44, 30 (2011): 1, 30.

34. *See Nova Scotia (Workers' Compensation Board) v. Martin; Nova Scotia (Workers' Compensation Board) v. Laseur* [2003] 2 SCR 504, 559; 2003 SCC 54; 2003 SCR LEXIS 572; [2003] (disability); *Quebec (Commission des Droits de la Personne et des Droits de la Jeunesse) v. Montreal (City); Quebec (Commission des Droits de la Personne et des Droits de la Jeunesse) v. Boisbriand (City)*, File No.: 26583, Supreme Court of Canada, [2000] 1 SCR 665; 2000 SCC 27; 2000 SCR LEXIS 27 (handicap); *Lavoie v. Canada* [2002] 1 SCR 769, 2002 SCC 23 (citizenship); *Sauvé v. Canada (Chief Electoral Officer)* 2002 Can. Sup. Ct. LEXIS 77; 2002 SCC 68 ("Denial of the right to vote on the basis of attributed moral unworthiness is inconsistent with the respect for the dignity of every person that lies at the heart of Canadian democracy and the Charter") (imprisonment) (decided on right to vote, not equality, grounds); *Dunmore v. Ontario (Attorney General)* 2001 Can. Sup. Ct. LEXIS 94; 2001 SCC 94 (right to organize) (decided on right of association, not equality, grounds); *Trociuk v. British Columbia (Attorney General)* [2003] 1 SCR 835; 2003 SCC 34; 2003 SCR LEXIS 552; [2003] SCJ 32 (6 June 2003) (gender); *Little Sisters Book and Art Emporium v. Canada (Minister of Justice)* 2000 Can. Sup. Ct. LEXIS 66; 2000 SCC 69; *M v. H.* 1999 Can. Sup. Ct. LEXIS 28 (sexual orientation); *Corbiere v. Canada (Minister of Indian and Northern Affairs)* 1999 Can. Sup. Ct. LEXIS 25 (Indian band members).

35. *R. v. Kapp* [2008] 2 SCR 483, 2008 SCC 41, paras. 19–25.

36. *Minister of Home Affairs v. Fourie*, 2006 (3) BCLR 355 (CC), 72 (S. Afr.).

37. Ibid., 94–95.

38. *Nat'l Coal. for Gay and Lesbian Equality v. Minister of Justice*, 1999 (1) SA 6 (CC); 1998 (12) BCLR 1517 (CC), 99, 100 (S. Afr.).

39. HCJ 6427/02, *The Movement for Quality Government in Israel v. The Knesset*, para. 43.

40. Decision 20/1999 (VI. 25.) AB, citing Decision 61/1992 (XI. 20.) AB, ABH 1992, 280–82; Decision 963/B/1993 AB, ABH 1996, 437–45 (concerning regulations of sexual conduct).

41. Sentencia T-1258/08 (Colombia 2008).

42. "Fine Property Situation," Pl US 38/02, at III.2.A.b (Mar. 9, 2004): "In any case, the examination of one's property situation is established in the Czech legal order (similarly to the legal orders of other developed countries) in a number of contexts (not only as a criterion for the proportionality of an imposed penalty), and in the opinion of the Constitutional Court it cannot be interpreted a limine as unconstitutional because it introduces inequality in dignity and rights."

43. See *Univ. of California Regents v. Bakke*, 438 U.S. 265 (1978); *Metro Broad. Inc. v. FCC*, 497 U.S. 547 (1990); *Richmond v. J.A. Croson Co.*, 488 U.S. 469 (1989); *Adarand Constructors v. Peña*, 515 U.S. 200 (1995). These cases do not rely on the individuation aspect of dignity or on dignity generally.

44. See, e.g., Schedule B Constitution Act, 1982, Part I Ch. 11 (U.K.), reprinted in R.S.C., No. 5, §15(2) (Canadian Charter of Rights & Freedoms) (provision guaranteeing equal protection of the law "does not preclude any law, program or activity that has as its object the amelioration of conditions of disadvantaged individuals or groups including those that are disadvantaged because or race, national or ethnic origin, colour, religion, sex, age, or mental or physical disability"); Grundegesetz fur die Bundesrepublik Deutschland [GG] [Constitution], Article 3(2) ("Men and women shall have equal rights. The state shall promote the actual implementation of equal rights for women and men and take steps to eliminate disadvantages that now exist"); India Constitution, Art. 15, §3 ("Nothing in this article shall prevent the State from making any special provision for women and children"); India Constitution, Art. 15, §4 ("Nothing in this article . . . shall prevent the State from making any special provision for the advancement of any socially and educationally backward classes of citizens or for the Scheduled Castes and the Scheduled Tribes"); South African Constitution, §9 (2) ("Equality includes the full and equal enjoyment of all rights and freedoms. To promote the achievement of equality, legislative and other measures designed to protect or advance persons, or categories of persons, disadvantaged by unfair discrimination may be taken").

45. *EV Chinnaiah v. State of Andhra Pradesh & Ors* (2005) 1SCC 294, 88.

46. Ibid., 89.

47. *Maneka Ghandi v. Union of India* (1978) 2 SCR 621, 692 (emphasis added).

48. *Whitney v California*, 274 U.S. 357 (1927) (Brandeis, J., concurring).

49. See Decision 39/2007 (VI. 20) AB, 375 at 13: "the Constitutional Court has adopted several decisions on the basis of the *right to self-determination* and the right to privacy as 'special personality rights' deriving from Article 54 para. (1) of the Constitution." See Decision 57/1991 (XI. 8.) AB, ABH 1991, 279; Decision 1/1994 (I. 7.) AB, ABH 1994, 29, 35–36; Decision 75/1995 (XII. 21.) AB, ABH 1995, 376, 380; Decision 5/1996 (II. 23.) AB, 14 ABH 1996, 47; Decision 11/1996 (III. 13.) AB, ABH 1996, 240; Decision 20/1997 (III. 19.) AB, ABH 1997, 85; Decision 4/1998 (III. 1.) AB, ABH 1998, 71; Decision 10/2001 (IV. 12.) AB, ABH 2001, 123; Decision 36/2000 (X.27.)

50. *Roe v. Wade*, 410 U.S. 113, 152 (1973).

51. *Planned Parenthood v. Casey*, 505 U.S. 833, 852 (1992).

52. Aborto en Caso de Violacion, Inseminacion Artificial o Trasferencia de Ovulo no Consentida—Supone la relativización del principio de dignidad humana (S.V. C-355/06): "penalizar ésta conducta no es coherente con la doctrina del núcleo esencial al derecho al libre desarrollo de la personalidad y autonomía como máxima expresión de la dignidad humana. En otras palabras, al considerar a la persona autónoma y libre, como lo preceptúa la Constitución, se hacen inviables todas aquellas normas en donde el legislador desconoce la condición mínima del ser humano como ser capaz de decidir sobre su propio rumbo y opción de vida."

53. *Minister of Home Affairs v. Fourie*, 2006 (3) BCLR 355 (CC), 49–50 (S. Afr.).

54. Decision 48/1998 (XI. 23.) AB (Hungary) (abortion decision) (noting that a law

that permits abortion when the woman is in "serious crisis" requires her to reveal "details of the situation of crisis and having it assessed by a third party [may] violate the woman's privacy and may in some cases violate her right to human dignity as well").

55. Sentencia T-009/09, para 3.2 (Colombia Constitutional Court (2009)): "No ser tratado como un objeto sobre el cual otros toman decisiones trascendentales para el proyecto de vida de la persona, en este caso la mujer, hace parte del derecho a la dignidad humana. Una decisión de tan alta importancia como la de interrumpir o continuar un embarazo, cuando este representa riesgo para la vida o la salud de la mujer, es una decisión que puede adoptan únicamente ella, bajo su propio criterio y dentro del respeto de las reglas vigentes, ya que será quien deberá soportar las consecuencias que se deriven de dicha decisión."

56. EXP.N.º 02005-2009-PA/TC, Lima ONG, "Acción De Lucha Anticorrupcion, para. 6 (Peru Constitutional Tribunal (2009)): "El derecho a la autodeterminación reproductiva es un derecho implícito contenido en el más genérico derecho al libre desarrollo de la personalidad. Este derecho consiste en la autonomía para decidir en los asuntos que sólo le atañen a la persona. Pero también puede afirmarse que el derecho a la autodeterminación reproductiva se desprende del reconocimiento de la dignidad de la persona humana y del derecho general de libertad que le es inherente. Dignidad y libertad concretizadas a partir de la necesidad de poder optar libremente y sin ninguna interferencia en el acto de trascender a través de las generaciones. Libertad para poder decidir como ser racional, con responsabilidad, sobre: 1) el momento adecuado u oportuno de la reproducción; 2) la persona con quién procrear y reproducirse; y, 3) la forma o método para lograrlo o para impedirlo [STC 7435-2006-PC/TC, fundamento de voto del Magistrado Mesía Ramírez]. En consecuencia, toda mujer tiene derecho a elegir libremente el método anticonceptivo de su preferencia, lo que está directamente relacionado con su decisión acerca de cuántos hijos quiere tener, con quién y cuándo."

57. Ibid., para 5, "En cuanto a lo que es materia del presente proceso, el derecho a la información sobre los distintos métodos anticonceptivos que se constituye en el presupuesto básico para el ejercicio de los derechos reproductivos de la mujer, consagrados en el artículo 6º de la Constitución. Pero es también un auténtico principio constitucional que obliga al Estado a brindar la información necesaria para que tanto la paternidad y maternidad se desarrollen en condiciones de responsabilidad, obligando a que las personas asuman a conciencia las implicancias y la trascendencia de traer un hijo a la sociedad. En consecuencia, el derecho a la información sobre los métodos anticonceptivos constituye una forma de concretizar el principio de dignidad de la persona humana y forma parte de los elementos esenciales de una sociedad democrática, porque posibilita el ejercicio de los derechos sexuales de modo libre, consciente y responsable" (The right to information about different methods of birth control that are a basic part of the exercise of women's reproductive rights, enshrined in article 6 of the Constitution. But it is also an authentic constitutional principle that obligates the State to bring necessary information so that paternity and maternity decisions can be made in conditions of

responsibility, obligating people to consider in a conscientious way the implications and significance of bringing a child into society)

58. BVerfG, 2 BvF 2/90 vom 28.5.1993, paras. 145, 146 (quoting BVerfGE 39, 1 [41]).

59. BVerfG, 2 BvF 2/90 vom 28.5.1993, commenting on abortion decision, BVerfGE 39, 1 (1975).

60. Ibid., 184.

61. CFH 2401/95, *Nahmani v. Nahmani*, (1996) Piskei Din 50(4) 661 (Supreme Court sitting as the Court of Civil Appeals).

62. *Minister of Home Affairs v. Fourie*, 2006 (3) BCLR 355 (CC), 10 (S. Afr.).

63. See, e.g., Decision 23/1999 (VI. 30) AB (concerning access to the historical archives). The Hungarian Constitutional Court stated: "Just as violations of the right to (informational) self-determination require that everyone may gain access to secret service files concerning them so that they may understand the true extent to which the past regime influenced their personal fate, and in this way, at least, temper the transgression against their human dignity, so the nagging issue of the past in the larger sense, too, as it concerns the nation as a whole, can be resolved only if the secrecy of former secret service records is not further maintained" (citations omitted).

64. James Q. Whitman, "The Two Western Cultures of Privacy: Dignity Versus Liberty," *Yale Law Journal* 113 (2004): 1151.

65. On private accusation and on the right of the person, against whom the institution of a criminal case is refused, to lodge a complaint against the decision of the prosecutor: Ruling 16 January 2006; Case No. 7/03-41/03-40/04-46/04-5/05-7/05-17/05.

66. EXP.N.º 06817-2008-AA/TC Lambayeque José Alberto Asunción Reyes, para. 15: "Al respecto, como este Tribunal Constitucional ya ha expresado, el 'fundamento último del reconocimiento del derecho a la buena reputación es el principio de dignidad de la persona, del cual el derecho en referencia no es sino una de las muchas maneras como aquélla se concretiza. El derecho a la buena reputación, en efecto, es en esencia un derecho que se deriva de la personalidad y, en principio, se trata de un derecho personalísimo. Por ello, su reconocimiento (y la posibilidad de tutela jurisdiccional) está directamente vinculado con el ser humano'" (case involving a notice published in a newspaper about disciplinary actions taken against an attorney).

67. Corte Suprema de Justicia [CSJN] [Supreme Court of Justice], 7/7/1992, "Ekmedjian v. Sofovich," Fallos (1992-315-1492) (Arg.), reprinted in Oquendo, *Latin American Law*, 245.

68. See e.g., Stasi dispute case, BVerfG, 1 BvR 1696/98 vom 25.10.2005, para.34: "If the statement is a factual claim, it is decisive whether it is possible to prove its veracity. It will be material in the case of value judgments whether they are to be regarded as abuse, a formal insult or a violation of human dignity, and hence should cease, or if this is not the case, whether they prevail over the protection of personality when weighing up these interests" (citation omitted).

69. *Kanawagi A/l Seperumaniam v. Dato' Abdul Hamid Bin Mohamad* [2004] 5 MLJ 495, 506 (High Court of Malaysia—Kuala Lumpur) (Fiaza Tamby Chik J.).

70. Bundesverfassungsgericht [BVerfGE], [Federal Constitutional Court, First Division], Feb. 24, 1971, 30 BVerfG 173 (FRG) (translation by J. A. Weir).

71. CA 294/91 *Jerusalem Community Jewish Burial Society v. Kestenbaum* (1992) IsrSC 46(2) 464.

72. Geneva Convention Relative to the Treatment of Prisoners of War, Art. 130, Aug. 12, 1949, 6 UST 3316, 75 UNTS 135.

73. Whitman, "The Two Western Cultures of Privacy."

74. *R. v. Morgentaler* [1988] 1 SCR 30, 158 (opinion of Wilson, J.).

75. *Fleming v. Starson* [2003] Can. Sup. Ct. LEXIS 33; [2003] SCC 32, 60.

76. *Indiana v. Edwards*, 128 S. Ct. 2379, 2393 (2008) (Scalia, J., dissenting).

77. England, "Human Dignity," 918, quoting Immanuel Kant, *Foundations of the Metaphysics of Morals*, 2nd ed. (1786).

78. Air Transport Security Case, para. 119.

79. Christoph Möllers, "Democracy and Human Dignity: Limits of a Moralized Conception of Rights in German Constitutional Law," *Israel Law Review* 42 (2009): 416, 427. Möllers notes that the emphasis has always been on Kant's *moral* rather than his legal philosophy.

80. Bundesverfassungsgericht [BVerfG], [Federal Constitutional Court], Feb. 15, 2006, 59 Neue Juristiche Wochenschrift (NJW) 751 (FRG); Oliver Lepsius, "Human Dignity and the Downing of Aircraft: The German Federal Constitutional Court Strikes Down a Prominent Anti-terrorism Provision I: The New Air-Transport Security Act," *German Law Journal* 7 (2006): 762, 767.

81. Air Transport Security Case, paras. 121–22.

82. Lepsius, "Human Dignity and the Downing of Aircraft," 761. For further discussion of the German approach, see Baer, "Dignity, Liberty, Equality."

83. Decision 58/2001 (III. 2.) (Hungary) (regarding change of names). See Constitution of the Republic of Hungary, Art. 54, para. (1): "In the Republic of Hungary everyone has the inherent right to life and to human dignity. No one shall be arbitrarily denied of these rights."

84. Aborto en Caso de Violacion, Inseminacion Artificial o Trasferencia de Ovulo no Consentida-Supone la relativización del principio de dignidad humana (S.V. C-355/06): "La dignidad de la mujer es subyugada por la fuerza necesaria para convertirla en objeto del que ejerce poder sobre ella. También se desconoce su dignidad como ser humano, cuando el legislador le impone a la mujer, igualmente contra su voluntad, servir de instrumento efectivamente útil para procrear al penalizar el aborto sin ninguna excepción. . . . En estos casos se estaría cosificando a la mujer como puro vientre desligado de la conciencia."

85. *Mohamad Bin Senik v. Public Prosecutor* [2005] 4 MLJ 164 (High Court Malaysia—Seremban).

86. HCJ 5432/03, *Shin v. Council for Cable TV and Satellite Broadcasting* [2004] IsrSC 58(3) 65.

87. Constitutional Court Decision on Privacy Rights, 91CH0650A Budapest Magyar

Kozlony No. 30, 13 Apr. 91, pp. 805-14 [Constitutional Court Decision No. 15-AB of 13 April].

88. Decision 36/2000 (X. 27.) AB, ABH 2000, 241; Decision 56/2000 (XII. 19.) AB, ABH 2000, 527, 529–30; Decision 684/B/1997 AB, ABH 2002, 813, 828; Decision 43/2005 (XI. 14.) AB, ABH 2005, 536, 560.

89. EXP.N.° 2945-2003-AA/TC, Meza García, para. 17: "Partiendo de la máxima kantiana, la dignidad de la persona supone el respeto del hombre como fin en sí mismo . . ."

90. Don Juan Carlos Díaz Montes y 8,971 ciudadanos (demandante) c. Congreso de la República (demandado), Sentencia del Pleno Juridiccional, Tribunal Constitucional 00033-2007-PI/TC (13/2/09), para. 34: "Finalmente, es necesario recordar que detrás de los fines del régimen penitenciario se encuentra necesariamente una concreción del principio dignidad de la persona (artículo 1º de la Constitución) y, por tanto, este constituye un límite para el legislador penal. Dicho Principio, en su versión negativa, impide que los seres humanos puedan ser tratados como cosas o instrumentos (sino como sujetos de derechos y obligaciones), sea cual fuere el fin que se persiga alcanzar con la imposición de determinadas medidas, pues cada uno, incluso los delincuentes, debe considerarse como un fin en sí mismo. (STC 0010-2002-AI)."

91. Constitutional Court of Slovenia, Up-143/97-14 (19.6.1997), para. 10.

92. Constitutional Court of Slovenia, U-II-1/10-26 (10.6.2010), para. 21 (on regularization of citizenship).

93. State v. Makwanyane, Case No. CCT/3/94 (1995), para. 26.

94. BVerfG, 2 BvR 2259/04 vom 6.7.2005, para 31 (see BVerfGE 45, 187 (245).

95. Life Imprisonment Case, Bundesverfassungsgericht [BVerfG] [Federal Constitutional Court], June 21, 1977, 45 BVerfGE 187 (FRG), reprinted in Norman Dorsen, Michael Rosenfeld, András Sajó, and Susanne Baer, Comparative Constitutionalism: Cases and Materials, (St. Paul, Minn.: Thompson West, 2003), 516.

96. Ibid., 515. David Currie has translated the German passage as follows: "It is contrary to human dignity to make the individual the mere tool of the state. The principle that 'each person must always be a end in himself' applies unreservedly to all areas of law; the intrinsic dignity of the person consists in acknowledging him as an independent personality." David Currie, The Constitution of the Federal Republic of Germany (Chicago: University of Chicago Press, 1995), 314, quoted in Lepsius, "Human Dignity and the Downing of Aircraft," 761, 771 n. 27.

97. Armenia Constitution (1995), Art. 19.

98. Vaccination Case, citing Decision 21/1996 (V. 17.) and Decision 43/2005 (XI. 14.) AB, ABH 2005, 536, 541–43.

99. Head Scarf Case, BVerfG, 2 BvR 1436/02 vom 24.9.2003, paras. 34, 119–23; cf. BVerfGE 41, 29 (50).

100. Harvard College v. Canada Commissioner of Patents), [2002] 4 S.C.R. 45, 2002 SCC76.

101. Decision 39/2007 (VI. 20.) AB, paras. 16–17 (vaccination case).

102. Constitutional Court of Slovenia, Up-143/97-14 (19.6.1997), para. 16.

103. See Bendor and Sachs, "Human Dignity as a Constitutional Concept," 34–35 (noting that German courts have held that human dignity was violated regardless of the consent of the people in question, as in cases concerning peep shows, dwarf throwing, or laser dromes [citing cases]).

104. Mathias Reimann, "Prurient Interest and Human Dignity: Pornography Regulation in West Germany and the United States," *University of Michigan Journal of Law Reform* 21 (1988): 201, discussing Decision of Dec. 15, 1981, Entscheidungen des Bundesverwaltungsgerichts (Decisions of the Federal Supreme Administrative Court) 64 [BVerwG]:274. See also David Feldman, "Human Dignity as a Legal Value—Part I," *Public Law* (1999): 682 (discussing CE (*Conseil d'Etat*), ass., 27 oct. 1995, *Cne de Mor-san-sur-Orge*, Dalloz Jur. 1995, p. 257; CE, ass., 27 oct. 1995, *Ville d'Aix-en-Provence, Rec.* C.E., p. 372; Dalloz Jur. 1996, p. 177).

105. These ideas are elaborated in Stéphanie Hennette-Vauchez, "A Human Digni-tas? Remnants of the Ancient Legal Concept in Contemporary Dignity Jurisprudence," *International Journal of Constitutional Law* 9, 1 (2011): 32–57; Hennette-Vauchez, "A Human Dignitas? The Contemporary Principle of Human Dignity as a Mere Reap-praisal of an Ancient Legal Concept," EUI Working Papers, LAW 2008/18; and Hen-nette-Vauchez, "When Ambivalent Legal Principles Prevail: Leads for Explaining Western Legal Orders' Infatuation with the Human Dignity Principle," EUI Working Papers, LAW 2007/37.

Chapter 3. "The Minimum Necessities of life"

1. Christoph Möllers, "Democracy and Human Dignity: Limits of a Moralized Con-ception of Rights in German Constitutional Law," *Israel Law Review* 42 (2009): 416, 433.

2. Constitution of Finland (1999) (731/1999, amendments to 802/2007 included), Art. 19.

3. Constitution of the German Reich (Weimar Constitution) (1919), Art. 151.

4. Decision 32/1998 (VI. 25.) AB (Hungary) (social welfare case).

5. *Danial Latifi & Anor v. Union of India and Other Petitions* (2002) 4 LRI 36, citing *Olga Tellis v. Bombay Municipal Corp* (1985) 3 SCC 545; and *Maneka Gandhi v. Union of India* (1978) 1 SCC 248. See also *Chairman, Railway Board & Ors v. Chandrima Das & Ors* (2000) 2 LRI 273, 33 (noting that previously the court had "held that the term 'life' indicates something more than mere animal existence. . . . The inhibitions contained in art 21 against its deprivation extends even to those faculties by which life is enjoyed. In *Bandhua Mukti Morcha v. UOI*, it was held that the right to life under art 21 means the right to live with dignity, free from exploitation") (internal citation omitted). Moreover, "The fundamental right to life which is the most precious human right and which forms the arc of all other rights must therefore be interpreted in a broad and expansive spirit so as to invest it with significance and vitality which may endure for years to come and enhance the dignity of the individual and the worth of the human person." *Francis*

Coralie v. Union of India AIR 1981 SC 746 (Bagwhati J.), quoted in *Lembaga Tatatertib Perkhidmatan Awam, Hospital Besar Pulau Pinang v. Utra Badi A/l K Perumal* (2000) 3 MLJ 281 (Court of Appeal—Kuala Lumpur).

6. *Francis Coralie v. Union of India* (1981 1 SCC 60.

7. *Bandhua Mukti Morcha v. Union of India & Ors*, AIR 1984 SC 802, 811–12, quoted in *Tan Tek Seng v. Suruhanjaya Perkhidmatan Pendidikan & Anor* (1996) 1 MLJ 261, 287 (Malaysia). The reference in the Indian cases to the Directive Principles, however, poses a problem for the court, since those principles, while enumerated in the constitution, are not judicially enforceable. India Constitution, Art. 37: "Application of the principles contained in [Part IV: Directive Principles of State Policy]: The provisions contained in this Part shall not be enforced by any court, but the principles therein laid down are nevertheless fundamental in the governance of the country and it shall be the duty of the State to apply these principles in making laws." Thus, the court has held that notwithstanding the lack of judicial power to require the government to recognize those rights, where the state has legislated to promote "these basic requirements to the workmen and thus investing their right to live with basic human dignity, with concrete reality and content," it can be required to ensure that such legislation would not amount to a "denial of the right to live with human dignity enshrined in art 21." *Bandhua Mukti Morcha v. Union of India & Ors*, 802. Through this sleight of hand, the right to life has become an enforceable guarantee of human dignity, which the government is under an obligation to promote through its socioeconomic policies. Still, the Indian Supreme Court has not accepted all claims that government action violates human dignity. See, e.g., *John Vallamattom & Anor v. Union of India* (2003) 3 LRI 169 (rejecting the argument that human dignity requires an allowance of a testamentary disposition to a religious institution), and *AK Bindal & Anor v. Union of India & Ors* (2003) 2 LRI 837, para. 18 (rejecting the argument that diminution in pay by a government company results in denial of human dignity, unless "wholly inadequate to lead a life with human dignity").

8. "On this principle, even those who are not citizens of this country and come here merely as tourists or in any other capacity will be entitled to the protection of their lives in accordance with the Constitutional provisions. They also have a right to life in this country. Thus, they also have the right to live, so long as they are here, with human dignity, just as the State is under an obligation to protect the life of every citizen in this country, so also the State is under an obligation to protect the life of the persons who are not citizens." *Chairman, Railway Board & Ors v. Chandrima Das & Ors* (2000) 2 LRI 273, para. 34.

9. EXP.N.° 05913-2007-PA/TC (2009) (Peruvian Constitutional Tribunal): "3. Que, en el presente caso, este Tribunal considera pertinente señalar que la suspensión de la pensión de la que ha sido objeto el demandante indudablemente lo priva de su derecho al mínimo vital necesario para su subsistencia, lo que impide que satisfaga sus necesidades básicas, atentándose de forma directa contra su dignidad."

10. *Meza Garcia*, EXP.N.° 2945-2003-AA/TC, para. 17 ("en el Estado social el respeto a la dignidad se refiere esencialmente a lograr una mejor calidad de vida de las personas").

11. Colombian Constitution, Art. 51.

12. Ibid., Art. 21. See also Art. 70: "Culture in its diverse manifestations is the basis of nationality. The state recognizes the equality and dignity of all those who live together in the country. The state will promote research, science, development, and the diffusion of the nation's cultural values."

13. Sentencia T-292/09 (Constitutional Court of Colombia), para II.2: "The denial of the health service in supplying this element, rendered the applicant's existence undignified and without quality of life. . . . The right to life implicates as well the safeguarding of tolerable conditions, which permit a person to live with dignity; indeed, for her protection, it is not necessary that she confront a situation of imminent death, rather, her protection emerges when her existence becomes undignified, as occurs when an older person can no longer control her bladder and needs disposable diapers." ("Se consideró, que la negativa de la EPS para suministrar tal elemento, tornaba indigna y sin calidad de vida la existencia de la actora . . . el derecho a la vida implica también la salvaguardia de unas condiciones tolerables, que permitan subsistir con dignidad y, por tanto, para su protección no se requiere estar enfrentada una situación inminente de muerte, sino que al hacerse indigna la existencia ha de emerger la protección constitucional, tal como ocurre cuando una persona mayor no puede controlar sus esfínteres y necesita pañales desechables" [citation omitted].)

14. Sentencia T-649/08 "(v) la cirugía será ordenada por la Sala de Revisión, con el fin de proteger los derechos fundamentales a la salud y a la vida en condiciones dignas de Juan Andrés López Díaz, para la Sala es claro, que el costo del procedimiento quirúrgico deberá ser cubierto." The court went on to say that "for the court, the adequate, efficient, and continuing provision of health services must be implemented as a real program of state action and of those who offer the public health service. And this program must be aimed at offering to people, where appropriate, a life of dignity and quality, which is why it is not admissible to suspend the delivery of services [on the basis of unsupportable reasons]." ("Para la Corte, la adecuada, eficiente y continua prestación del servicio de salud tiene que convertirse en un propósito real de la acción estatal y de los particulares que prestan el servicio público de salud, y está orientada a brindar a las personas condiciones apropiadas para llevar una vida digna y de calidad, razón por la cual no es admisible suspender la prestación del servicio.")

15. Sentencia T-212/09. See also Sentencia T-148/09, also concerning provision of colostomy bags.

16. Sentencia T-274/09: "Unjustified delay in attention to ordinary illnesses, occasioned by the failure of diagnosis, is an illegitimate disrespect of the right to human dignity." ("La demora injustificada en la atención de las enfermedades ordinarias, ocasionada por la falta de diagnóstico, supone un ilegítimo irrespeto al derecho a la dignidad humana."). See also Sentencia 159/09 (deciding whether periodontal services should be covered under the government health plan).

17. Sentencia T-110/09 (ordering government health service to recommend special therapy for patient with skin disease).

18. Sentencia T-082/09.

19. Sentencia T-244/08: "El ser humano necesita mantener niveles apropiados de salud, no solo para sobrevivir sino para desempeñarse adecuadamente, de modo que la presencia de ciertas afecciones, así no tengan el carácter de enfermedad grave, causan desmedro y pueden poner en peligro la dignidad; es válido pensar, entonces, que el paciente tiene derecho a abrigar esperanzas de recuperación y, en efecto, conseguir alivio a sus dolencias y procurar una vida acorde con su condición humana."

20. Sentencia T-220/09, para. 3.1.4 (holding that an energy company was not constitutionally required to provide electricity in a poor neighborhood, so that a five-year-old boy with severe disabilities, including asthma, would not be subjected to extreme temperature variations, as required by his doctors): "Por otra esta Corporación ha precisado que el derecho a la salud puede ser protegido acudiendo al juez constitucional cuando se halla íntimamente ligado con el derecho a la vida, la integridad y la dignidad, y en tal virtud 'el concepto de vida que ha guiado la jurisprudencia de esta Corte, no se limita a la protección de una mera existencia biológica, sino que debe fundarse en el principio de la dignidad humana, lo cual implica el derecho a una vida saludable. En este orden, la Sala precisa que el derecho a la salud en conexión con el derecho a la vida, no solo debe ampararse cuando se está frente a un peligro de muerte, o de perder una función orgánica de manera definitiva, sino ante eventos que pueden ser de menor gravedad pero que puedan llegar a desvirtuar claramente la calidad de vida de las personas, en cada caso específico. En efecto se trata de casos en los que se compromete la posibilidad que les asiste a todas las personas de desarrollar dignamente todas las facultades inherentes al ser humano, así como sus determinados proyectos de vida'."

21. See, e.g., Sentencia T-504/08 (holding that the right of an employee to dignified work warrants the reinstatement of an employee who became disabled into a job that is appropriate for his condition and capacity).

22. Shylashri Shankar and Pratap Bhanu Mehta, "Courts and Socioeconomic Rights in India," in *Courting Social Justice: Judicial Enforcement of Social and Economic Rights in the Developing World*, ed. V. Gauri and D. M. Brinks (Cambridge: Cambridge University Press, 2008), 154.

23. Azanca Alhelí Meza García, EXP.N.º 2945-2003-AA/TC, para. 10. "Es ahí donde se hace necesaria la exigencia de los derechos sociales y económicos, también llamados derechos prestacionales, como la seguridad social, salud pública, vivienda, educación y demás servicios públicos, pues ellos representan los fines sociales del Estado a través de los cuales el individuo puede lograr su plena autodeterminación."

24. *Danial Latifi & Anor v. Union of India and Other Petitions* (2002) 4 LRI 36, 21. See also *Hassam v. Jacobs*, Case CCT 83/08 (2009) ZACC 19 (holding that a law that disinherited women in a polygynous Muslim marriage violated their dignity).

25. Azanca Alhelí Meza García, EXP.N.º 2945-2003-AA/TC, para. 22: "Es en este último caso donde la dignidad, la libertad y la autonomía de la persona se ven afectadas a consecuencia del deterioro de la salud y riesgo de vida del paciente, tornando a estos

individuos en una suerte de parias sociales, lo que de ninguna manera puede ser admitido desde el punto de vista constitucional."

26. *Islamic Academy of Educ. & Anr v. State of Karnataka*, W.P. (Civil) No. 350/1993 (2008).

27. *Republic of South Africa v. Grootboom*, 2000 (11) BCLR 1169 (CC), 23 (S. Afr.).

28. Id., 25 (S. Afr.), quoting *Soobramoney v. Minister of Health, KwaZulu-Natal* 1998 (1) SA 765 (CC), 8 (S. Afr.).

29. CESCR General Comment 3 "The nature of States parties obligations" (Art. 2, par.1) 14/12/90 para 10.

30. *Minister of Health v. Treatment Action Campaign*, 2002 (5) SA 721 (CC), 19 (S. Afr.), at 21.

31. Id. at 19 (S. Afr.). At para. 37.

32. *Mazibuko v. City of Johannesburg*, Case CCT 39/09 (2009) ZACC 28, para. 61.

33. *Minister of Health v. Treatment Action Campaign*, 2002 (5) SA 721 (CC), 19 (S. Afr.) para 26, quoting CESCR General Comment 3.

34. Sentencia T-291/09 (Colombia 2009), para. 4.2: "Progressivism justifies the impossibility of judicially requiring, in individual and concrete cases, an immediate accomplishment of all the obligations that derive from the ambit of protection of a constitutional right, but it does not authorize the state to fail to adopt adequate and necessary means to accomplish the constitutional rights in question, even progressively." ("La progresividad justifica la imposibilidad de exigir judicialmente en casos individuales y concretos, el inmediato cumplimiento de todas las obligaciones que se derivarían del ámbito de protección de un derecho constitucional, pero no es un permiso al Estado para que deje de adoptar las medidas adecuadas y necesarias orientadas a cumplir las obligaciones en cuestión, valga repetir, progresivamente.")

35. *Republic of South Africa v. Grootboom*, 2000 (11) BCLR 1169 (CC), 30 (S. Afr.).

36. Decision 42/2000 (XI. 8.) AB (Hungary) (place to live case).

37. Constitutional Court of Colombia T-616/10 at para 2.7,

38. *Asahi v. Minister of Health and Welfare*, 21 Minshu 1043 (Sup. Ct., G.B., May 24, 1967), reprinted in the *Constitutional Case Law of Japan: Selected Supreme Court Decisions, 1961–1970*, ed. Hiroshi Itoh and Lawrence W. Beer (Seattle: University of Washington Press, 1978), 131–47. See KENPO, Art. 25 (Welfare Rights): "(1) All people shall have the right to maintain the minimum standards of wholesome and cultured living. (2) In all spheres of life, the State shall use its endeavors for the promotion and extension of social welfare and security, and of public health."

39. *Minister of Health v. Treatment Action Campaign*, 2002 (5) SA 721 (CC), 23 (S. Afr.).

40. Id., 25 (S. Afr.): "As the Bill of Rights indicates, their function in respect of socio-economic rights is directed towards ensuring that legislative and other measures taken by the state are reasonable. As this Court said in *Grootboom*, 'It is necessary to recognise that a wide range of possible measures could be adopted by the State to meet its obligations.'"

41. *Minister of Health v. Treatment Action Campaign*, 2002 (5) SA 721 (CC), 26 (S. Afr.)

42. Constitution of the Republic of Maldives (2008), Art. 57.

43. Jutta Stender-Vorwachs, "The Decision of the Federal Constitutional Court of 3 March 2004 on Acoustic Supervision of Housing Space," *German Law Journal* 5 (2004): 1337, 1344.

44. See, e.g., *Golan v. Prisons Service* [1996] lsr SC PPA 4463/94 (opinion of Justice E. Mazza), 17: "We must remember and recall that the human dignity of a prisoner is like the dignity of every person. Imprisonment violates a prisoner's liberty, but it must not be allowed to violate his human dignity."

45. Constitution of Yemen (1991, 2001), Art. 48(a).

46. PPA 4463/94 *Golan v. Prisons Service* (1996) IsrSC 50(4) 136, 149–50, quoting HCJ 355/79 *Katlan v. Prisons Service* (1980) IsrSC 34(3) 294, 298.

47. HCJ 5100/94 *Public Committee Against Torture in Israel v. Israel* (1999) 53(4) 817.

48. Don Juan Carlos Díaz Montes y 8,971 ciudadanos (demandante) c. Congreso de la República (demandado), Sentencia del Pleno Jurisdiccional, Tribunal Constitucional 00033-2007-PI/TC (13/2/09), para. 34: "Finalmente, es necesario recordar que detrás de los fines del régimen penitenciario se encuentra necesariamente una concreción del principio dignidad de la persona (artículo 1º de la Constitución) y, por tanto, este constituye un límite para el legislador penal. Dicho Principio, en su versión negativa, impide que los seres humanos puedan ser tratados como cosas o instrumentos (sino como sujetos de derechos y obligaciones), sea cual fuere el fin que se persiga alcanzar con la imposición de determinadas medidas, pues cada uno, incluso los delincuentes, debe considerarse como un fin en sí mismo." And see para. 35: "Este fin constitucional que busca la resocialización de los internos genera en algunos casos una antinomia con la obligación del Estado de proteger a la población de las amenazas contra su seguridad. Así el Estado al desarrollar la política criminal y otorgarle una finalidad intimidatoria a la pena, desarrolla también medidas en cumplimiento de su obligación de "protección" dentro de las cuales se encuentra la restricción de algunos beneficios penitenciarios. Esta medida grave por la que opta el legislador necesariamente debe estar fundado en fines relevantes y dentro del marco de la Constitución. Así, este Tribunal considera *prima facie* que la negación total de los beneficios penitenciarios vacía de contenido el principio "resocializador" de la pena y la dignidad misma de los internos. Pero para determinar cuál es el motivo por el que el Estado restringe beneficios penitenciarios es necesario desarrollar la obligación que la Constitución le ha otorgado para proteger a la población."

49. HCJ 3278/02 (2002), reprinted in Israel Ministry of Foreign Affairs, *Judgments of the Israel Supreme Court: Fighting Terrorism Within the Law* (2005), 86, 101.

50. See, e.g., CRO-2008-2-007 (Croatian Constitutional Court: 23-04-2008 / U-III-1437/2007 / Narodne novine [Official Gazette]), 55/08 (finding that prison conditions providing for inadequate space, light, and access to toilets violate the inmate's dignity, since, as the Constitutional Court emphasized, "Modern democratic states particularly protect the personal rights of every human being, and non-pecuniary damage includes

three forms of damage: biological (bodily injury), moral (mental injury) and existential (injury to all other personal rights i.e., injury to the human spirit)," according to the précis, http://www.codices.coe.int/NXT/gateway.dll/CODICES/full/eur/cro/eng/cro-2008 -2-007?f=templates$fn=document-frame.htm$3.0#JD_Full_ENG_CRO-2008-2-007).

51. HCJ 3278/02 *Center for the Defense of the Individual v. Commander of the IDF Forces* (2002), 101.

52. See, e.g., *Lai Hung Wai v. Superintendent of Stanley Prison* (2003) 969 HKCU 1 (CFI) (holding that indeterminate sentencing is not violative of any provision in Bill of Rights). In the United States, see *O'Lone v. Estate of Shabazz*, 482 U.S. 342 (1987) (prohibition against attending weekly prayer session does not violate First Amendment), and *Beard v. Banks*, 126 S. Ct. 2572 (2006) (upholding restriction on reading materials for certain prisoners).

53. *Safford Unified School District #1 et Al. v. Redding*, 557 U.S. 364, 129 S.Ct. 2633, 2642 (2009) (internal citations omitted); see also *R. v. Golden*, 2001 Can. Sup. Ct. LEXIS 84; 2001 SCC 83 (strip searches violate the right to dignity absent exigent circumstances such as police or public protection or the preservation of evidence).

54. Constitution of Hungary (1989), §54(1); and see generally Wojciech Sadurski, *Constitutional Courts in the Process of Articulating Constitutional Rights in the Post-Communist States of Central and Eastern Europe: Part II, Personal, Civil, and Political Rights and Liberties,* quoting Decision 23/1990, October 31, 1990, Section IV of the Opinion of the Court at 122.

55. *State v. Makwanyane*, Case No. CCT/3/94 (1995), para. 95. The opinion of the court canvasses death penalty jurisprudence from around the world.

56. *Joseph Kindler v. Canada* (1992) 6 CRR (2d) 193 SC, 241 (per Cory, J, dissenting with Lamer, CJC, concurring), quoted in *Makwanyane*, paras. 60–62.

57. *Baze v. Rees*, 553 U.S. 35, 40 (2008).

58. *Salt & Light Development Inc. & Ors. v. SJTU Sunway Software Industry Ltd.* (2006) 2 HKLRD 279, 72 (CA). See also, e.g., *R. v. Amway Corp.* (1989) 1 SCR 21.

59. Judgment of 12 December 2005, K 32/04 (Police Surveillance) (Constitutional Court of Poland).

Chapter 4. "Master of one's fate"

1. 2 U.S. 419, 450–51.

2. Id. at 451.

3. In 1854, Justice Campbell described the reaction to *Chisholm* as follows: "One month after, January, 1794, the senate was moved . . . to adopt the eleventh amendment to the constitution, declaring that the constitution should not be construed to authorize such suits. Various attempts were made in both branches of congress to limit the operation of the amendment, but without effect. It was accepted without the alteration of a letter, by a vote of 23 to 2 in the senate, and 81 to 9 in the house of representatives, and received the assent of the state legislatures. Georgia ratified the amendment as 'an

explanatory article,' her legislature concurring therewith, deeming the same to be the only just and true construction of the judicial power by which the rights and dignity of the several States can be effectively secured." *Florida v. Georgia*, 58 U.S. 478, 520 (Campbell, J., dissenting). But other cases have noted that the affront to dignity might have been a convenient way to prevent a more troublesome assault on state treasuries. "When Chisholm dared to sue the 'sovereign state' of Georgia, all the states were so indignant that Congress moved with vehement speed to prevent subsequent affronts to the dignity of states. More than the dignity of a sovereign state was probably at issue, however. When the Eleventh Amendment was proposed many states were in financial difficulties and had defaulted on their debts. The states could therefore use the new amendment not only in defense of theoretical sovereignty but also in a more practical way to forestall suits by individual creditors!" Marian Doris Irish and James Warren Prothro, *The Politics of American Democracy* (Englewood Cliffs, N.J.: Prentice-Hall, 1959), 123; *Petty v. Tennessee-Missouri Bridge Comm'n*, 359 U.S. 275, 277 (1959). For a discussion of the relationship between dignity and the evolution of the court's Eleventh Amendment jurisprudence, see Judith Resnik and Julie Chi-hye Suk, "Adding Insult to Injury: Questioning the Role of Dignity in Conceptions of Sovereignty," *Stanford Law Review* 55 (2003): 1921; for an evaluation of the court's Eleventh Amendment jurisprudence as protecting the expressive nature of indignity to states, see Evan H. Caminker, "Judicial Solicitude for State Dignity," *Annals* 81 (2001): 574.

4. 2 U.S. 419, 455.

5. Id. at 470–71.

6. Cases from Canada follow a similar path, attaching dignity first to the Crown, then other instruments of government, then individuals. See, e.g., *R. v. Belleau*, 1881 Carswell Nat 4, 7 SCR 53, The Supreme Court of Canada, February 10, 1881 (referring to the "dignity and honor of the Crown"); and *Lenoir v. Ritchie*, 1879 Carswell NS 7, 3 SCR 575, 1 Cart. 488, The Supreme Court of Canada, November 4, 1879 (noting that only the Crown can confer dignities and honors). As with the American cases, the concept of dignity would also soon attach to inchoate interests, particularly those related to the law. See, e.g., *R. v. Doutre*, 1882 Carswell Nat 8, 6 SCR 342, The Supreme Court of Canada, May 18, 1882 (giving effect to the "Dignity and standing in court which is supposed to appertain to a barrister"); and *R. v. Howland*, 1889 Carswell Alta 1, 16 SCR 197, The Supreme Court of Canada (referring to the dignity of the court). For a useful analysis of the relationship between sovereignty and dignity, particularly with regard to the emergence of state sovereignty in Supreme Court jurisprudence, see Resnik and Suk, "Adding Insult to Injury," 1921.

7. 11 U.S. 116 (1812).

8. *The Schooner Exchange v. M'Faddon*, 137–38 (1812). Elsewhere in the case, Marshall explained that a public armed ship (as distinguished from private property) "constitutes a part of the military force of her nation; acts under the immediate and direct command of the sovereign; is employed by him in national objects. He has many and powerful motives for preventing those objects from being defeated by the interference

of a foreign state. Such interference cannot take place without affecting his power and his dignity."

9. See also *National City Bank v. Republic of China*, 348 U.S. 356, 362 (1955: "As expounded in *The Schooner Exchange*, the doctrine is one of implied consent by the territorial sovereign to exempt the foreign sovereign from its 'exclusive and absolute' jurisdiction, the implication deriving from standards of public morality, fair dealing, reciprocal self-interest, and respect for the 'power and dignity' of the foreign sovereign"). And see *Boos v. Barry*, 485 U.S. 312, 324 (1988) (acknowledging the dignitary interests of foreign embassies and assuming the obligation of the United States to recognize such interests).

10. 14 U.S. 238 (1816)

11. Id. at 254.

12. Id. at 254–56.

13. 92 U.S. 520, 524 (1876).

14. 29 U.S. 410, 437–38 (1830).

15. 19 U.S. 264, 291 (1821).

16. Art. III, §2. See *Virginia v. Rives*, 100 U.S. 313, 337 (1880) (the Constitution's "framers seemed to have entertained great respect for the dignity of a State which was to remain sovereign, at least in its reserved powers, notwithstanding the new government, and therefore provided that when a State should have occasion to seek the aid of the judicial power of the new government, or should be brought under its subjection, that power should be invoked only in its highest tribunal"); and see *Virginia v. West Virginia*, 206 U.S. 290 (1907) (Supreme Court has original jurisdiction over case involving debts owed by West Virginia to Virginia on formation of the former as a state, notwithstanding the Eleventh Amendment).

17. 521 U.S. 261, 268 (1997).

18. *Alden v. Me.*, 527 U.S. 706, 715 (1999).

19. *FMC v. S.C. State Ports Auth.*, 535 U.S. 743, 760 (2002).

20. Id. at 770 (Stevens, J. dissenting).

21. For discussion of the operation of the Eleventh Amendment in federal court, see *Hess v. Port Auth. Trans-Hudson Corp.*, 513 U.S. 30, 52 (1994) (noting that the concerns that underpin the Eleventh Amendment are the solvency and dignity of the states). See also *Idaho v. Coeur D'Alene Tribe*, 521 U.S. 261, 268, 287–88 (1997) ("the dignity and respect afforded a State, which the immunity is designed to protect, are placed in jeopardy whether or not the suit is based on diversity jurisdiction"; "The dignity and status of its statehood allows Idaho to rely on its Eleventh Amendment immunity and to insist upon responding to these claims in its own courts, which are open to hear and determine the case"; "The dignity and status of its statehood allows Idaho to rely on its Eleventh Amendment immunity and to insist upon responding to these claims in its own courts, which are open to hear and determine the case"); *Kimel v. Fla. Bd. of Regents*, 528 U.S. 62 (2000). See also *FMC v. S.C. State Ports Auth.*, 535 U.S. 743, 760 (2002) ("The preeminent purpose of state sovereign immunity is to accord States the dignity that is consistent with their status as sovereign entities").

22. The Eleventh Amendment does not exist solely to "preven[t] federal-court judgments that must be paid out of a State's treasury," *Hess v. Port Authority Trans-Hudson Corporation*, 513 U.S. 30, 48, 130 L. Ed. 2d 245, 115 S. Ct. 394 (1994); it also serves to avoid "the indignity of subjecting a State to the coercive process of judicial tribunals at the instance of private parties," *Puerto Rico Aqueduct and Sewer Authority Metcalf & Eddy*, 506 U.S. 139, 146 (1993) (internal quotation marks omitted); *Seminole Tribe v. Fla.*, 517 U.S. 44, 58 (1996). While the court was willing, in 1996, to acknowledge both these underpinnings for state immunity from suit, by 2002 it wrote that "the primary function of sovereign immunity is not to protect State treasuries, but to afford the States the dignity and respect due sovereign entities." *FMC v. S.C. State Ports Auth.*, 535 U.S. 743, 769 (2002).

23. See, e.g., *Florida v. Georgia*, 58 U.S. 478, 495 (1854).

24. For examples of suits brought by and against states, see, e.g., *California v. Nevada*, 447 U.S. 125 (1980) and *Florida v. Georgia*, 58 U.S. 478 (1854).

25. *Ex Parte Young*, 209 U.S. 123 (1908) (Harlan, J., dissenting: "I am justified . . . in now saying that the men who framed the Constitution and who caused the adoption of the Eleventh Amendment would have been amazed by the suggestion that a State of the Union can be prevented by an order of a subordinate Federal court from being represented by its Attorney General in a suit brought by it in one of its own courts; and that such an order would be inconsistent with the dignity of the States as involved in their constitutional immunity from the judicial process of the Federal courts (except in the limited cases in which they may constitutionally be made parties in this court) and would be attended by most pernicious results." States' immunity from suits by other states is more limited. Because such a claim of immunity "necessarily implicates the power and authority of a second sovereign; its source must be found either in an agreement, express or implied, between the two sovereigns, or in the voluntary decision of the second to respect the dignity of the first as a matter of comity." *Nevada v. Hall*, 440 U.S. 410, 416 (1979).

26. *Edelman v. Jordan*, 415 U.S. 651, 663 (1974).

27. 322 U.S. 47, 51 (1944).

28. Id.

29. This also distinguishes the states from their political subddivisions. The states, the court explains in *Alden v. Maine*, "thus retain 'a residuary and inviolable sovereignty.' They are not relegated to the role of mere provinces or political corporations, but retain the dignity, though not the full authority, of sovereignty." *Alden v. Me.*, 527 U.S. 706, 715 (1999).

30. *Edelman v. Jordan*, 415 U.S. 651, 673 (1974), quoting *Great Northern Life Insurance Co. v. Read*, 322 U.S. at 54.

31. *Printz v. U.S.*, 521 U.S. 898, 925 (1997); see also *New York v. United States*, 505 U.S. 144 (1992).

32. On the dignity of the United States, see *Thomas v. City of Richmond*, 79 U.S. 349, 358 (1871), *Snow v. United States*, 85 U.S. 317, 321 (1873); on the obligations that

dignity imposes on the United States, see *U.S. v. Hosmer*, 76 U.S. 432, 435 (1869), *Mesarosh v. United States*, 352 U.S. 1, 9 (1956); on threats to the federal government's dignity caused by the commission of federal crimes, see, e.g., *Ex Parte Virginia*, 100 U.S. 339, 340 (1880); *Ex Parte Siebold*, 100 U.S. 371, 378 (voting rights offense is against the peace and dignity of the United States); *Adair v. United States*, 208 U.S. 161(1908) (firing an employee for participation in labor organization is an offense against the peace and dignity of the United States, according to the charge filed).

On the dignity of Congress, see *Kilbourn v. Thompson*, 103 U.S. 168, 184–85 (1881). See also *Anderson v. Dunn*, 19 U.S. 204, 226 (1821): "But if there is one maxim which necessarily rides over all others, in the practical application of government, it is, that the public functionaries must be left at liberty to exercise the powers which the people have intrusted to them. The interests and dignity of those who created them, require the exertion of the powers indispensable to the attainment of the ends of their creation"). Federal laws in some cases have dignity. See *Gozlon-Peretz v. United States*, 498 U.S. 395, 408 (1990) (noting that "the Sentencing Reform Act . . . had all the weight and dignity of a deliberate, considered enactment of the Congress, presented to, and approved by, the President"), and see *Marshall v. Gordon*, 243 U.S. 521 (1917). On the dignity of the presidency, see, e.g., *Nixon v. Warner Communications*, 435 U.S. 589, 616 (Stevens, J., dissenting) (recognizing dignity interest in President's tape recordings but arguing nonetheless that suppression of trial exhibits was not required); *Ky. v. Dennison*, 65 U.S. 66, 76–77 (1861) (C. J. Taney); see also *Monell v. Dep't of Soc. Servs.*, 436 U.S. 658, 678 (1978). The dissent in *INS v. Chadha* also recognized the dignity of decisions by the executive branch. *INS v. Chadha*, 462 U.S. 919, 1001 (1983) (White J. dissenting). On the dignity of the courts, see *Ex Parte Secombe*, 60 U.S. 9 (1857) (C. J. Taney). This applies to the courts of appeal: "In establishing the Courts of Appeals, Congress intended to create courts of great dignity and ability whose decisions were to be final except in the very limited instances where the Supreme Bench should pronounce for the whole nation." *NLRB v. Mexia Textile Mills, Inc.*, 339 U.S. 563, 572 (1949) (Frankfurter, J., dissenting). The dignity of the magistracy has also been recognized. *Franks v. Delaware*, 438 U.S. 154, 169–170 (1978). The purpose of the original jurisdiction of the United States Supreme Court was to "match . . . the dignity of the parties to the status of the court" (i.e., states and diplomatic or commercial representative of a foreign government). *California v. Arizona*, 440 U.S. 59, 66 (1979). Other attributions of judicial dignity include *United States v. Wilson*, 421 U.S. 309 (1975), *Degen v. United States*, 517 U.S. 820, 829 (1996) (disallowing the sanction of civil disentitlement [against a party who was a fugitive in a related criminal case] because it "could disserve the dignitary purposes for which it is invoked"). On the dignity of specific types of courts, see *Nations v. Johnson*, 65 U.S. 195 (1861) (courts of equity); *Ex Parte Lothrop*, 118 U.S. 113 (1886) (territorial courts), *Crescent City Live Stock Co. v. Butchers' Union Slaughter-House Co.*, 120 U.S. 141 (1887) (state and federal courts); *The Robert W. Parsons*, 191 U.S. 17 (1903) (admiralty courts). In *Sisson v. Ruby*, 497 U.S. 358, 375 n. 5 (1990), Justice Scalia noted that, historically, cases involving vessels powered by oars were beneath the dignity of the admiralty courts (Scalia, J., concurring); and *Humphrey's Executor v. United States*, 295 U.S. 602, 625 (1935) (Article I courts, noting that the House Report intended to create a "board or commission of dignity, permanence, and ability, independent of executive authority, except in its selection, and independent in character").

33. See *Tennessee v. Davis*, 100 U.S. 257, 268 (1880) (citing the chairman of the House Judiciary Committee who introduced the bill); *Burgess v. Seligman*, 107 U.S. 2, 21–22 (1883); see also *Freeport Water Co. v. Freeport City*, 180 U.S. 587 (1901) (quoting same); and see *Kuhn v. Fairmont Coal Co.*, 215 U.S. 349 (1910). In *Darr v. Burford*, 339 U.S. 200 (1950), the court split on the question of whether the dignity of state courts required a habeas petitioner to seek certiorari in the Supreme Court prior to bringing a claim in the lower federal court. The majority held that "Since the states have the major responsibility for the maintenance of law and order within their borders, the dignity and importance of their role as guardians of the administration of criminal justice merits review of their acts by this Court before a prisoner, as a matter of routine, may seek release from state process in the district courts of the United States." 339 U.S. 217. Justices Frankfurter and Black wrote in dissent that it would not be any "more respectful of the dignity of a State court for the District Court to disagree with the State court's view of federal law if such disagreement came after this Court had denied certiorari rather than before." Id. at 228. Conversely, Justice Souter has recently written that it "is neither prudent nor natural to see [federal court review of a state court determination of federal law] as impugning the dignity of the State or implicating the States' sovereign immunity in the federal system." *Verizon Md., Inc. v. PSC*, 535 U.S. 635, 653 (2002) (Souter, J., concurring).

34. "The right not to have property taken without just compensation has, so far as the scope of judicial power is concerned, the same constitutional dignity as the right to be protected against unreasonable searches and seizures, and the latter has no less claim than freedom of the press or freedom of speech or religious freedom." *West Virginia Bd. Of Educ. v. Barnette* 319 U.S. 624, 648 (1943) (Frankfurter, J., dissenting); see also *Dick v. United States*, 208 U.S. 340 (1908) (constitutional principles that states control everything within their territory and that Congress has exclusive authority to regulate commerce with the Indian tribes have equal dignity).

35. *Slaughter-House Cases*, 83 U.S. 36, 125 (1876) (Swayne, J., dissenting).

36. *Texas v. Johnson*, 491 U.S. 397, 420 (1989) ("We can imagine no more appropriate response to burning a flag than waving one's own, no better way to counter a flag burner's message than by saluting the flag that burns, no surer means of preserving the dignity even of the flag that burned than by—as one witness here did—according its remains a respectful burial. We do not consecrate the flag by punishing its desecration, for in doing so we dilute the freedom that this cherished emblem represents").

37. See *Plessy v. Ferguson*, 163 U.S. 537, 555 (1896); *Marchie Tiger v. Western Inv. Co.*, 221 U.S. 286 (1911) (holding that restrictions on the ability of Indians to dispose of their land did not "detract in the slightest degree from the dignity or value of citizenship"); *Buchanan v. Warley*, 245 U.S. 60 (1917); *Mandoli v. Acheson*, 344 U.S. 133, 139 (1952);

United States v. Minker, 350 U.S. 179, 199 (1956) (Douglas, J., concurring); *Schneider v. Rusk*, 377 U.S. 163, 165 (1964) (noting that the only difference is that "only the 'natural born' citizen is eligible to be president. Art. II, §1"). See also *Rogers v. Bellei*, 401 U.S. 815 (1971); *Vance v. Terrazas*, 444 U.S. 252 (1980); *Zelman v. Simmons-Harris*, 536 U.S. 639, 678 (2002) (Thomas, J., concurring).

38. *United States v. Grace*, 461 U.S. 171 (1983). Other public buildings also have dignity. *United States v. Kokinda*, 497 U.S. 720, 738 (1990) (Kennedy, J., concurring).

39. *Stark v. Wickard*, 321 U.S. 288, 304 (1944).

40. *Wyoming v. Oklahoma*, 502 U.S. 437, 451 (1992); see also *Mississippi v. Louisiana*, 506 U.S. 73 (1992) and *Nebraska v. Wyoming*, 507 U.S. 584, 593 (1993) (referring to the character and dignity of a claim to render it justiciable in the Supreme Court's original jurisdiction).

41. *Palmer v. Low*, 98 U.S. 1, 13 (1878); see also *Wright v. Roseberry*, 121 U.S. 488 (1887).

42. *Langdeau v. Hanes*, 88 U.S. 521, 529 (1877); see also *Wisconsin C. R. Co. v. Price County*, 133 U.S. 496 (1890). A patent privilege also has dignity. *Louisiana ex rel. Francis v. Resweber*, 329 U.S. 459, 463 (1947).

43. *Deseret Salt Co. v. Tarpey*, 142 U.S. 241, 252 (1891) ("It is a conveyance by the government, when the government has any interest to convey; but where it is issued upon the confirmation of a claim of a previously existing title it is documentary evidence, having the dignity of a record").

44. *The Wren*, 73 U.S. 582, 587 (1868) ("We cannot think that it needs any argument to show that [the proofs relied on to disprove the evidence] do not rise to the character or dignity of testimony in any court that respects the law of evidence").

45. *Xenia Bank v. Stewart*, 114 U.S. 224, 232 (1885) (a statement that is unlikely to be true "does not rise to the dignity of evidence, and was properly excluded").

46. *Luria v. United States*, 231 U.S. 9, 12 (1913).

47. See *McLean v. Clapp*, 141 U.S. 429, 433 (1891) ("Were this all that appeared in the case, there would be nothing rising to the dignity of a question"). Even a constitutional question may be "simple, uncomplicated and of no great dignity." *Republic Natural Gas Co. v. Oklahoma*, 334 U.S. 62, 73 (1948) (Douglas, J., concurring).

48. *Smith v. Gale*, 144 U.S. 509, 527 (1892) ("there is nothing above the dignity of a suspicion to contradict her").

49. *Fleitas v. Richardson*, 147 U.S. 538, 546 (1893).

50. See *Tate v. Norton*, 94 U.S. 746, 751 (1876) (a claim allowed and classified by the Probate Court has "the dignity and effect of a judgment"); see also *Arizona v. California*, 530 U.S. 392, 415 (2000), quoting *United States v. International Building Co.*, 345 U.S. 502, 505–6 (1953).

51. *Barber v. Barber*, 323 U.S. 77, 87 (1944) (alimony order has no less dignity than any other contract).

52. *Leggett v. Standard Oil Co.*, 149 U.S. 287 (1893).

53. 148 U.S. 547 (1893).

54. 155 U.S. 47 (1894).

55. *Mast, Foos & Co. v. Stover Mfg. Co.*, 177 U.S. 485 (1900).

56. See also *Werk v. Parker*, 249 U.S. 130, 133 (1919) ("mechanical adaptation of familiar materials and methods, not rising to the dignity of invention"); *Berlin Mills Company v. Procter & Gamble Company*, 254 U.S. 156 (1920) (process for producing lard substitutes does not rise to the dignity of an invention).

57. Dissenters in *Farrell v. United States* thought service in the merchant marines had dignity. 336 U.S. 511, 524 (1949) (Douglas, J., dissenting).

58. *Indiana v. Kentucky*, 136 U.S. 479 (1890).

59. *Packer v. Bird*, 137 U.S. 661 (1891).

60. *Ecker v. Western P. R. Corp.*, 318 U.S. 448 (1943).

61. *Schick v. U.S.*, 195 U.S. 65, 67–68 (1904).

62. *McConaughey v. Morrow*, 263 U.S. 39, 48 (1923).

63. *B. Altman Co. v. U.S.*, 224 U.S. 583, 601 (1912).

64. *Illinois v. Michigan*, 409 U.S. 36 (1972).

65. *Watters v. Wachovia Bank, N.A.*, 127 S. Ct. 1559, 1579 (2007) (Stevens, J., dissenting).

66. *California State Auto. Asso. Inter-Insurance Bureau v. Maloney*, 341 U.S. 105, 111 (1951).

67. *The Three Friends*, 166 U.S. 1, 77 (1897) (Harlan, J., dissenting).

68. *Gray v. Sanders*, 372 U.S. 368, 380 (1963). See also *Bush v. Gore*, 531 U.S. 98, 104 (2000) (recognizing the "equal weight accorded to each vote and the equal dignity owed to each voter").

69. *United States v. Drayton*, 536 U.S. 194, 207 (2002).

70. *United States v. Raynor*, 302 U.S. 540, 552 (1937); see also *White v. Winchester Country Club*, 315 U.S. 32 (1942).

71. *Stark v. Wickard*, 321 U.S. 288, 306 (1944).

72. See, e.g., *Straus v. Foxworth*, 231 U.S. 162, 172 (1913) (statutory provision does not assume the dignity of an essential element of due process); *California State Auto. Asso. Inter-Insurance Bureau v. Maloney*, 341 U.S. 105, 111 (1951) (diminution in value has never mounted to the dignity of a taking in the constitutional sense); *Harisiades v. Shaughnessy*, 342 U.S. 580, 599 (1952) (Douglas, J., dissenting) (Justice Douglas would have held that the "right to remain here" has the dignity of a constitutional protection); *Bode v. Barrett*, 344 U.S. 583, 586 (1953) (vagaries of the law do not rise to the dignity of an Equal Protection violation); *United States v. Agurs*, 427 U.S. 97, 109 n. 15 (1976); *Lehman v. Shaker Heights*, 418 U.S. 298, 304 (1974) (limits on advertising on public buses do not rise to the dignity of a First Amendment claim).

73. *United States v. Wood*, 299 U.S. 123 (1936); *United States v. Butler*, 297 U.S. 1, 87 (1936) (Stone, J., dissenting).

74. *Paterno v. Lyons*, 334 U.S. 314, 332 (1948) (Frankfurter, J., concurring).

75. *Arlington Cent. Sch. Dist. Bd. of Educ. v. Murphy*, 126 S. Ct. 2455, 2466 (2006) (Souter, J., dissenting). See also *United States v. Vonn*, 535 U.S. 55, 65 (2002) (two rules of federal civil procedure having equal dignity).

76. *United States v. International Union United Auto.*, 352 U.S. 567, 596 (1957) (Douglas, J., dissenting). Some courts have even recognized that the opportunity to fish is "an interest of sufficient dignity and importance to warrant certain protections." *Idaho ex rel. Evans v. Oregon*, 462 U.S. 1017, 1030 (1983) (O'Connor, J., dissenting).

77. 107 U.S. 265, 266, 267 (1883). See also *United States v. Shipp*, 214 U.S. 386 (1909) (considering whether the lynching of a man convicted of rape to prevent his appeal to the United States Supreme Court is an offense against the dignity of that court).

78. *Deck v. Missouri*, 544 U.S. 622 (2005).

79. 544 U.S. 622, 631 (2005). Justice Breyer continued: "As this Court has said, the use of shackles at trial 'affront[s]' the 'dignity and decorum of judicial proceedings that the judge is seeking to uphold.' Allen, at 344, 25 L. Ed. 2d 353, 90 S. Ct. 1057; see also *Trial of Christopher Layer*, 16 How. St. Tr., at 99 (statement of Mr. Hungerford) ('[T]o have a man plead for his life' in shackles before 'a court of justice, the highest in the kingdom for criminal matters, where the king himself is supposed to be personally present' undermines the 'dignity of the Court'"). Id. at 631–32. See also *Illinois v. Allen*, 397 U.S. 337, 344 (1970) ("Not only is it possible that the sight of shackles and gags might have a significant effect on the jury's feelings about the defendant, but the use of this technique is itself something of an affront to the very dignity and decorum of judicial proceedings that the judge is seeking to uphold").

80. Id. at 656 (Thomas J., dissenting).

81. Id. Thomas wrote: "This is why a defendant who proves himself incapable of abiding by the most basic rules of the court is not entitled to defend himself, or to remain in the courtroom" (citations omitted).

82. *Bessette v. W. B. Conkey Co.*, 194 U.S. 324, 328 (1904); see also *United States v. Barnett*, 376 U.S. 681 (1964); *Ex Parte Bradley* 74 U.S. 364 (1869) (referring to a "court, which possessed ample powers itself to take care of its own dignity and punish the offender"). See also *Ex Parte Terry*, 128 U.S. 289, 308 (1888) ("A breach of the peace in facie curioe is a direct disturbance and a palpable contempt of the authority of the court. It is a case that does not admit of delay, and the court would be without dignity that did not punish it promptly and without trial"). See also *Pounders v. Watson*, 521 U.S. 982, 988 (1997) ("Where misconduct occurs in open court, the affront to the court's dignity is more widely observed, justifying summary vindication"); *Fisher v. Pace*, 366 U.S. 155, 165 (1949) (Douglas, J., dissenting). Cf. *Secretary for Justice V. Choy Bing Wing*, Hcmp 4694/2003 (High Court of the Hong Kong Special Administrative Region—Court of First Instance), 2005 HKCU Lexis 1623; [2005] 1678 HKCU 1, para. 41: "It has long been recognised that the purpose of using the discipline of contempt of court is not to protect the dignity of judges individually; that is, to protect their feelings, but is instead to prevent undue interference with the administration of justice." Moreover, in the British system, it has been noted that "When such unjustifiable interference is suppressed, it is not because those charged with the responsibilities of administering justice are concerned for their own dignity, it is because the very structure of ordered life is at risk if the recognized courts of the land are so flouted that their authority wanes and is supplanted."

Re Zainur Zakaria [1999] 2 MLJ 577 (High Court of Malaysia—Kuala Lumpur), quoting *Attorney General v. Times Newspapers Ltd* [1974] AC 273, 302.

83. Attorneys and the legal profession have also been held to have dignity. See *Zauderer v. Office of Disciplinary Counsel of Supreme Court*, 471 U.S. 626 (1985); see also *Florida Bar v. Went For It, Inc.*, 515 U.S. 618, 639 (1995) (Kennedy, J., dissenting).

84. *Brown v. Walker*, 161 U.S. 591, 632 (1896). To the same effect is the court's decision in *United States v. White*, 322 U.S. 694, 698 (1944): "The constitutional privilege against self-incrimination is essentially a personal one, applying only to natural individuals. It grows out of the high sentiment and regard of our jurisprudence for conducting criminal trials and investigatory proceedings upon a plane of dignity, humanity and impartiality."

85. *Tumey v. Ohio*, 273 U.S. 510, 526 (1927).

86. See *Mobile v. Bolden*, 446 U.S. 55, 89 (1980) (Blackmun, J., concurring) ("the members of each [group] go to the polls with equal dignity and with an equal right to be protected from invidious discrimination").

87. 316 U.S. 535, 542 (1942). See also *Poe v. Ullman*, 367 U.S. 497, 554 (1961) (Harlan, J., dissenting).

88. The principle had also been mentioned in a concurring opinion in *Glasser v. United States*, 315 U.S. 60 (1942), decided earlier the same term. Justice Frankfurter wrote that "The guarantees of the Bill of Rights are not abstractions. Whether their safeguards of liberty and dignity have been infringed in a particular case depends upon the particular circumstances," suggesting that both liberty (which is of course textually guaranteed in the Constitution) and dignity (which is not) must be constitutionally safeguarded. The reference comes in the context of a separate opinion arguing that a lawyer who was a defendant had not proven ineffective assistance of counsel. The comment about dignity was not central to Justice Frankfurter's opinion. In *Carter v. Illinois*, 329 U.S. 173, 175 (1946) Justice Frankfurter again intimated, without elaboration, that the Constitution protects "the dignities of man" ("The Constitution commands the States to assure fair judgment. Procedural details for securing fairness it leaves to the States. It is for them, therefore, to choose the methods and practices by which crime is brought to book, so long as they observe those ultimate dignities of man which the United States Constitution assures"). See also *Louisiana ex Rel. Francis v. Resweber*, 329 U.S. 459 (1947) (Frankfurter, J., concurring) (the Fourteenth Amendment "did mean to withdraw from the States the right to act in ways that are offensive to a decent respect for the dignity of man, and heedless of his freedom" (although agreeing with the court that electrocuting a man twice for the same crime—the first did not result in death—did not violate due process).

89. In *McNabb v. United States*, Justice Frankfurter set aside a conviction where the defendants had not been brought before a judicial officer. He wrote that "The purpose of this impressively pervasive requirement of criminal procedure is plain. A democratic society, in which respect for the dignity of all men is central, naturally guards against the misuse of the law enforcement process. Zeal in tracking down crime is not in itself an

assurance of soberness of judgment." 318 U.S. 332, 343 (1943); see also *Gerstein v. Pugh*, 420 U.S. 103, 118 (1975) (quoting same).

90. *Korematsu v. United States*, 323 U.S. 214, 240 (1944) (Murphy, J., dissenting).

91. 323 U.S. 192, 208 (1944) (Murphy, J., concurring).

92. *United States v. Screws*, 325 U.S. 91 (1945) (Murphy, J., dissenting).

93. UN Charter, Preamble.

94. Id.

95. 327 U.S. 1 (1946).

96. 327 U.S. 759 (1946).

97. 327 U.S. 1, 26–27.

98. Id.

99. 327 U.S. 759, 759–60 (Murphy, J., dissenting). In both cases, although there was no doubt that the atrocities happened, and no doubt that the defendants commanded the military forces that committed the atrocities, there were serious questions about the legal responsibility that the defendants bore for the crimes.

100. See also *Cox v. Louisiana*, 332 U.S. 442, 458 (1947) (Murphy, J., dissenting) ("If respect for human dignity means anything, only evidence of a substantial nature warrants approval of the draft board classification in a criminal proceeding.").

101. 327 U.S. 304 (1946).

102. *Duncan v. Kahanamoku*, 327 U.S. 304, 334 (1946) (Murphy, J., concurring).

103. See *Oyama v. California*, 332 U.S. 633 (1947) (Murphy, J., concurring) (in finding unconstitutional California's Alien Land Law, which prohibited people of Japanese descent from owning land, Justice Murphy wrote: "The Constitution of the United States, as I read it, embodies the highest political ideals of which man is capable. It insists that our government, whether state or federal, shall respect and observe the dignity of each individual, whatever may be the name of his race, the color of his skin or the nature of his beliefs. It thus renders irrational, as a justification for discrimination, those factors which reflect racial animosity").

104. 339 U.S. 763, 798 (1950) (Black, J., dissenting).

105. *Carter v. Illinois*, 329 U.S. 173, 175 (1946).

106. "The Fourteenth Amendment did not mean to imprison the States into the limited experience of the eighteenth century. It did mean to withdraw from the States the right to act in ways that are offensive to a decent respect for the dignity of man, and heedless of his freedom." *Louisiana ex rel. Francis v. Resweber*, 329 U.S. 459, 468 (1947).

107. "If the basis of selection is merely that those provisions of the first eight Amendments are incorporated which commend themselves to individual justices as indispensable to the dignity and happiness of a free man, we are thrown back to a merely subjective test," wrote Justice Frankfurter. *Adamson v. California*, 332 U.S. 46, 65 (1947) (Frankfurter, J., concurring).

108. *Irvine v. California*, 347 U.S. 128, 146 (1954).

109. 338 U.S. 160 (1949).

110. Id. at 180–81.

111. *United States v. Carignan*, 342 U.S. 36 , 47 (1951) (Douglas, J., dissenting) (Fifth Amendment violation).

112. *Rochin v. California*, 342 U.S. 165, 174 (1952) (the court could not sanction a "force so brutal and so offensive to human dignity in securing evidence from a suspect as is revealed by this record") (where police forced a suspect to vomit evidence).

113. 384 U.S. 436 (1966).

114. Id. at 457.

115. Id. at 460. The court explained: "To maintain a 'fair state-individual balance,' to require the government 'to shoulder the entire load,' 8 Wigmore, Evidence 317 (Mc-Naughton rev. 1961), to respect the inviolability of the human personality, our accusatory system of criminal justice demands that the government seeking to punish an individual produce the evidence against him by its own independent labors, rather than by the cruel, simple expedient of compelling it from his own mouth." Id. See also *Schmerber v. California*, 384 U.S. 757, 767 (1966) ("The overriding function of the Fourth Amendment is to protect personal privacy and dignity against unwarranted intrusion by the State," though upholding a compulsory blood test and the admission thereof); *Kentucky Dep't of Corrections v. Thompson*, 490 U.S. 454, 467 n. 1 (1989) (Marshall, J., dissenting).

116. Id. at 537 (White, J., dissenting).

117. Id. at 542 (White, J., dissenting). See also *Ashe v. Swenson*, 397 U.S. 436, 469 (1970) (Burger, J., dissenting) (noting the individual dignity of the victims: "No court that elevates the individual rights and human dignity of the accused to a high place—as we should—ought to be so casual as to treat the victims as a single homogenized lump of human clay. I would grant the dignity of individual status to the victims as much as to those accused, not more but surely no less").

118. See, e.g., *Skinner v. Railway Labor Executives' Ass'n*, 489 U.S. 602, 613–14 (1989) (Recognizing that the Fourth Amendment "guarantees the privacy, dignity, and security of persons against certain arbitrary and invasive acts by officers of the Government or those acting at their direction," but finding that unwarranted drug and alcohol tests of railroad workers were not sufficiently intrusive to violate their Fourth Amendment rights).

119. *Florence v. Board of Chosen Freeholders*, slip op. at 6 (April 12, 2012) (Breyer, d., dissenting). See also *Schmerber v. California*, 384 U.S. 757 (1966) supra (Douglas, J., dissenting); *Wainwright v. New Orleans*, 392 U.S. 598, 607 (1968) (Warren, J., dissenting) ("using a minor and imaginary charge to hold an individual . . . is a technique which makes personal liberty and dignity contingent upon the whims of a police officer, and can serve only to engender fear, resentment, and disrespect of the police in the populace which they serve"); *Osborn v. United States*, 385 U.S. 323, 343 (1966) (Douglas, J., dissenting) ("These examples and many others demonstrate an alarming trend whereby the privacy and dignity of our citizens is being whittled away by sometimes imperceptible steps. Taken individually, each step may be of little consequence. But when viewed as a whole, there begins to emerge a society quite unlike any we have seen—a society in which government may intrude into the secret regions of man's life at will"); *United*

States v. Wade, 388 U.S. 218, 261–62 (1967) (Fortas, J., concurring in part and dissenting in part) ("To permit [the insidious doctrine of Schmerber] to extend beyond the invasion of the body, which it permits, to compulsion of the will of a man, is to deny and defy a precious part of our historical faith and to discard one of the most profoundly cherished instruments by which we have established the freedom and dignity of the individual. We should not so alter the balance between the rights of the individual and of the state, achieved over centuries of conflict"); *Hurtado v. United States*, 410 U.S. 578, 595 (1973) (Brennan, J., dissenting) (noting the severe assault on the dignity of a material witness held in custody for want of bail). But see *Spinelli v. United States*, 393 U.S. 410, 435 (1969) (Fortas, J., dissenting) ("We may well insist upon a sympathetic and even an indulgent view of the latitude which must be accorded to the police for performance of their vital task; but only a foolish or careless people will deduce from this that the public welfare requires or permits the police to disregard the restraints on their actions which historic struggles for freedom have developed for the protection of liberty and dignity of citizens against arbitrary state power"); *Meachum v. Fano*, 427 U.S. 215, 233 (1976) (Stevens, J., dissenting) (transfer of prisoners not violating due process clause; Justice Stevens arguing in dissent that "even the inmate retains an unalienable interest in liberty—at the very minimum the right to be treated with dignity—which the Constitution may never ignore"); *United States v. Leon*, 468 U.S. 897, 979 (1984) (Stevens, J., dissenting) ("[The] forefathers thought this was not too great a price to pay for that decent privacy of home, papers and effects which is indispensable to individual dignity and self-respect. They may have overvalued privacy, but I am not disposed to set their command at naught." *Harris v. United States*, 331 U.S. 145, 198 (1947) (Jackson, J., dissenting)."); *Segura v. United States*, 468 U.S. 796 (1984) (Stevens, J., dissenting) (citing same); *Colorado v. Connelly*, 479 U.S. 157, 176 (1986) (Brennan, J., dissenting) (confession admissible where no police coercion, even though suspect claimed mental illness; Justice Brennan noting in dissent that the right against self-incrimination "requires vigilant protection if we are to safeguard the values of private conscience and human dignity"); *O'Lone v. Estate of Shabazz*, 482 U.S. 342, 368 (1987) (Brennan, J., dissenting) (disallowing inmates from attending weekly congregational services held not to violate First Amendment; Justice Brennan noting in dissent that "To deny the opportunity to affirm membership in a spiritual community, however, may extinguish an inmate's last source of hope for dignity and redemption"); *Doe v. United States*, 487 U.S. 201, 219 n. 1 (1988) (Stevens, J., dissenting) ("The forced execution of a document that purports to convey the signer's authority, however, does invade the dignity of the human mind; it purports to communicate a deliberate command. . . . [That] the assertions petitioner is forced to utter by executing the document are false, causes an even greater violation of human dignity"); *Walton v. Arizona*, 497 U.S. 639, 675 (1990) (Brennan, J., dissenting) ("Even if I did not believe that the death penalty is wholly inconsistent with the constitutional principle of human dignity, I would agree that the concern for human dignity lying at the core of the Eighth Amendment requires that a decision to impose the death penalty be made only after an assessment of its propriety in each individual case"); *Bell v. Wolfish*, 441 U.S. 520 (1979) (upholding rules regarding body cavity searches, double-bunking, mail, and access to books all of which dissenters claim violate individual dignity); *Hudson v. Palmer*, 468 U.S. 517, 553 (1984) (Stevens, J., dissenting from ruling upholding searches in jail cells, on ground that such searches violate dignity and reduce prisoners to slaves); *Hewitt v. Helms*, 459 U.S. 460 (1983) (Stevens, J., dissenting from ruling upholding process accorded for administrative detention); *Arizona v. Evans*, 514 U.S. 1, 23 (1995) (Stevens, J., dissenting) ("The offense to the dignity of the citizen who is arrested, handcuffed, and searched on a public street simply because some bureaucrat has failed to maintain an accurate computer data base strikes me as equally outrageous"); *Autry v. McKaskle*, 465 U.S. 1090, 1091 (1984) (Brennan, J., dissenting); *Spaziano v. Florida*, 468 U.S. 447, 471 (1984) (imposition of death penalty violates human dignity); *Stanford v. Kentucky*, 492 U.S. 361 (1989), overruled by *Roper v. Simmons*, 543 U.S. 551 (2005); *Washington v. Harper*, 494 U.S. 210, 258 (1990) (Stevens, J., dissenting) (finding no due process violation where state administers antipsychotic drugs to competent, unconsenting inmate); *Vernonia Sch. Dist. 47J v. Acton*, 515 U.S. 646, 672 (1995) (O'Connor, J., dissenting from ruling upholding random drug testing for student athletes); *United States v. Balsys*, 524 U.S. 666, 713 (1998) (Breyer, J., dissenting from decision to make Fifth Amendment protection against self-incrimination unavailable with regard to foreign prosecution).

120. For instance, the court has held that "The right to appear *pro se* exists to affirm the dignity and autonomy of the accused and to allow the presentation of what may, at least occasionally, be the accused's best possible defense." *McKaskle v. Wiggins*, 465 U.S. 168, 176–77 (1984). See also *Jones v. Barnes*, 463 U.S. 745, 759, 763 (1983) (Brennan, J., dissenting) (noting that the Sixth Amendment right to counsel "is predicated on the view that the function of counsel under the Sixth Amendment is to protect the dignity and autonomy of a person on trial by *assisting* him in making choices that are his to make, not to make choices for him, although counsel may be better able to decide which tactics will be most effective for the defendant," and recognizing "the values of individual autonomy and dignity central to many constitutional rights, especially those Fifth and Sixth Amendment rights that come into play in the criminal process." See also *Portuondo v. Agard*, 529 U.S. 61, 76 (2000) (Stevens, J., concurring) ("The defendant's Sixth Amendment right 'to be confronted with the witnesses against him' serves the truth-seeking function of the adversary process. Moreover, it also reflects respect for the defendant's individual dignity and reinforces the presumption of innocence that survives until a guilty verdict is returned").

121. *Irvin v. Doud* (1961): "England, from whom the Western World has largely taken its concepts of individual liberty and of the dignity and worth of every man, has bequeathed to us safeguards for their preservation, the most priceless of which is that of trial by jury."

122. *Dothard v. Rawlinson*, 433 U.S. 321, 346 n. 5 (1977) (Marshall, J., dissenting).

123. *Trop v. Dulles*, 356 U.S. 86, 100 (1957); see, e.g., *Autry v. McKaskle*, 465 U.S. 1090, 1091 (1984) (Brennan, J., dissenting from denial of cert. and of stay of execution

on the ground that the death penalty, particularly under the circumstances of this case "inevitably amounts to an inexcusable affront to 'the dignity of man'").

124. See *Furman v. Georgia*, 408 U.S. 238 (1972) (invalidating capital punishment) and *Gregg v. Georgia*, 428 U.S. 153 (1976) (upholding capital punishment). See also, e.g., *Glass v. Louisiana*, 471 U.S. 1080, 1093–94 (1985) (Brennan, J., dissenting from denial of cert.: "For me, arguments about the 'humanity' and 'dignity' of *any* method of officially sponsored executions are a constitutional contradiction in terms") (examining in detail the procedure for execution); *De Garmo v. Texas*, 474 U.S. 973, 974 (1985) (Brennan, J., dissenting from denial of cert.: "In my view, the constitutional infirmity in the punishment of death is that 'it treats "members of the human race as nonhumans, as objects to be toyed with and discarded"' and is thus 'inconsistent with the fundamental premise of the [Eighth Amendment] that even the vilest criminal remains a human being possessed of common human dignity.'"); *Roach v. Aiken*, 474 U.S. 1039, 1042 (1985) (Brennan, J., dissenting from denial of stay of execution and denial of cert.: "Neither this Court nor the State of South Carolina is now in a position to ascertain whether Roach is indeed sufficiently competent to face his execution with the dignity that is the final right we allow even the most heinous criminals"); *Campbell v. Wood*, 511 U.S. 1119, 2129 (1994) (Blackmun, J., dissenting from the denial of stay of execution and the denial of cert.: "A person who slowly asphyxiates or strangulates while twisting at the end of a rope unquestionably experiences the most torturous and 'wanton infliction of pain,' *Gregg v. Georgia*, 428 U.S. at 173 [opinion of Stewart, Powell, and Stevens, JJ.], while partial or complete decapitation of the person, as blood sprays uncontrollably, obviously violates human dignity"); *Beard v. Banks*, 126 S. Ct. 2572, 2591 (2006) (Stevens, J., dissenting). In *Davidson v. Cannon*, 474 U.S. 344, 356 (1986), the court held that the due process clause was not violated by prison officials' failure to protect inmates from assaults by other inmates. Dissenting, Brennan wrote that "excusing the State's failure to provide reasonable protection to inmates against prison violence demeans both the Fourteenth Amendment and individual dignity."

125. *Brown v. Plata*, 131 S.Ct 1910, 1928 (2011). But see *Atiyeh v. Capps*, 449 U.S. 1312, 1315 (1981) (Rehnquist, J., staying an injunction ordering Oregon prisons to reduce prison population, dismissive of district court's reliance on this phrase).

126. *Estelle v. Gamble*, 429 U.S. 97, 102–3 (1976). See also *Hudson v. McMillian*, 503 U.S. 1 (1992).

127. *Hope v. Pelzer*, 536 U.S. 730, 745 (2002).

128. *Brown v. Plata*. 131 S.Ct. 1910, 1928 (2011).

129. *Roper v. Simmons*, 543 U.S. 551, 561 (2005).

130. 543 U.S. 551, 589 (2005), citing *Trop v. Dulles*.

131. The court intimated that the recognition of the constitutional right to human dignity is grounded in the original (Madisonian) vision of the Constitution, while reflecting the evolution of constitutional rights "from one generation to the next," and that it is grounded in the "American experience" while being consistent with the weight of authority from other countries. 543 U.S. 551, 578. *Roper* recognized that many foreign

courts have found the death penalty (and particularly the juvenile death penalty) to violate human dignity and, moreover, that congruence between American jurisprudence and that of the rest of the Western world should not be grounds for disqualification. The court explained, "It does not lessen our fidelity to the Constitution or our pride in its origins to acknowledge that the express affirmation of certain fundamental rights by other nations and peoples simply underscores the centrality of those same rights within our own heritage of freedom." Id.

132. 459 U.S. 460 (1983).

133. 459 U.S. at 484 (Stevens, J., dissenting) Justice Stevens argued that due process must accompany changes in that status that are "sufficiently grievous." See also *Bell v. Wolfish* (upholding 4 rules: body cavity searches, double-bunking, no packages, limited access to books against dissenters' argument that the rules violate dignity); *Hudson v. Palmer*, 468 U.S. 517, 553 (1984) (upholding search in jail cells against Justice Stevens's argument in dissent that rules violate dignity and reduce prisoners to slaves).

134. 489 U.S. 656, 680 (1989) (Scalia, J., dissenting).

135. *Goldberg v. Kelly*, 397 U.S. 254, 264–65 (1970) ("From its founding the Nation's basic commitment has been to foster the dignity and well-being of all persons within its borders. We have come to recognize that forces not within the control of the poor contribute to their poverty"). But see *Wyman v. James*, 400 U.S. 309, (1971) (Marshall, J., dissenting) (acknowledging the "severe intrusion upon privacy and family dignity" effected by welfare visits to the home).

136. *Wiseman v. Massachusetts*, 398 U.S. 960, 962 (1970) (Harlan, J., dissenting from denial of cert.). See also *Whisenhunt v. Spradlin*, 464 U.S. 965 (1983) (dissenting from the denial of cert. on the question of whether there was sufficient notice to justify termination of public employment, Justice Brennan wrote: "The requirement that the government afford reasonable notice of the kinds of conduct that will result in deprivations of liberty and property reflects a sense of basic fairness as well as concern for the intrinsic dignity of human beings").

137. *Gibson v. Florida Legislative Investigation Committee*, 372 U.S. 539, 561 (1963) (Douglas, J., concurring: "Today review of both federal and state action threatening individuals' rights is increasingly important if the Free Society envisioned by the Bill of Rights is to be our ideal. For in times of crisis, when ideologies clash, it is not easy to engender respect for the dignity of suspect minorities and for debate of unpopular issues").

138. *Hampton v. Mow Sun Wong*, 426 U.S. 88, 107 (1976) ("it must be acknowledged that in 1883 there was no doubt a greater inclination than we can now accept to regard 'foreigners' as a somewhat less desirable class of persons than American citizens. A provincial attitude toward aliens may partially explain the assumption that they would not be employed in the federal service by the new Civil Service Commission. But since that attitude has been implicitly repudiated by our cases requiring that aliens be treated with the dignity and respect accorded to other persons . . ."); *United States v. Martinez-Fuerte et al.*, 428 U.S. 543, 573 (1976) (Brennan, J., dissenting.) (objecting to unwarranted stops at border checkpoints in part because of insult to dignity of Mexican Americans who are targeted).

139. "The ancient foundations for so sweeping a privilege have long since disappeared. Nowhere in the common-law world—indeed in any modern society—is a woman regarded as chattel or demeaned by denial of a separate legal identity and the dignity associated with recognition as a whole human being. Chip by chip, over the years those archaic notions have been cast aside so that '[no] longer is the female destined solely for the home and the rearing of the family, and only the male for the marketplace and the world of ideas.' *Stanton v. Stanton*, 421 U.S. 7, 14–15 (1975)." *Trammel v. United States*, 445 U.S. 40, 52 (1980).

140. *W. Air Lines v. Criswell*, 472 U.S. 400, 410 (1985).

141. In *City of Cleburne v. Cleburne Living Ctr.*, only a dissenting Justice Marshall acknowledged the dignity of people who are mentally retarded, noting that "For the retarded, just as for Negroes and women, much has changed in recent years, but much remains the same; outdated statutes are still on the books, and irrational fears or ignorance, traceable to the prolonged social and cultural isolation of the retarded, continue to stymie recognition of the dignity and individuality of retarded people." 473 U.S. 432, 467 (1985) (Marshall, J., dissenting). In *Olmstead v. L. C. by Zimring*, 527 U.S. 581, 609 (1999), the court (with the help of the Americans with Disabilities Act) finally assumed that dignity attaches, or should attach, to people with mental disabilities ("The so-called 'deinstitutionalization' has permitted a substantial number of mentally disabled persons to receive needed treatment with greater freedom and dignity") (Kennedy, J., concurring). See also *Tennessee v. Lane*, 541 U.S. 509 (2004).

142. *Brinegar v. United States*, 338 U.S. 160, 181 (1949).

143. *NAACP v. Claiborne Hardware Co.*, 458 U.S. 886, 918 (1982).

144. *Heart of Atlanta v. United States*, 379 U.S. 241, 291 (1964) (Goldberg, J., concurring). See also *Roberts v. United States Jaycees*, 468 U.S. 609, 625 (1984). Justice Souter has more recently argued that Title VII "arguably vindicates an interest in dignity as a human being entitled to be judged on individual merit." *United States v. Burke*, 504 U.S. 229, 247 (1992) (Souter, J., concurring).

145. *Roberts v. United States Jaycees*, 468 U.S. 609, 625 (1984).

146. 476 U.S. 89 (1986).

147. *Powers v. Ohio*, 499 U.S. 400, 402 (1991): "racial discrimination in the qualification or selection of jurors offends the dignity of persons and the integrity of the courts" (citing *Strauder v. West Virginia*, 100 U.S. 303 (1880); *Virginia v. Rives*, 100 U.S. 313 (1880); *Ex Parte Virginia*, 100 U.S. 339 (1880) (prosecutor excluding African American jurors in trial of white defendant prohibited)). See also *Georgia v. McCollum*, 505 U.S. 42 (1992) (invalidating Georgia's purposeful racial discrimination of jurors). With respect to gender-based exclusion, the court has likewise explained that such practice violates the Fourteenth Amendment because "It denigrates the dignity of the excluded juror, and, for a woman, reinvokes a history of exclusion from political participation." *J.E.B. v. Ala. ex rel. T.B.*, 511 U.S. 127, 142 (1994).

148. *Edmonson v. Leesville Concrete Co.*, 500 U.S. 614 , 631 (1991): "And if a litigant believes that the prospective juror harbors the same biases or instincts, the issue can be

explored in a rational way that consists with respect for the dignity of persons, without the use of classifications based on ancestry or skin color" (defense attorney excluding white jurors from civil case involving African American plaintiff).

149. *City of Richmond v. Croson*, 488 U.S. 469 (1989); *Adarand Constructors v. Peña*, 515 U.S. 200 (1995).

150. *Rice v. Cayetano*, 528 U.S. 495, 517 (2000).

151. *Frank v. Maryland*, 359 U.S. 360, 376 (1959) (Douglas, J., dissenting). See also *Stanford v. Texas*, 379 U.S. 476 (1965) (Justice Stewart's opinion for the court adopting this language); *Walter v. United States*, 447 U.S. 649, 655 n. 6 (Justice Stevens's judgment of the court adopting this language).

152. *Ullmann v. United States*, 350 U.S. 422, 449 (1954) (Douglas, J., diss). Douglas also wrote: "The guarantee against self-incrimination contained in the Fifth Amendment is not only a protection against conviction and prosecution but a safeguard of conscience and human dignity and freedom of expression as well. My view is that the Framers put it beyond the power of Congress to *compel* anyone to confess his crimes. The evil to be guarded against was partly self-accusation under legal compulsion. But that was only part of the evil. The conscience and dignity of man were also involved. So too was his right to freedom of expression guaranteed by the First Amendment. The Framers, therefore, created the federally protected right of silence and decreed that the law could not be used to pry open one's lips and make him a witness against himself." See also *Slochower v. Board of Higher Education*, 350 U.S. 551, 557 (1954) (prohibiting New York and other states from terminating public employees because of their refusal to testify before Congress) ("At the outset we must condemn the practice of imputing a sinister meaning to the exercise of a person's constitutional right under the Fifth Amendment. The right of an accused person to refuse to testify, which had been in England merely a rule of evidence, was so important to our forefathers that they raised it to the dignity of a constitutional enactment, and it has been recognized as 'one of the most valuable prerogatives of the citizen'"). In *Watkins v. United States*, 354 U.S. 178, 187 (1957), the only dignity recognized, however, was that of Congress, which demanded that witnesses answer questions (so long as they are notified of the subject matter of the investigation).

153. This concern also had a cognitive dimension. As the information age dawned, the court became increasingly aware of the effect on individual dignity of government efforts to learn more about citizens. See *Tarver v. Smith*, 402 U.S. 1000 (1971) (Douglas, J., dissenting from denial of cert.) ("The ability of the Government and private agencies to gather, retain, and catalogue information on anyone for their unfettered use raises problems concerning the privacy and dignity of individuals"); *United States v. White*, 401 U.S. 745, 763 (1971) (Brennan, J., dissenting) ("The sheer numbers in our lives, the anonymity of urban living and the inability to influence things that are important are depersonalizing and dehumanizing factors of modern life. To penetrate the last refuge of the individual, the precious little privacy that remains, the basis of individual dignity, can have meaning to the quality of our lives that we cannot foresee. In terms of present

values, that meaning cannot be good"). In *Oncale v. Sundowner Offshore Servs.*, 523 U.S. 75, 78 (1998), Justice Scalia in an opinion for the court declined to set out in detail the factual basis of a male employee's same-sex sexual harassment claim "in the interest of both brevity and dignity."

154. 476 U.S. 747, 772 (1986). The court continued: "A woman's right to make that choice freely is fundamental. Any other result, in our view, would protect inadequately a central part of the sphere of liberty that our law guarantees equally to all."

155. 505 U.S. 833 (1992).

156. Id. at 851.

157. Stevens, J. at 916. As a judge on the Seventh Circuit, Justice Stevens argued that "privacy" was an unfortunate misnomer for that class of cases: "The character of the Court's language in these cases brings to mind the origins of the American heritage of freedom—the abiding interest in individual liberty that makes certain state intrusions on the citizen's right to decide how he will live his own life intolerable. Guided by history, our tradition of respect for the dignity of individual choice in matters of conscience and the restraints implicit in the federal system, federal judges have accepted the responsibility for recognition and protection of these rights in appropriate cases." *Fitzgerald v. Porter Memorial Hospital*, 523 F.2d 716, 719–20 (1975) (7th Cir. 1975) (Stevens, J.).

158. 539 U.S. 558, 567 (2003).

159. 539 U.S. 558, 573–74. I have elsewhere written about *Lawrence*'s reference to dignity; see Erin Daly, "The New Liberty," *Widener Law Review* (2005):221, as have others. See Christopher A. Bracey, "Race Jurisprudence and the Supreme Court: Where Do We Go from Here?: Dignity in Race Jurisprudence," *University of Pennsylvania Journal of Constitutional Law* 7, 669 (2005): 705–10; Maxine D. Goodman, "Human Dignity in Supreme Court Constitutional Jurisprudence," *Nebraska Law Review* 84 (2006): 740–94.

160. *Cohen v. California*, 403 U.S. 15, 24 (1971), citing *See Whitney v. California*, 274 U.S. 357, 375–77 (1927) (Brandeis, J., concurring). See also *Herbert v. Lando*, 441 U.S. 153, 199 (1979) (Brennan, J., dissenting) ("Freedom of speech is . . . intrinsic to individual dignity. This is particularly so in a democracy like our own, in which the autonomy of each individual is accorded equal and incommensurate respect"). See also *Simon & Schuster, Inc. v. Members of the N.Y. State Crime Victims*, 502 U.S. 105, 116 (1991).

161. 548 U.S. 521, 553 (Stevens, J., dissenting).

162. Id., quoting *Wooley v. Maynard*, 430 U.S. 705, 715 (1977).

163. *Beard v. Banks*, 548 U.S. 521, 552–553 (2006) (Stevens, J., dissenting). Justice Stevens continued: "Similarly, the ban on personal photographs, for at least some inmates, interferes with the capacity to remember loved ones, which is undoubtedly a core part of a person's 'sphere of intellect and spirit.' Moreover, it is difficult to imagine a context in which these First Amendment infringements could be more severe; LTSU-2 inmates are in solitary confinement for 23 hours a day with no access to radio or television, are not permitted to make phone calls except in cases of emergency, and may only have one visitor per month. They are essentially isolated from any meaningful contact with the outside world. The severity of the constitutional deprivations at issue in this

case should give us serious pause before concluding, as a matter of law, that the challenged regulation is consistent with the sovereign's duty to treat prisoners in accordance with 'the ethical tradition that accords respect to the dignity and worth of every individual.' *Overton v. Bazzetta,* 539 U.S. 126, 138, 123 S. Ct. 2162, 156 L. Ed. 2d 162 (2003)" (Stevens, J., concurring) (citation and internal quotation marks omitted).

164. *Citizens United v. FEC,* 130 S. Ct. 876 (U.S. 2010).

165. *Chaplinsky v. New Hampshire,* 315 U.S. 568 (1942)

166. *Gertz v. Robert Welch,* 418 U.S. 323 (1974) (White, J., dissenting).

167. Id.: See also *Miami Herald v. Tornillo,* 418 U.S. 241 (1974).

168. *Rosenblatt v. Baer,* 383 U.S. 75, 92 (1966). See also *Time v. Firestone,* 421 U.S. 448, 471–72 (1976) (Brennan J., dissenting); *Dun & Bradstreet v. Greenmoss Builders,* 472 U.S. 749 (1984); *Philadelphia Newspapers v. Hepps,* 475 U.S. 767, 781 (Stevens J., dissenting) (1986); *Milkovich v. Lorain Journal,* 497 U.S. 1, 22 (1990) (citing same).

169. Estes v. Texas, 381 U.S. 532 (1965).

170. 347 U.S. 483 (1954).

171. 410 U.S. 113 (1973).

172. 381 U.S. 479 (1965).

173. 538 U.S. 343 (2003) (authorizing state prohibition of cross-burning in certain circumstances).

174. 536 U.S. 304 (2002) (invalidating death penalty for people with mental retardation).

175. See *Watters v. Wachovia Bank, N.A.,* 550 U.S. 1, 32 (U.S. 2007) (Stevens, J., dissenting) (noting that a particular interpretation would "give Congress' silence greater statutory dignity than an express command"); *Arlington Cent. Sch. Dist. Bd. of Educ. v. Murphy,* 548 U.S. 291 (2006) (Souter, J., dissenting) (referring to two statutory provisions as having equal dignity); *Gonzales v. Oregon,* 546 U.S. 243 (2006) (mentioning Oregon's Death with Dignity Act).

176. See *Carey v. Musladin,* 127 S. Ct. 649, 657 (2006) (referring to the calm and dignity of a court); *Baze v. Rees,* 553 U.S. 35 (2008) (referring to the dignity of the lethal injection procedure, not of the individual, "especially where convulsions or seizures could be misperceived as signs of consciousness or distress"); *Wellons v. Hall,* 130 S. Ct. 727, 728 (2010) ("From beginning to end, judicial proceedings conducted for the purpose of deciding whether a defendant shall be put to death must be conducted with dignity and respect"); *Beard v. Kindler,* 130 S. Ct. 612, 620 (2009) ("There is no justification for an unlawful escape, which 'operates as an affront to the dignity of [a] court's proceedings'"); *Holingsworth v. Perry,* 130 S. Ct. 705, 714 (2010) (noting that broadcasts of trials are generally forbidden "unless 'there is no interference with the due process, the dignity of litigants, jurors and witnesses, or with other appropriate aspects of the administration of justice'").

177. Dignity of Indian tribes: see *Wagnon v. Prairie Band Potawatomi Nation,* 546 U.S. 95, 121 (2005) (referring to an Indian tribe's independence and dignity); *Plains Commerce Bank v. Long Family Land & Cattle Co.,* 128 S. Ct. 2709, 2727 (2008)

(referring to tribal self-rule and dignity). Dignity of states: *Massachusetts v. EPA*, 549 U.S. 497, 519 (2007) (noting that states "retain the dignity, though not the full authority, of sovereignty"); *South Carolina v. North Carolina*, 130 S. Ct. 854, 862 (2010) (referring repeatedly to the "sovereign dignity" of states). Dignity of foreign nations: *Philippines v. Pimentel*, 553 U.S. 851 (2008) ("Giving full effect to sovereign immunity promotes the comity and dignity interests that contributed to the development of the immunity doctrine").

178. See *Hudson v. Michigan*, 547 U.S. 586, 594 (2006) (finding the exclusionary rule inapplicable to a violation of the "knock-and-announce" rule, noting that the rule "protects those elements of privacy and dignity that can be destroyed by a sudden entrance"); *Kennedy v. Louisiana*, 128 S. Ct. 2641, 2649 (2008) (invalidating the death penalty for nonfatal crimes, noting that "Evolving standards of decency must embrace and express respect for the dignity of the person, and the punishment of criminals must conform to that rule" and citing *Trop v. Dulles*); *Virginia v. Moore*, 553 U.S. 164 (2008) (noting that the state chose to protect "dignity and privacy"); *Parents Involved in Cmty. Sch. v. Seattle Sch. Dist. No. 1*, 551 U.S. 701, 746 (2007) (noting that "One of the principal reasons race is treated as a forbidden classification is that it demeans the dignity and worth of a person to be judged by ancestry instead of by his or her own merit and essential qualities," citing *Rice v. Cayetano*, 528 U.S. 495, 517 (2000)).

179. *Herring v. United States*, 129 S. Ct. 695, 709 (2009) (Ginsburg, J., dissenting); *Gonzales v. Carhart*, 550 U.S. 124, 170 (2007) (Ginsburg, J., dissenting) (citing the "dignity and autonomy" language of *Planned Parenthood v. Casey*); *Florence v. Board of Chosen Freeholders*, 556 U.S. (2012) (Breyer, J. dissenting).

180. See Peggy Cooper Davis, "The Second Founding: Responsive Constitutionalism and the Idea of Dignity," *University of Pennsylvania Journal of Constitutional Law* 11 (2009): 1373, 1376 ("The Court has never related this idea about human dignity and human rights to our national history of slavery, emancipation, and constitutional reconstruction. Still, if we were to read, in light of our history, the guarantees contained in our Reconstruction Amendments, we would see a notion of individual worth and the accompanying belief in a right of self-definition intentionally, and responsively, implanted").

181. *Boos v. Barry*, 485 U.S. 312, 322 (1988): "A 'dignity' standard, like the 'outrageousness' standard that we [previously rejected] is so inherently subjective that it would be inconsistent with 'our longstanding refusal to [punish speech] because the speech in question may have an adverse emotional impact on the audience.'"

182. 554 U.S. 164, 176 (2008).

183. 554 U.S. 164, 187 (2008) (Scalia, J., dissenting).

184. *Seminole Tribe*, 517 U.S. 44, 58 (1996): "We think it follows *a fortiori* from this proposition that the type of relief sought is irrelevant to whether Congress has power to abrogate States' immunity. The Eleventh Amendment does not exist solely in order to 'preven[t] federal-court judgments that must be paid out of a State's treasury,' *Hess v. Port Authority Trans-Hudson Corporation*, 513 U.S. 30, 48, 115 S.Ct. 394, 404, 130 L.Ed.2d

245 (1994); it also serves to avoid 'the indignity of subjecting a State to the coercive process of judicial tribunals at the instance of private parties,' *Puerto Rico Aqueduct and Sewer Authority*, 506 U.S., at 146, 113 S.Ct., at 689" (internal quotation marks omitted).

185. Thus, the conflict between what Resnick and Chi-hye Suk call "role dignity" and individual dignity may be more apparent than real. Judith Resnik and Julie Chi-hye Suk, "Adding Insult to Injury: Questioning the Role of Dignity in Conceptions of Sovereignty," *Stanford Law Review* 5 (2003): 1921. Nonetheless, from a political perspective, it may be hard to reconcile the two, as conservatives (on and off the court) would typically favor institutional dignity claims, while liberals (both on and off the court) would tend to be more sympathetic to individual dignity claims. True to form, the jurisprudence of Justices O'Connor and Kennedy sits happily on the fence, embracing state claims of sovereign immunity as well as individual claims of human dignity.

186. To suggest that the abortion decisions have always been about autonomy and dignity flies in the face of the language and tone of *Roe*, which was more concerned with the physician's autonomy than the woman's: "This means, on the other hand, that, for the period of pregnancy prior to this 'compelling' point, the attending physician, in consultation with his patient, is free to determine, without regulation by the State, that, in his medical judgment, the patient's pregnancy should be terminated. If that decision is reached, the judgment may be effectuated by an abortion free of interference by the State." *Roe v. Wade*, 410 U.S. 113, 163 (1973). Other substantive due process cases more strongly support the claim that the court had all along been concerned with autonomy.

187. *Gonzales v. Oregon*, 546 U.S. 243 (2006).

188. *Frontiero v. Richardson*, 411 U.S. 677 (1973).

189. See Bracey, "Race Jurisprudence and the Supreme Court," 669, 698–700.

190. *Hope v. Pelzer*, 536 U.S. 731 (2002).

191. Cooper Davis, "The Second Founding," 1373, 1374–75. In this way, it is perhaps connected to the African notion of *ubuntu*, popularized by Archbishop Desmond Tutu in the course of the South African Truth and Reconciliation Commission. See, e.g., Erin Daly and Jeremy Sarkin, *Reconciliation in Divided Societies: Finding Common Ground* (Philadelphia: University of Pennsylvania Press, 2007).

192. It is in this sense that dignity is used in the French Declaration of the Rights of Man and of the Citizen: "Tous les citoyens étant égaux à ses yeux, sont également admissibles à toutes dignités, places et emplois publics, selon leur capacité, et sans autre distinction que celle de leurs vertus et de leurs talents." Art. 6 (All citizens, being equal in the eyes of the law, are equally eligible to all dignities and to all public positions and occupations, according to their abilities, and without distinction except that of their virtues and talents.).

193. "During the past thirty-five years, the Court has typically reversed lower court decisions favoring the poor. These rulings reflect that, constitutionally speaking, the state need not take affirmative steps to protect and preserve human dignity." Goodman, "Human Dignity in Supreme Court Constitutional Jurisprudence," 740, 786 (citation omitted).

Chapter 5. "What Respect Is Due"

1. Of the 36 new constitutions adopted since 2000, only 3 make no reference at all to dignity (Qatar, Rwanda, and Senegal). The remaining 33 refer to it, usually emphatically and repeatedly (Afghanistan, Angola, Bahrain, Bhutan, Bolivia, Burundi, Central African Republic, Comoros, Democratic Republic of Congo, Côte d'Ivoire, Ecuador, East Timor, Finland, Greenland, Guinea, Hungary, Iraq, Kenya, Kosovo, Kyrgyzstan, Libya, Madagascar, Maldives, Montenegro, Morocco, Myanmar, Serbia, Slovakia, South Sudan, Swaziland, Thailand, Turkmenistan, Venezuela).

2. Of the 33 constitutions since 2000 that refer to dignity, 14 refer to it in the preamble, 15 as a value, and 25 as a right at least once. Only 4 refer to it only once.

3. Ariel L. Bendor and Michael Sachs, "Human Dignity as a Constitutional Concept in Germany and in Israel (January 19, 2011)," *Israel Law Review* 44 (2011): 26.

4. Constitution of Kenya (2010), Art. 19.

5. Bendor and Sachs, "Human Dignity as a Constitutional Concept," 28, quoting Justice Zamir, HCJ 453/94 *Israel Women's Network v. Government of Israel* 48(5) PD 501 [1994] (Isr.).

6. Christoph Möllers, "Democracy and Human Dignity: Limits of a Moralized Conception of Rights in German Constitutional Law," *Israel Law Review* 42 (2009): 416, 416.

7. Peggy Cooper Davis, "The Second Founding: Responsive Constitutionalism and the Idea of Dignity," 11 U. Pa. J. Const. L. 1373, 1374 (2009).

8. Ibid.

9. U-I-60/03-4-12-2003 | Official Gazette RS, No. 131/2003 and OdlUS XII, 93 at para. 1.

10. *Planned Parenthood v. Casey*, 505 U.S. 833, 851 (1992).

11. Sentincia T-244/08.

12. George Kateb, *Human Dignity* (Cambridge, Mass.: Belknap Press of Harvard University Press, 2011), 8–9.

13. HCJ 6427/02 *The Movement for Quality Government in Israel v. The Knesset* [2006] (Judgment of C. J. Aharon Barak), para. 35. See also Bendor and Sachs, "Human Dignity as a Constitutional Concept," 32, quoting Justice Aharon Barak; see HCJ 7052/03 *Adalah v. Minister of Interior*, Tak-Al 2006 (2) 1754 (Isr.): "The basis of human dignity is the autonomy of personal will, freedom of choice and the liberty to act as a free being."

14. *Fleming v. Starson*, 2003 Can. Sup. Ct. LEXIS 33; 2003 SCC 32, 60.

15. Robert Post, "Dignity, Autonomy, and Democracy" (Inaugural Richard Daub Lecture, J. W. Goethe Universität, Frankfurt/M., November 1999), http://igs.berkeley.edu/publications/working_papers/WP2000-11.pdf.

16. Möllers, "Democracy and Human Dignity," 433.

17. *Sauvé v. Canada (Chief Electoral Officer)*, (2002) 3 SCR 519; 2002 SCC 68 (Gonthier, J., dissenting at para. 73).

18. Bendor and Sachs, "Human Dignity as a Constitutional Concept," 20 n.66.

19. Ngaire Naffine, *Law's Meaning of Life: Philosophy, Religion, Darwin and the Legal Person* (Oxford: Hart, 2009), 79.

20. Ibid., 62–65 (mentioning that Locke described the person as someone who is "capable of law"). See also Walter F. Murphy, *Constitutional Democracy: Creating and Maintaining a Just Political Order* (Baltimore: Johns Hopkins University Press, 2006), 8.

21. Naffine, *Law's Meaning of Life*, 83

22. Ibid., 62.

23. Susanne Baer, "Dignity, Liberty, Equality: A Fundamental Rights Triangle of Constitutionalism," *University of Toronto Law Journal* 59, 4 (Fall 2009): 417-68.

24. Constitución de la República de Cuba (1976): "16.-El Estado organiza, dirige y controla la actividad económica nacional conforme a un plan que garantice el desarrollo programado del país, a fin de fortalecer el sistema socialista, satisfacer cada vez mejor las necesidades materiales y culturales de la sociedad y los ciudadanos, promover el desenvolvimiento de la persona humana y de su dignidad, el avance y la seguridad del país."

25. Constitution of the People's Republic of China (1982), Art. 38.

26. Islamic Republic of Iran Constitution (1979), Art. 22.

27. See, e.g., Azerbaijan Constitution (1995), Art. 17 [Family and the State]: "I. The family as the foundation of society is under special protection of the State"; Art. 46 [Protection of Honor and Dignity]: "I. Everyone has the right to protect his or her honor and dignity. II. The State shall protect personal dignity. Nothing can justify humiliation of personal dignity." See also the Constitution of Brazil (1988), which is founded on "human dignity" (Art. I [III]) but whose social assistance programs are designed to protect the family (Art. 203) and whose national minimum wage is fixed at a level that is "capable of meeting a worker's basic living needs and those of his family, for housing, nourishment, education, health, leisure, clothing, hygiene, transportation and social security, with periodic adjustments to maintain its purchasing power" (Art. 7 [IV]).

28. Constitutional Court of Slovenia, Up-2155/08-10 (01.10.2009), para. 5.

29. For an extended examination of the rationality of nonhuman animals, see Susan Hurley and Matthew Nudds, eds., *Rational Animals?* (Oxford: Oxford University Press, 2006).

30. Federal Constitution of the Swiss Confederation of 18 April 1999 (status as of 7 March 2010), Art. 120.

31. Naffine, *Law's Meaning of Life*, 69. See also *Citizens United v. Federal Election Commission*, 558 U.S. 50 (2010).

32. "Reverence is respect for and the memory of the personality of the deceased, which individuals cherish in accordance with their convictions. As a personality right to one's mental integrity, it is part of the individual's privacy. Within this framework, personal feelings and one's inner spiritual life are protected." Up-2155/08-10 (01.10.2009), para. 5.

33. "The structure, then, on which the self is built is this response which is common to all, for one has to be a member of a community to be a self." George Herbert

Mead, *Mind, Self, and Society*, ed. Charles W. Morris (Chicago: University of Chicago Press, 1962), 162, quoted in Post, "Dignity, Autonomy, and Democracy." See also Jennifer Nedelsky, *Law's Relations: A Relational Theory of Self, Autonomy and Law* (Oxford University Press, 2011).

34. Magdalena Sepulveda, "Colombia: The Constitutional Court's Role in Addressing Social Injustice," in *Social Rights Jurisprudence: Emerging Trends in International and Comparative Law*, ed. Malcolm Langford (Cambridge: Cambridge University Press, 2008), 144, 147–48, citing cases as well as R. Arango and J. Lemaitre, eds., *Jurisprudencia constitucional sobre ele derecho al minimo vital* (Bogota: Uniandes, 2002), 7.

35. Sepulveda, "Colombia," 151–52.

36. BVerfG, 1 BVL 1/09, 1 BVL 3/09, 1 BVL 409 of 9 Feb. 2010 (Hartz IV).

37. HCJ 7052/03 *Adalah Legal Centre for Arab Minority Rights in Israel and Others v. Minister of Interior*.

38. Baer, "Dignity, Liberty, Equality," 460.

39. Kateb, *Human Dignity*, 5.

40. *Luis Alejandro Lobatón Donayre y más de cinco mil ciudadanos contra el Poder Ejecutivo*, EXP.N.° 0042-2004-AI/TC: "el hecho que la Constitución de 1993 reconozca el derecho fundamental de las personas a su identidad étnica y cultural, así como la pluralidad de las mismas, supone que el Estado social y democrático de Derecho está en la obligación de respetar, reafirmar y promover aquellas costumbres y manifestaciones culturales que forman parte de esa diversidad y pluralismo cultural."

41. EXP.N.° 0042-2004-AI/TC, para. 2: "Ahora bien, esta perspectiva social que la Constitución otorga a la persona humana, permite, por otro lado, afirmar que la Constitución no sólo es *ratio*, sino también *emotio*. Esto quiere decir que, si bien las Constituciones democráticas han presupuesto personas racionales y dispuestas a hacer armonizar sus legítimos intereses con los de los demás, no podemos negar esa dimensión emocional o 'irracional' que es también inherente a su naturaleza. Es precisamente en atención a esta dimensión emocional que la Constitución reconoce las diversas manifestaciones culturales que realizan las personas ya sea individualmente o como miembros de una comunidad más amplia y diversa culturalmente." The court then provided examples of the constitutional protection for the nonrational dimension of human beings: "En efecto, la Constitución (artículo 1), al reconocer que la defensa de la persona humana y el respeto de su dignidad son el fin supremo de la sociedad y del Estado, capta al ser humano no sólo como ser 'racional', sino también aprehende la *conditio humana* desde el lado emocional o 'irracional.'"

42. Constitution of Republic of South Korea (1987), Art. 10.

43. *Bangladesh Society for the Enforcement of Human Rights and Ors v. Government of Bangladesh and Ors*, 53 DLR (2001) 1, judgment dated 14 March 2000, cited in Langford, *Social Rights Jurisprudence*, 140–41.

44. Constitution of Guyana (1980), Preamble.

45. Constitution of India (1950), Art. 39(f).

46. David Luban has defined dignity *solely* in relational and not in individualistic

terms: Dignity, he says, "consists in relationships among human beings in which they do not humiliate and degrade each other. Respectful relationships honor human dignity; humiliating relationships violate it; and institutions honor human dignity when they do not humiliate people." David J. Luban, "The Rule of Law and Human Dignity: Reexamining Fuller's Canons," *Hague Journal of the Rule of Law* 2, 1 (2010): 29–47.

47. HCJ 7052/03 *Adalah v. Minister of Interior*, para. 32 (opinion of A. Barak) (citation omitted).

48. *Minister of Home Affairs and Another v. Fourie and Another*, Case CCT 60/04 [2005] ZACC 19; 2006 (3) BCLR 355 (CC); 2006 (1) SA 524 (CC) (1 December 2005) (Sachs, J.), para 50.

49. Colombia Constitutional Court, Sentencia C-793/09.

50. Colombia Constitutional Court, Sentencia T-881/02. "El agua que usan las personas es indispensable para garantizar la vida física y la dignidad humana, entendida esta como la posibilidad de gozar de condiciones materiales de existencia que le permitan desarrollar un papel activo en la sociedad."

51. *Acción de Inconstitucionalidad* 2/2010 (Mexico, 2101).

52. ADI 3510 (Brazil, 2008).

53. HCJ 366/03 *Commitment to Peace and Social Justice Society v. Minister of Finance*, 60(3) PD 464 [2005] (Isr.), 2617, quoted in Bendor and Sachs, "Human Dignity as a Constitutional Concept," 41–42.

54. Press release no. 5/2009 of 9 February 2010 concerning Judgment of 9 February 2010—1 BvL 1/09, 1 BvL 3/09, 1 BvL 4/09, http://www.bundesverfassungsgericht.de/en/press/bvg10-005en.html, 4.

55. Slovenian Involuntary Mental Commitment Case, U-I-60/03 (04.12.2003), para 4.

56. Jeremy Waldron, 2009 Oliver Wendell Holmes Lectures: "Dignity and Defamation: The Visibility of Hate," *Harvard Law Review* 123 (2010): 1596, 1646.

57. HC 821.424QQ, Rel. p/o ac. Min, Mauricio Corrêa, julgamento em 17-9-2003, Plenário DJ. 19-3-2004.

58. HCJ 6427/02 *The Movement for Quality Government in Israel v. The Knesset*, para. 43.

59. Terry L. Anderson and J. Bishop Grewell, "It Isn't Easy Being Green: Environmental Policy Implications for Foreign Policy, International Law, and Sovereignty," *Chicago Journal of International Law* 2 (2001): 427–34.

60. Bendor and Sachs, "Human Dignity as a Constitutional Concept," 36–37, quoting HCJ 7357/95 *Berki Petta Humphries Ltd v. State of Israel* 50(2) PD 769 [1996] (Isr.), 780–82.

61. *Meza Garcia v. Ministry of Health*, Exp.N. 2945-2003-AA/TC, Resolution & 2 (Apr. 20, 2004) (Peru Constitutional Tribunal), para 25: "Como bien lo ha señalado Jorge Adame (op.cit. pág. 82), reconocer los derechos sociales como deberes de solidaridad sirve a su vez para que cada individuo enfoque sus máximos esfuerzos en obtener aquellos bienes que representan sus derechos sociales, superando de este modo la visión paternalista que exige que la satisfacción de necesidades esté enfocada en manos del

Estado. Para este Tribunal, conseguir bienestar y un nivel de vida digno es un deber conjunto, tanto de la sociedad como del propio individuo y el Estado, pero no exclusivamente de este."

62. Donald S. Lutz, *Principles of Constitutional Design* (Cambridge: Cambridge University Press, 2006), 23.

63. Cindy Skach, Review of Walter F. Murphy, *Constitutional Democracy: Creating and Maintaining a Just Political Order* (Baltimore: Johns Hopkins University Press 2007) and Donald S. Lutz, "Principles of Constitutional Design," *International Journal of Constitutional Law* 7, 1(2009): 175.

64. Murphy, *Constitutional Democracy*, 377.

65. Declaration of the Rights of Man and of the Citizen (1789).

66. *Olmstead v. United States*, 277 U.S. 438 (1928) (Brandeis, J., dissenting).

67. But this, of course, paints with much too broad a stroke. There are *many* examples in American jurisprudence (and even in conservative American jurisprudence) where the state is allowed to meddle and control, even at the expense of rationalist human dignity. The deference the Supreme Court has given to the state's imposition of the death penalty is but one example. Another comes, somewhat ironically, from the area of freedom of religion, where the court has deferred to state and federal assertions of control over religion, explicitly at the expense of individual choice. See *Employment Division v. Smith*, 494 U.S. 872 (1990).

68. It may be worth noting that America's closest ideological allies are similar in this regard. The United Kingdom, of course, has no official written constitution; Australia has a constitution with no bill of rights; and Canada has a relatively new bill of rights, which, though ample, does not mention dignity. Nor does the more recently enacted United Kingdom Human Rights Act (1998).

69. Naffine, *Law's Meaning of Life*, 68.

70. Constitutional Complaint of A. A., of Ž. and B. B., of Z., Up-555/03-41, Up-827/04-26 (06.07.2006), para. 25 (Slovenian Constitutional Court on accidental deaths in police custody).

71. HCJ 355179 *Katalan v. Prison Services* 34(3) PD 294 [1980] (Isr.), quoted in Bendor and Sachs, "Human Dignity as a Constitutional Concept," 8.

72. *Minister of Home Affairs v. Fourie and Another*, Case CCT 60/04 (2005), para. 78.

73. Christoph Möllers, "Democracy and Human Dignity: Limits of a Moralized Conception of Rights in German Constitutional Law," *Israel Law Review* 42 (2009): 416, 422.

74. Jurisprudence du Conseil constitutionnel, Tables d'analyses au 25 février 2010, available at http://www.conseil-constitutionnel.fr/conseil-constitutionnel/root/bank_ mm/Tables/tables_analytiques.pdf, citing 94-343/344 DC, 27 juillet 1994, Journal officiel du 29 juillet 1994, p. 11024, cons. 2, Rec. p. 100.

75. *Whitney v. California* (1927) (Brandeis, J., concurring).

76. *Olmstead v. United States*, 277 U.S. 438, 478 (1928) (Brandeis, J., dissenting).

77. Daniel J. Whelan, *Indivisible Human Rights: A History* (Philadelphia: University of Pennsylvania Press, 2010), 209–10.

78. *Francis Coralie v. Union of India*, AIR 1981 SC 746 (Bagwhati J.).

79. Waldron, "Dignity and Defamation," 1596, 1617–18.

80. Ibid.

81. Interim National Constitution of The Republic of the Sudan (2005), Art. 185 (1).

Chapter 6. "The Beginning and the End of the State"

1. *Asociación Lucha por la Identidad Travesti-Transexual v. Inspección General de Justicia* (2006): "[8°) Que en igual sentido el voto disidente del juez Fayt (Fallos: 314:1531) subrayó que frente a la existencia de un grupo de personas que desea organizarse a efectos de preservar su dignidad ante posibles afectaciones, la protección constitucional de ese derecho legitima la asociación perseguida. Con esa comprensión,] se enfatizó que la protección de un valor rector como la dignidad humana implica que la ley reconozca, en tanto no ofenda el orden y la moral pública, ni perjudique a un tercero, un ámbito íntimo e infranqueable de libertad, de modo tal que pueda conducir a la realización personal, posibilidad que es requisito de una sociedad sana. La protección del ámbito de privacidad, se concluyó, resulta uno de los mayores valores del respeto a la dignidad del ser humano y un rasgo de esencial diferenciación entre el estado de derecho y las formas autoritarias de gobierno."

2. Ronald Dworkin has written: "Collective coercive government is essential to our dignity. We need the order and efficiency that only coercive government can provide to make it possible for us to create good lives and to live well. Anarchy would mean the end of dignity altogether." Ronald Dworkin, *Justice for Hedgehogs* (Cambridge, Mass.: Belknap Press of Harvard University Press, 2011), 320.

3. Ibid.

4. David Bilchitz, "Constitutionalism, the Global South and Economic Justice," in *Constitutionalism of the Global South,* ed. Daniel Bonilla (Cambridge University Press, 2012). Bilchitz cites Dworkin, *Is Democracy Possible Here? Principles for a New Political Debate* (Princeton, N.J.: Princeton University Press, 2006), 97, for the argument that "for a legal system to be legitimate, 'it must treat all those over whom it claims dominion not just with a measure of concern but with *equal* concern'"—or, in other words, with dignity.

5. EXP.N.º 0030-2005-PI/TC (Peru Constitutional Tribunal): "El principio democrático como principio articulador en el Estado social y democrático de derecho. La democracia se fundamenta pues, en la aceptación de que la persona humana y su dignidad son el inicio y el fin del Estado (artículo 1º de la Constitución), por lo que su participación en la formación de la voluntad político-estatal es presupuesto indispensable para garantizar el máximo respeto a la totalidad de sus derechos constitucionales."

6. Hannah Arendt, "The Preplexities of the Rights of Man," in *The Portable Hannah Arendt,* ed. Peter Baehr (New York: Penguin 2000).

7. Christoph Möllers, "Democracy and Human Dignity: Limits of a Moralized Conception of Rights in German Constitutional Law," *Israel Law Review* 42 (2009): 416, 433.

8. Robert Post: "Dignity, Autonomy, and Democracy," Inaugural Richard Daub Lecture at J. W. Goethe Universität, Frankfurt/M, November 1999: "Democracy requires us to sustain a social and institutional structure that empowers we, as a people, to choose our destiny, to decide our fate, to make ourselves into what we wish to be. That is what self-determination means." Post, however, views the relationship between dignity and democracy as paradoxical, unless one unpacks the various strands of dignity that exist even within the Kantian conception of the term: the majority can assert its will on the minority, as it is wont to do in a pure democracy, without doing violence to the dignity of the outvoted minority only insofar as dignity is " 'the social entitlement to value and regard' or as an 'entitlement to respect . . . in the social sphere' but not insofar as dignity is 'a way of describing the worth of a being that is autonomous' or a signifier of 'the value that such a being bears' " (citing decisions of the German Federal Constitutional Court).

9. Constitution of the Principality of Andorra (1993), Art. 4.

10. Constitution of Bulgaria (1991, 2007), Art. 4.

11. I am grateful to an anonymous reader of this manuscript for the foregoing taxonomy.

12. Arendt, "The Perplexities of the Rights of Man," 37.

13. John Helis, "Hannah Arendt and Human Dignity: Theoretical Foundations and Constitutional Protection of Human Rights," *Journal of Politics and Law* 1, 3 (September 2008).

14. Arendt, "The Perplexities of the Rights of Man," 41. See also Jeffrey C. Isaac, "Human Dignity and the Politics of Human Rights," *American Political Science Review* 90, 1 (1996): 61–63.

15. Arendt appeals not "to a doctrine of natural rights before which men are passive recipients but [instead emphasizes] the *activity* of human beings, who can only achieve their dignity by *doing something about it.*" Isaac, "Human Dignity and the Politics of Human Rights," 63.

16. Constitution of the Republic of Poland (1997), Art. 30.

17. Walter F. Murphy, *Constitutional Democracy: Creating and Maintaining a Just Political Order* (Baltimore: Johns Hopkins University Press, 2007), 5.

18. Linda S. Bosniak, "Persons and Citizenship in Constitutional Thought," *International Journal of Constitutional Law* 8, 1 (2010): 9–29, 21–23.

19. Ibid., 22.

20. Donald S. Lutz, *Principles of Constitutional Design* (Cambridge: Cambridge University Press, 2006), 196.

21. By "jurisprudence of dignity" I mean the body of cases built up over time by a constitutional court dealing with the right to dignity; in the aggregate, these cases offer a sense of what dignity means in constitutional terms.

22. Lutz, *Principles of Constitutional Design*, 202.

23. Constitution of Bangladesh (1972), Art. 11.

24. See *BSEHR (Bangladesh Society for the Enforcement of Human Rights) v. Bangladesh,* (2001) 53 Dhaka Law Reports 1, 10 (Karim, J.) (finding that sex workers, *as*

citizens, had the right to enforce their dignity-related rights under Arts. 11, 31, and 32 of the constitution).

25. Case CCT 8/99 [1999] ZACC 3; 1999 (3) SA 1; 1999 (4) BCLR 363 (1 April 1999).

26. *August and Another v. The Electoral Commission*, Case CCT 8/99 [1999] ZACC 3; 1999 (3) SA 1; 1999 (4) BCLR 363 (1 April 1999), opinion of J. Sachs at para. 17.

27. In *Justice for Hedgehogs*, 384, Ronald Dworkin writes: "The partnership conception of democracy . . . holds that self-government means government not by the majority of people exercising authority over everyone but by the people as a whole acting as partners. This must inevitably be a partnership that divides over policy, of course, since unanimity is rare in political communities of any size. But it can be a partnership nevertheless if the members accept that in politics they must act with equal respect and concern for all the other partners in the joint enterprise of self-governance. . . . That is, . . . if each accepts a standing obligation not only to obey the community's law but to try to make that law consistent with his good faith understanding of what every citizen's dignity requires."

28. *Doctors for Life International v. Speaker of the National Assembly and Others* (CCT12/05) [2006] ZACC 11; 2006 (12) BCLR 1399 (CC); 2006 (6) SA 416 (CC) (17 August 2006) at 115. Justice Ngcobo continued: "It encourages citizens of the country to be actively involved in public affairs, identify themselves with the institutions of [64] government and become familiar with the laws as they are made. It promotes a spirit of democratic and pluralistic accommodation calculated to produce laws that are likely to be widely accepted and effective in practice. It strengthens the legitimacy of legislation in the eyes of the people. Finally, because of its open and public character it acts as a counterweight to secret lobbying and influence peddling. Participatory democracy is of special importance to those who are relatively disempowered in a country like ours where great disparities of wealth and influence exist."

29. *Matatiele Municipality and Others v. President of the Republic of South Africa and Others*, Case CCT 73/05 (2006) (J. Ngcobo), para. 67.

30. *Matatiele Municipality and Others v. President of the Republic of South Africa and Others*, Case CCT 73/05 (2006) (J. Ngcobo), para. 66, citing Philip L. Bryden, "Public Interest Intervention in the Courts," *Canadian Bar Review* 66 (1987): 490–513, 509, cited with approval by the Court of Appeals of Quebec, Canada, in *Caron v. R*, 20 Q.A.C. 45 [1988] R.J.Q. 2333, para. 14. Section 118 provides for "Public access to and involvement in provincial legislatures" by requiring that provincial legislatures "facilitate public involvement" and conduct their "business in an open manner," among other things. See also Ariel L. Bendor and Michael Sachs, "Human Dignity as a Constitutional Concept in Germany and in Israel (January 19, 2011)," *Israel Law Review* 44 (2011): 24: "Most recently the Federal Constitutional Court [in Germany] has added the free and equal participation in public power to be founded in the human dignity of Art. 1 Sect. 1," citing 123 BVerfGE 267 (341).

31. Lisbon Case, BVerfG, 2 BvE 2/08, vom 30.6.2009, para. 211. For an analysis of

the case and a discussion of the implications of linking equal suffrage to dignity, see Christoph Schönberger, "Lisbon in Karlsruhe: Maastricht's Epigones at Sea," *German Law Journal* 10 (2009): 1201.

32. Decision No. 7 of June 4, 1996 on CC No. 1/96, section I (Bulgaria, 1996).

33. Exp. No. 02005-2009-PA/TC (Peru 2009), Para. 5: "En cuanto a lo que es materia del presente proceso, el derecho a la información sobre los distintos métodos anticonceptivos que se constituye en el presupuesto básico para el ejercicio de los derechos reproductivos de la mujer, consagrados en el artículo 61 de la Constitución. Pero es también un auténtico principio constitucional que obliga al Estado a brindar la información necesaria para que tanto la paternidad y maternidad se desarrollen en condiciones de responsabilidad, obligando a que las personas asuman a conciencia las implicancias y la trascendencia de traer un hijo a la sociedad. En consecuencia, el derecho a la información sobre los métodos anticonceptivos constituye una forma de concretizar el principio de dignidad de la persona humana y forma parte de los elementos esenciales de una sociedad democrática, porque posibilita el ejercicio de los derechos sexuales de modo libre, consciente y responsable." (. . . The right to information about different methods of birth control that are a basic part of the exercise of women's reproductive rights, enshrined in Art. 6 of the Constitution. But it is also an authentic constitutional principle that obligates the State to bring necessary information so that paternity and maternity decisions can be made in conditions of responsibility, obligating people to consider in a conscientious way the implications and significance of bringing a child into society. . . .)

34. *Planned Parenthood of Southeastern Pennsylvania v. Casey*, 505 U.S. 833 (1992). In fact, in a single sentence, the joint opinion in *Casey* recognized multiple facets of human dignity; reaffirming the constitutional right to choose to terminate a pregnancy, the opinion says: "The destiny of the woman must be shaped to a large extent on her own conception of her spiritual imperatives and her place in society."

35. *R. v. Beaulac*, [1999] 1 SCR 768, para. 16, quoting *Reference re Manitoba Language Rights*, [1985] 1 SCR 721, 744.

36. Sentencia T-820/07: "Sobre el derecho fundamental de salud, la Corte Constitucional ha reconocido que la vida comprende el respeto de la dignidad humana y por ello, una afectación de la salud que altere la vida en condiciones dignas debe ser protegida mediante los mecanismos constitucionales dispuestos para la protección de derechos fundamentales. Así, mediante la acción de tutela es posible proteger el derecho constitucional a la salud cuando su vulneración o amenaza afecte la vida digna de las personas."

37. See *Allen v. Wright*, 468 U.S. 737 (1984) (requiring civil rights plaintiffs to show that they have been injured "in fact," that their injuries are traceable to the defendants' conduct, and that a successful outcome is likely to redress their personal injuries); *Lujan v. Defenders of Wildlife*, 504 U.S. 555 (1992) (further restricting standing in environmental litigation).

38. Allan R. Brewer-Carías, *Constitutional Protection of Human Rights in Latin America: A Comparative Study of Amparo Proceedings* (Cambridge: Cambridge University Press, 2009).

39. *M. C. Mehta and Anr. v. Union of India & Ors.*, 1987 AIR 1086, 1987 SCR (1) 819, 828.

40. The French Constitution of 1946 establishes that: "Any person persecuted because of his action in the struggle for liberty has a right to asylum in the territories of the [French] Republic." ("Tout homme persécuté en raison de son action en faveur de la liberté a droit d'asile sur les territoires de la République.") Le Préambule de la Constitution du 27 octobre 1946.

41. See, e.g., *Sauvé v. Canada (Chief Electoral Officer)*, [2002] 3 SCR 519, 2002 SCC 68, paras. 35 and 44 ("denying citizens the right to vote runs counter to our constitutional commitment to the inherent worth and dignity of every individual. . . . Denial of the right to vote on the basis of attributed moral unworthiness is inconsistent with the respect for the dignity of every person that lies at the heart of Canadian democracy and the Charter").

42. PPA 4463/94 *Golan v. Prisons Service* Supreme Court of Israel (1996) (opinion of Justice E. Mazza), 19.

43. *Asociación Lucha por la Identidad Travesti-Transexual v. Inspección General de Justicia* (2006): "la esencia misma de nuestra carta de derechos que con la incorporación de los tratados internacionales en materia de derechos humanos ha sido fortalecida y profundizada es el respeto de la dignidad y libertad humanas, y si la regla estructural de un estilo de vida democrático reside en la capacidad de una sociedad para resolver sus conflictos mediante el debate público de las ideas, el umbral de utilidad exigido por la Ley Suprema es indiscutiblemente satisfecho por toda agrupación voluntaria de personas que, por vías pacíficas y sin incitación a la violencia, convenga en la obtención de cualquiera de los múltiples objetos o pretensiones que, respetando los principios del sistema democrático, no ofendan al orden, la moral pública ni perjudiquen de modo cierto y concreto bienes o intereses de un tercero."

44. Lietuviškai Case No. 44/01, The Constitutional Court of the Republic of Lithuania, Ruling Regarding the Regulations on Granting the Social Allowance and Payment Thereof, Case 5 March 2004 No. 44/01, para. 3, (citing European (Communities) Council Recommendation 92/441/EEC "On common criteria concerning sufficient resources and social assistance in social protection system" of 24 June 1992).

45. Bosniak, "Persons and Citizenship in Constitutional Thought," 22.

46. Möllers, "Democracy and Human Dignity," 433–34: "Put negatively, human dignity expresses the prohibition to reduce those who have been recognized in this way to their body. To do so would violate their human dignity as well as the democratic integrity of the political community."

47. See, e.g., *Griswold v. Connecticut*, 381 U.S. 479, 511 (1965) (Black, J., dissenting) (arguments based on Fourteenth and Ninth Amendments are "merely using different words to claim for this Court and the federal judiciary power to invalidate any legislative act which the judges find irrational, unreasonable or offensive").

48. *Divisional Manager, Aravali Golf Course & Anr. v. Chander Hass*, JT 2007(3) SC 221, 31.

49. Abraham Lincoln, First Inaugural Address (1861), http://avalon.law.yale.edu/19th_century/lincoln1.asp.

50. Aharon Barak, *The Judge in a Democracy* (Princeton, N.J.: Princeton University Press, 2006), 25–26.

51. The judgment in the landmark ruling *Citizens United v. FEC*, holding that the constitutional words "Congress shall make no law . . . abridging the freedom of speech" applies equally to corporations and to people, consisted of 183 pages of analysis in six separate opinions. The remedy, given at the end of the opinion of the court, is as follows: "The judgment of the District Court is reversed with respect to the constitutionality of 2 U. S. C. §441b's restrictions on corporate independent expenditures. The judgment is affirmed with respect to BCRA's disclaimer and disclosure requirements. The case is remanded for further proceedings consistent with this opinion. *It is so ordered.*"

52. Miguel Schor, "Mapping Comparative Judicial Review," *Washington University Global Legal Studies Law Review* 7 (2008): 271–75 (though criticizing those who fall into both camps).

53. Ibid.

54. Mark Tushnet, *Weak Courts, Strong Rights: Judicial Review and Social Welfare Rights in Comparative Constitutional Law* (Princeton, N.J.: Princeton University Press, 2009).

55. See, e.g., Constitution of India, Sec. 37: "The provisions contained in this Part shall not be enforceable by any court, but the principles therein laid down are nevertheless fundamental in the governance of the country and it shall be the duty of the State to apply these principles in making laws."

56. Brinks and Gauri, "A New Policy Landscape," in Varun Gauri and Daniel M. Brinks, *Courting Social Justice: Judicial Enforcement of Social and Economic Rights in the Developing World* (Cambridge: Cambridge University Press, 2008), 304.

57. Gauri and Brinks, *Courting Social Justice*, 132 (commenting on Brazilian case allowing reimbursement for irregular medical procedure).

58. Optional Protocol for ICCPR, http://www2.ohchr.org/english/law/ccpr-one.htm; running tally of signatories and parties, http://treaties.un.org.

59. ICESCR, Art. 2.

60. Sentencia T-291/09 (Constitutional Court of Colombia), para. 4.1: "Para la jurisprudencia constitucional, cuando el goce efectivo de un derecho constitucional fundamental depende del desarrollo progresivo, *lo mínimo que debe hacer* [la autoridad responsable] *para proteger la prestación de carácter programático derivada de la dimensión positiva de* [un derecho fundamental] *en un Estado Social de Derecho y en una democracia participativa, es, precisamente, contar con un programa o con un plan encaminado a asegurar el goce efectivo de sus derechos.*" (case involving livelihood of recyclers).

61. Ibid. para. 4.1: "Concretamente, la jurisprudencia constitucional ha precisado tres condiciones básicas, a la luz de la Constitución Política, que debe observar toda política pública orientada a garantizar un derecho constitucional: (i) que la política

efectivamente exista; (ii) que la finalidad de la política pública debe tener como prioridad garantizar el goce efectivo del derecho; y (iii) que los procesos de decisión, elaboración, implementación y evaluación de la política pública permitan la participación democrática."

62. Ibid. para. 5: "por intermedio de sus Secretarías de Educación, Salud y Bienestar Social, adoptar dentro de los seis (6) meses siguientes a la notificación de la presente sentencia, las medidas necesarias para asegurar a los recicladores de Navarro censados en el año 2003 y carnetizados en el año 2006 el goce efectivo de sus derechos constitucionales a la salud, a la educación, a la vivienda digna y a la alimentación, verificando en cada caso concreto la afiliación o vinculación al sistema de seguridad social en salud, el acceso a la educación para los hijos menores de edad, y su inclusión en los programas sociales de la alcaldía en materia de alimentación y vivienda."

63. Sandra Liebenberg, *Socio-Economic Rights: Adjudication Under a Transformative Constitution* (Claremont, S.A.: Juta 2010), 33, citing T. Roux, "Democracy," in *Constitutional Law of South Africa*, 2nd ed., ed. Stu Woolman et al. (Juta. Original Service, September 2006), chap. 10, 15–18.

64. "Courts are likely to be most effective, and therefore most attractive to strategic litigants, when they resolve obstacles to achieving genuinely popular policies. As a result, their behavior is likely to be more dialogical than monological, drawing on and incorporating the views of a variety of social and political actors." Gauri and Brinks, *Courting Social Justice*, 26.

65. *S v. Mahlungu* (1995) (3) SA 867 (CC), 1995 (7) BCLR 793 (CC), para. 129, cited in Liebenberg, *Socio-Economic Rights*, 33 n. 46.

66. See Constitution of Ecuador (2008), Art. 436(10), authorizing the Constitutional Court to provisionally write legislation if the government fails to do so: "Si transcurrido el plazo la omisión persiste, la Corte, de manera provisional, expedirá la norma o ejecutará el acto omitido, de acuerdo con la ley."

67. Brinks and Gauri, "A New Policy Landscape," 306.

68. *Minister of Health and Another v. New Clicks South Africa (Pty) Ltd and Others* (CCT 59/2004) [2005] ZACC 14; 2006 (8) BCLR 872 (CC); 2006 (2) SA 311 (CC) (30 September 2005) (Opinion of J. Sachs) para. 627. See also Liebenberg: "All groups should be able to participate in deliberative processes as peers or political equals," Liebenberg, "Socio-Economic Rights," 32, citing Nancy Fraser's notion of 'participatory parity' developed in "Social Justice in the Age of Identity Politics: Redistribution, Recognition, and Participation," in Nancy Fraser and Axel Honneth, *Redistribution or Recognition? A Political-Philosophical Exchange* (London: Verso, 2003).

69. Florian F. Hoffmann and Fenando R. N. M. Bentes, "Accountability for Social and Economic Rights in Brazil," in Gauri and Brinks, *Courting Social Justice*, 120.

70. Lincoln, First Inaugural Address, March 4, 1861.

71. Brinks and Gauri, "A New Policy Landscape," 304.

72. Malcolm Langford, "Domestic Adjudication and Economic, Social and Cultural Rights: A Socio-Legal Review," *Sur—International Journal on Hman Rights* 6, 11 (December 2009): 91–121.

73. BVerfG 1 BvL 1/09, 1 BvL 3/09, 1 BvL 4/09 of 9 Feb. 2010—Standard benefits paid according to the Second Book of the Code of Social Law ("Hartz IV legislation").

74. See Möllers, "Democracy and Human Dignity," 433: "Those who cannot participate in the act of constitutional law giving due to their different nationality participate in this recognition as well. The constitution protects their human dignity and recognizes them as possible, maybe future participants in the democratic process. With human dignity, we thus do not promise ourselves a material extent of freedom and fraternity, but rather the preservation of the possibility to promise each other something. On a theoretical level, such an interpretation of human dignity questions the false but, at least in Germany, widespread idea of a contradiction between rule of law and democracy."

75. *Mazibuko and Others v. City of Johannesburg and Others* (CCT 39/09) [2009] ZACC 28; 2010 (3) BCLR 239 (CC); 2010 (4) SA 1 (CC) (8 October 2009), paras. 61–62.

76. Ibid., para. 71.

77. Brinks and Gauri, "A New Policy Landscape," 306.

78. Wojciech Sadurski, "Postcommunist Constitutional Courts in Search of Political Legitimacy," European University Institute Law Working Paper 2001/11, Department of Law, European University Institute, Florence,2001.

79. In some cases, however, this relationship can be turned on its head. In Slovenia, the court had previously found that the dignity of noncitizens and nonresidents who had been removed from residency rolls (and who therefore were prohibited from voting) had been violated. The legislative response was to submit the amended act (purporting to fix the indignity) to a referendum, where it would surely have failed. The court held it was necessary to diminish the democratic rights of the majority (to vote in the referendum and decide the contours of their polity) to vindicate the dignity rights of the noncitizen, nonresident minority to be included in the polity. The legislature had to simply implement the act. This would, the court said, "remedy all the established unconstitutionalities which have arisen as a result of the erasure of persons from the register of permanent residents; their human rights and fundamental freedoms will also be protected in a manner consistent with the Constitution, as the legislature has thereby fulfilled all obligations arising from the decisions of the Constitutional Court. In this case, it is therefore necessary to give priority to the rule of law (Art. 2), the right to equality before the law (second paragraph of Art. 14), the right to personal dignity and safety (Art. 34), the right to obtain redress for the violations of human rights (the fourth paragraph of Art. 15) as well as the authority of the Constitutional Court (Art. 2 and second paragraph of Art. 3) over the right to decision-making at a referendum." Constitutional Court of Slovenia, Up-II-1/10-26 10, June 2010, para. 46 (on regularization of citizenship).

80. Langford, "Domestic Adjudication and Economic, Social and Cultural Rights," 106: "More dexterous approaches can be seen by those adjudicatory bodies that have used two-track remedies. The Indian Supreme Court in cases on environmental health and food rights have issued continuing series of interim orders before they come to any

final order. For instance, authorities were forced to report back on orders that the court made for extending and efficiently implementing food ration schemes" (citing cases).

81. Langford, "Domestic Adjudication and Economic, Social and Cultural Rights," 106.

82. Brinks and Gauri, "A New Policy Landscape," 310.

83. Langford, "Domestic Adjudication and Economic, Social and Cultural Rights," 107.

84. Gauri and Brinks, *Courting Social Justice*, 14, quoting Hannah Pitkin, "Justice: On Relating Public and Private," *Political Theory* 9 (1981): 327–52, 14.

85. Arendt called this a "tremendous equalizing of differences which comes from being citizens of some commonwealth." Arendt, "The Perplexities of the Rights of Man," in *The Portable Hannah Arendt*, ed. Peter Baehr (New York: Penguin, 2000), 43.

INDEX

Wilson, James, 73
Women: India, 21, 58–59; Sudan, 21;
    United States, 90–91. *See also* Denial
    of rights, disenfranchised groups;
    Pornography
Women and pregnancy, 109; Colombia,
    40–41, 46; Germany, 41–42; Hungary,
40; Israel, 42; Malaysia, 46; Peru, 41,
    139; United States, 39–42, 92–93,
    98–99, 106, 139. *See also* Unborn hu-
    man life
Women and rationality, 115

Yemen, Constitution, 67

ACKNOWLEDGMENTS

I owe a debt of gratitude to many people who provided me with ideas, inspiration, support, and encouragement, including the H. Albert Young family, Linda Ammons and the Widener University School of Law, Peter Agree at the University of Pennsylvania Press for his continued commitment to this project, and Les Daly for reading every word, several times, as well as to President Aharon Barak, who offered encouragement and insights. I would also like to thank the organizers and participants at the VIIIth World Congress of the International Association of Constitutional Law, the International Association of Law Schools Conference on Constitutional Law, the Futures of Human Rights Conference at the University of South Carolina, the International Studies Association Annual Convention, the Lectures and Awards Series at the University of Oregon Law School, and the faculty at Widener Law School for opportunities to present some of the ideas that formed the basis of this book and for valuable feedback. And, as always, to David, Jasper, and Alex for their infinite forbearance, patience, support, and guidance.

www.ingramcontent.com/pod-product-compliance
Lightning Source LLC
Chambersburg PA
CBHW020345270326
41926CB00007B/316